Food for Thought

Food for Thought

AN ANTHOLOGY OF WRITINGS INSPIRED
BY FOOD

Edited by Joan and John Digby

COLLAGES BY JOHN DIGBY

THE ECCO PRESS

THE ECCO PRESS
100 West Broad Street
Hopewell, New Jersey 08525

Published simultaneously in Canada by
Penguin Books Canada Ltd., Ontario
Printed in the United States of America

Published by arrangement with William Morrow
and Company, Inc.
Pages 473–480 constitute an extension
of this copyright page.

Library of Congress Cataloging-in-Publication Data

Food for thought.
1. Food—Literary collections. I. Digby, Joan.
II. Digby, John, 1938–
PN6071.F6F6   1987   808.8'0355   86-33137
ISBN 0-88001-469-5

Designed by Dale Cotton

9 8 7 6 5 4 3 2 1

FIRST ECCO PAPERBACK EDITION

To Eunice Riedel

Preface

The easiest way to enjoy food without gaining weight or fretting over suspicious ingredients is to read about it. Food has been a staple literary subject in as many cultures as there are cuisines, and in their approach to food, authors have been as inspired as chefs. This collection of writings about food is offered as a kind of buffet—meant to suggest diversity and plenty without actually exhausting possibility. It is intended for readers with a sensual palate who can taste the flavor expressed by the printed word and savor the aroma aroused by sheer description. This is not a book of recipes but a book of ideas, organized as a menu of food for thought.

Acknowledgments

Our first and deepest acknowledgment of thanks is to our late editor, Eunice Riedel, whose vital intuition, wisdom, experience, kindness and encouragement gave life to our book. We dedicate this volume to her memory. At William Morrow we also wish to thank Randy Ladenheim, who has given us meticulous and caring assistance.

As the greatest dish owes most to its ingredients, we wish to express our sincere debt to all the authors and translators who have permitted their work to be included in this collection.

Finally, at the C. W. Post Campus of Long Island University, we wish to thank the reference librarians who helped us in diverse and laborious quests for information and the Faculty Research Committee for its generous grant in support of this project.

While it is said that too many cooks spoil the broth, it is our hope that we have had just the right number to create a *pièce de résistance*.

Contents

Meats

Fish

The Staff of Life

Vegetables

Fruits

Desserts

Introduction

Francis Bacon once said of books that some are to be tasted, some chewed, and some digested. The greatest number, he estimated, would bear only a casual reading and slip by the intellect as a kind of Renaissance fast food. Others revealed greater subtlety with rumination, while only a select few, the *haute cuisine* of verbal fare, would leave a lasting impression on the mind.

In choosing his metaphor from the table, Bacon was making a connection between physical and spiritual satisfaction that all people can appreciate who have a keen appetite either for food or for books or both. In fact, as he well illustrated, they are excellent metaphors for each other. We speak commonly of taste in reading even when we are not as literal as the angel of Revelation, who offered up the paradoxical little volume that was at once bitter to the stomach and sweet to the mouth. Its complex savor takes us back to the first garden and the irresistible fruit that tasted of knowledge, of divinity, and of death.

Here, indeed, is food for thought.

"Old wives" used to single out fish, in particular, as "brain food." But in a sense all food becomes brain food when it enters the cycle that metabolizes the external world and converts it into our bodies, our selves. The Upanishads interpret this as a sacred metamorphosis, identifying food, the elixir of life, with the chief of beings, Brahman. And among foods they distinguish those that are the finest and rise up to become mind—"brain food" again, the source of our human nature and the chemical link that bonds us to the universe.

Both by offering food and by eating it we express the human bond. There are rituals for both in every culture. They help define the identity of the tribe. The ancient Hebrews for example, enumerated elaborate procedures for offering meat and meal to secure peace and atone for sin. Their complexity would appeal to a God who gives precise instructions, the most famous culinary ones itemizing what may and may not be eaten. " 'Your belly is your God,' " says a character in John Gilgun's poem, "The Cosmos Has Teeth." The intimate relationship between food and worship is suggested by many of the opening selections. In Gilgun's poem it leads to a comic theory on the origin of the universe.

From the oldest texts to the most recent, all of the writing in the first section is an appetizer to the main fare, which we have structured like chapters in a cookbook. For, as Henry Fielding puts it, authors (even editors), like innkeepers, must provide their customers with enticing variety suited to diverse tastes so that they may order whatever satisfies their appetites and fancies. Food and service are metaphors for Fielding. In this collection they are content too. All of the pieces that we have chosen are inspired by particular foods that have aroused the writers' sensibilities. The opening is a *Vorspeise* of tangy savories to activate the taste buds. It consists of sweet and sour, sharp and pungent, reflections on food in many cultures and also on the manners and decorum, the anthropology of eating that we recognize as civilization.

Our own civilization has been named after a utensil—the melting pot. And as a mark of acceptance its cuisine is a fusion of many. In the ubiquitous Greek diner we can find not only spanakopita and baklava, but consommé, blintzes, veal alla parmigiana, sauerbraten, chili, and strawberry shortcake served without a flinch at the same booth. We can have a croissant for breakfast, stop for a quick sushi snack at lunch, and relax at a tapas bar for Attitude Adjustment Hour before some serious eating Cuban or Thai, Korean, Indian, or Middle Eastern style. And everyone knows what to order!

Many people know how to cook it all, too. Just look at the products on supermarket shelves where shiritake rubs cellophane with taco shells. What was once quite exotic is *nouvelle* home cooking, an original blending of ingredients and cuisines that reflects cultural sophistication, nutrition consciousness, and economics. The world traveler who serves up tostadas may connect the fragrant aroma of the chiles with fond memories of Oaxaca. The vegetarian maker of the same dish is probably more conscious of the chiles as a rich source of vitamins A, B, and C and of the extraordinary nutritional relationship by which the amino acid lysine in the beans contributes to the metabolism of the maize from which the tortillas are made.

For very different reasons these two cooks have developed a taste for what is essentially peasant food, and there is a nostalgia in that too. Think of the difference in cost between tostadas ordered by a Yuppie on a bar stool and made by a mother in a Mexican kitchen. The more complicated, frustrating, and expensive our culture becomes, the more we long for primal satisfactions that gratify us without making demands. Food is the essence of such satisfaction for John Updike, who interprets eating as a body building of ego: "Whatever is you, is pure," he writes. Certain foods have become identified with purity because they have an immediate association with roots, soil, and hard work—the simplicity we have drifted away from. These include stone-ground wheat, whole-meal bread, aged cheese, fresh produce, homemade pasta, and almost any peasant cuisine—whatever is natural, simple, and, with implicit ethical overtones, good.

Those who relish making things from scratch frequently enjoy reading about them. It is possible for such readers to anticipate the taste in the recipe. They blend the ingredients mentally, sensing the aromas, texture, and color, correcting the seasoning, perhaps adding a flourish that will transform it into something new. For such readers food is an inspiration, and cookery a kind of artistic medium.

It is not surprising that creative writers have, for centuries, been inspired by food. According to William Blake, "that call'd Body is a portion of the Soul discern'd by the five Senses," and through the senses—taste among them—we come to Eternal Delight. Poets express this delight in metaphors, comparing one thing to another and so connecting them, like pieces of a pie, into a perfect whole. Shakespeare called music "the food of love," but he might just as well have called food "the music of love," as Keats's Porphyro essentially did in "The Eve of St. Agnes" when he cast a love spell on Madeline by setting up a nocturnal banquet table of exotic sweets, which, though never eaten, were the lyrics of his accompanying lute song. The seduction worked, and away they rode.

But before we come to such sweet desserts, there are other courses to pursue. Food is not merely a metaphor but the basic ingredient of this collection. The book is about the meaning that has been attached to food by writers of diverse cultures, historic periods, and experience. For most, this meaning is filled with personal associations and values connected with a style of life.

Let us begin at the beginning. With great simplicity Clarence Day writes about the egg as "the source of all." Iriarte, the Spanish fabulist, sees the egg instead as the source of diversity, enumerating fanciful culinary embellishments invented by luxury. Simplicity and luxury are ever at odds with each other when we consider styles of life. So are the sacred and the profane. Erica Jong, for example, envisions cheeses as round prayer wheels; and while she feeds on divine mystery, Marvin Cohen cautions that a party and its hostess are, after all, only mortal, however divine the hors d'oeuvres may be.

Mortality is a constant theme in the opening section. We hear echoes of it in the imploring cries of Swift's street vendors, in the unsparing appetite of the Walrus and the Carpenter, and in the excruciating hunger of Chekhov's novitiate oyster eater. Hunger, like luxury, impels creativity, as any artist knows. And culinary creativity is no exception. There may, indeed, be more than thirteen ways to cook a snail—in Sicily there are perhaps as many as the shapes of macaroni. Between Elio Vittorini and Giuseppi Tomasi di Lampedusa we see the extremes of Italian poverty and Italian luxury, which together shaped an extraordinary national cuisine that owes much to economic contrasts. The same kind of contrast separates Louis Simpson's Russian deacon, who gorges on caviare at the funeral, from Turgenev's peasant mother, who feeds on cabbage soup.

The impact of contrasts is not only political, ethical, and economic but aesthetic as well. Contrast is an important principle of culinary style. Anyone realizes this who has tasted Chinese hot and sour soup—the soup perhaps prepared by Wang Chien's bride. There are many soups in the opening section, which we leave you to sample for their aesthetic and even philosophical contrasts. We begin, then, with metaphysical speculations on how the whole universe derives from a single egg and how a birthright might be sold for a mess of pottage.

In the matter of meat the great issue is whether or not to eat it. Starving people and traditional people, exhausted with gathering fodder, have not seen any choice. When meat presents itself, they eat, as Brecht suggests, "joyously." Repulsion only comes with complexity, with a connection made between lower animals and man and with reflection on murder as an ethical issue. We have included a full cross-section of pieces illustrating the moral dilemma raised by meat eating. What the reader will probably notice, above all, is the tonal range of the selections, which include large components of satire and propaganda. Once, in composing an antislave-trade ballad, William Cowper used the harsh title "Sweet Meat Has Sour Sauce." This is the prevailing irony from the satires of Samuel Butler and Ambrose Bierce to the more journalistic voices of Upton Sinclair and Dick Gregory.

The ambiguity of progress is a constant theme in the meat chapter. Most authors recognize that the refinement of carnivorous habits brings with it a decline in the impassioned relationship between man and beast. The earliest butcher is a ritual slaughterer, a priest of the tribe performing sacramental offerings; in time he is reduced to a heartless killer and finally to the operator of an impersonal machine, a conveyor belt of hooks and shrink-wrapped joints.

The history of carnivorous habits also includes a complication of taste from plain meat (the roast beef connected in Fielding's mind with Englishness and the steak connected in Barthe's with Frenchness) to ragouts, fricassees and other *pièces de résistances* of *haute cuisine*. For some eaters and writers, the elaboration is a sign of sophistication; for others, it implies trickery and disguise. This is best expressed in the English myth that French sauces conceal rottenness or ineptitude. Rivalry in cuisine is in many instances a form of nationalism. More than any other food, meat has patriotic significance. Irish stew is as distinctive a flag as Scottish haggis or the American Thanksgiving turkey. What is fair/fare in one country is often foul—or fowl—in another, as in the case of Voltaire's poultry-eating Egyptian, who was warned by an Indian holy man, "Your dead aunt's soul may have passed into this chicken's body." From the most sacramental to the most sarcastic selection, meat is clearly linked to veneration.

The veneration of Jesus is associated quite specifically with the fish, which became a symbol of membership among Christ's early followers. The eating of fish at Lent is a ritual commemoration of Christ's fast in the wilderness. Since meat is associated with Gluttony, one of the Deadly Sins, abstinence from meat, symbolized by the eating of fish, serves as an act of penance. In the medieval allegory by Juan Ruiz, Lady Lent commands the Virtues, represented as troops of fish, to take arms against the Vices, meats, marshaled by Lord Flesh. The sprightly (and also *sprat*-ly) mock epic is worthy of animation. The forces, armored for the battle in pots and pans, do combat according to their scale, from the herculean tuna to the quick-thinking sardine, who uses its full strength to choke a chicken to death!

Despite the serious theme, the comedic tone prevails here and in a number of other selections in the chapter on fish. Much of the comedy hinges on size—big fish, little fish—and on strategies of capture and evasion. Even where there is not comedy, there is something of *la Comédie Humaine*, an affirmation of the life-force that derives from the sea. Always associated with fish there is a kind of magic, a transformational power. The fish is a form of "souls who would be saved," like the "fishified" ghost of Thomas Hood's ballad, or the astonishing maiden concealed in Samuel Lover's white trout. This folktale, with its fusion of pagan mermaid and Christian icon, emphasizes the sexual potency of the female body as a spiritual power. Indeed, despite its symbolic connection with Christ, the fish is a widespread emblem of fertility, the body sleek and shining that releases its eggs into the ocean's receptive waters. No wonder the widow, Dona Flor, consumed by desire and longing, adds pungent spices to her vatapá. Female or male, the giving of fish is of self, essential substance so potent that from seven loaves and a few fishes multitudes are fed.

Grain, like fish, is associated with magical transformations that sustain life. On manna the Jews were fed in the desert. And on other crusts of earth around the globe the staff of life was made to grow, as if by miracle, from tiny seeds—wheat in Siberia, maize in the Americas, rice in the sodden marshes of the East. People who had not much more had these grains, except in times of famine, to stave off hunger and death. Together rice and wheat alone account for over forty percent of all foods consumed on earth—even now. And, as always, the breaking of bread and the sharing of rice are binding pledges to endure hardship and bless the harvest together as a community.

It is to be expected that the literature of staples has a stronger poetry of necessity than of ease. This does not mean it is without savor and richness, as Joel Barlow's "Hasty Pudding" readily attests. Much of that richness refers to human labor, the toil of production that is the most fundamental measure of our human worth. Grain revives our closeness to the land, if we have drifted from it, and to origins. Its magic is of the earth, of the goddess Persephone, who goes underground into the land of death to emerge resurrected in the new year's crop.

Those excluded from the harvest serve as awesome condemnations of society—Oliver Twist deprived of a second bowl of gruel; Shanker, the peasant, cheated of his land by an exacting, usurious priest. It is easy to understand how Gulliver, disgusted by the greed of the Yahoos, chose to live, like his Houyhnhnm masters, on simple oats and milk. "Justice is the bread of the people," Brecht asserts. According to Sholem Asch (who kept the bread of his own people by writing in Yiddish), justice, like God, often moves in a mysterious way.

The origins of the mystery are in Paradise. When Adam and Eve were found guilty in Eden, they were condemned to sow seed in less-fertile soil while Satan crawled on his belly between the rows. All their roads became crooked from that moment on, and the gardens of earth became forever seeded with sin and death. Eden was very different from the outlying land. It was copious with fruits only, no vegetables; the first we hear of them is when Cain is described as a tiller of the ground, to distinguish him from his brother Abel, the shepherd. So, vegetables in the first instance are unhappily the produce of a murderer. Most vegetarians would recoil at such a mystery.

Indeed, the vegetable section is rather a peaceful chapter in our collection, although Marge Piercy's, "Attack of the Squash People" is an amusing caution against aggressive gardeners who forcibly dispose of their crops. For the most part, earth's plenitude is greeted by writers with cheerful celebration, the main theme of which is variety. Their subjects are soft and crunchy by turns, also green and yellow, beet and tomato red. Dadie's yams parade "new shades of color, each hour taking on different tints." There is a poetry of every crop, expressed in language that is extremely metaphoric and quite often anthropomorphic as well. The poets unearth phallic parsnips, cauliflowers "all brains and ears," artichokes "of delicate heart," lentils hard like stones.

From the soil emerges a microcosm of life, an emblem, as Blake would have it, of Innocence and Experience. The earth itself is composed of clods and pebbles, soft yielding matter and defiant rocks. Vegetables share in the nature of these contraries; some are smooth and undisturbedly round, others twisted, prickly, and rootbound. Both elicit an intensity of passion from the writers, who take them to be symbols of human experience. Even the potato, which Richard Wilbur calls "blind and common brown," is a galaxy of private associations, remembrances of "the cold dark kitchens" in hard times that span centuries of starving peoples. For Nora Ephron, it is not famine but love that is called up by free association: "Whenever I fall in love, I begin with potatoes," she writes, and by their culinary metamorphoses they mark the stages of true romance.

From the first sprouting to the final stage of decay, the vegetable world is a biological clock, a gardener's calendar of natural and emotional seasons by which we measure out our works and days. "To every thing there is a season, and a time to every purpose under the heaven. A time to be born, and a time to die, a time to plant, and a time to pluck that which is planted." The author of Ecclesiastes, who gave us these words, also spoke out against human vanity: "For that which befalleth the sons of men befalleth beasts; even one thing befalleth them: as the one dieth, so dieth the other; yea, they have all one breath so that a man hath no preeminence above a beast."

This was not always the case. Adam at first was given the preeminent role of naming the beasts. It was part of his responsibility as chief gardener in Eden. But this status was altered by the first bite of forbidden fruit. Thus, even before vegetables had crossed his mind or come to stand for work and time, fruit had taken on the meaning of pleasure and of sin.

Sin came first. Eve fell and in her fall discovered fear—of loss, of death, or of a more unmentionable horror that might "separate us, linkt in Love so dear." Against Adam's scruples she employed the fruit as a charm to make love last. In one sense the charm worked; they were not sent their separate ways, and their eyes were opened to new worlds of sensual experience. But their glances, now lascivious and charged with carnal desire, also express a contest of selfish wills that was not part of their lovemaking before. In the eating of a

plum, Helen Chasin discovers "the luxury of self-love,"
which comes close to expressing the bittersweet nature of passion after the Fall, made conscious of flesh, skin, and seed.

The poetic meaning of all fruit is essentially sexual.
"Every fruit has its secret," D. H. Lawrence insists, its provocative mystery that plays upon our compelling desire to
open and to know. The sexual overtones are unmistakable,
and even when we speak innocently of getting to the "core"
of truth, our language makes unconscious reference to forbidden fruit.

In this language, fruit is feminine, a ripening womb that
contains generations. As such, it also contains paradox. The
dimpled flesh that conceals a wrinkled pit may be interpreted
as beauty containing truth or as youth that yields to age and
death. The mystery of the fruit's fertility is like a secret
geode that explodes in glittering crystal such as the hidden
rubies erupting from Paul Valéry's golden pomegranates.

The metaphoric connection between fruit and gems is
common to poetry of many cultural traditions. Wang I, writing in the second century, compares the peerless lychee to
rare jewels (the specific ones he names are as lost to us now as
the empire of Ozymandias, though the flavor of the fruit remains). In these comparisons the fruit and the gems are both
symbols of incomparable beauty and eternity. They are
meant to evoke the same wonder as our cosmic origins.

In prying open the secret of a fruit, as May Sarton puts it,
we dare "to eat a universe." This is the human gesture of
paring Tomlinson's apple or squeezing Neruda's lemon, full
of "creation's original juices . . . the diminutive fire of a
planet." These images catapult the imagination back to the
very beginnings of universal life and to the loss of paradise
that came with time.

Sins against Eden continue to occur in our fallen world;
now they are environmental acts, the burning of forests, the
spread of urban culture that makes the fruit fall far from the
tree. We feel this in the nostalgic longing of the Jamaican-born
poet Claude McKay, who weeps to discover on a New York

fruit stall displaced bananas and alligator pears—symbols of "the old familiar ways"—symbols of the lost paradise, of home.

Desserts are sweetened with a similar, though perhaps less tragic, nostalgia. From Proust's madeleine to the dissolving cotton candy of a summer's fair, sugar takes us back again to home and to the ephemera of childhood. We (those of us who are not diabetic, hypoglycemic, or on a diet) identify sugar with nurturing and resolution. Sweets come at the end—after we finish all our dinner, after pain, after the bitter pill.

This, of course, refers principally to Western culture, and then only to the last few centuries.* Classical and medieval fare included sweetened meats and fish that would defy all but the most adventurous and determined modern eater. By the medieval period, sweet and savory began their separation into complementary dishes. In an elaborate medieval meal, sweet tarts, jellies, fruit compotes, blancmange, and rice pudding were introduced as cheerful distractions from the insurmountable landscape of roasts, ragouts, fish, and fowl— rather like pawns among the knights and rooks on a chess-board.

The Medicis, who excelled in eating, as they did in all games, liked to begin at an hors d'oeuvre table set with dishes we would call desserts—cakes, custards, marzipan, and nuts—in order to work up an appetite and create a perfect symmetry with the final sweet course of preserves and candied fruits that followed the dozen or so overwhelming dishes in between. To the Italians we owe the invention of pastry and sweetmeats, and through Italy in the seventeenth century two important Turkish contributions made their way toward western Europe—coffee and sherbet *(sorbet)*—which have had a lasting impact on the modern palate.

The mingling of sweet and savory belonged to the sensibility of Shakespeare's age, to the tables of the Montagues and Capulets, where the scene was set for tragedy gently

*See Jean-François Revel, *Culture and Cuisine,* translated by Helen R. Lane (New York: Da Capo Press, 1982).

sweetened by a comic touch. Although Western culinary and literary traditions have both agreed on simplification over the centuries that followed, the taste for comic relief has not been lost in either. We thrill to desserts as we do to the happy ending—Bob Cratchit at last serving the Christmas pudding.

Even the Medici heirs now keep their pudding for what the English call "afters." The quivering rum jelly served in *The Leopard* with the final toast "To the health of our Tancredi" is a theatrical battlement garrisoned with candied fruit and nuts, like the Savoy fortress on the second tier of Madame Bovary's wedding surprise. They address their recipients in a language of pure sentiment. This is the same lyricism discovered by the pastry chef in *Cyrano de Bergerac* biting into a cream-filled *pâte à chou* harp. Exquisite and delicious when it is beaten to the lightest froth, airy cake elevates us, like Proust's madeleine, above the mediocre and the mortal, if only for a moment. Thus, we remember Madame Bovary at the triumph of her wedding, and Maupassant's Madame Anserre at the triumph of her salon, where the chosen one cuts the cake.

This feeling of transcendence is generally associated with art, and in cookery with the art of the *pâtissier* and confectioner, who are still trained to make cream-filled swans and spun-sugar castles. No wonder Thackeray's Trimmins sees the serving girls in a candy shop as divine creatures made angelic by living amid sweet ephemera. Among transcendent women, history has recently witnessed the creation of a life-size chocolate Statue of Liberty. The symbolic confection—part of the grand birthday *fête*—might be interpreted as a democratic challenge to the politics of privilege and status often connected with the meaning of sweets.

The haves and the have-nots emerge quite clearly in the final chapter. The Austrian-born restaurateur Ludwig Bemelmans sets the tone in his affecting anecdote of the convent-school child who comes to identify peaches with sin *(pêche, péché)* as a mark of his own deprivation. Class consciousness aroused in childhood by association with sweets is also the subject of Robert Graves's short story "Treacle Tart," which deals with an aristocratic schoolboy who defies regulations by refusing to eat a common dessert he despises.

Common desserts can cause a whole lot of trouble, William Goyen reiterates in his broadly comedic story "Tapioca Surprise." We rarely ever order dessert "with a twist," but it is served up here and again in Charles Fritch's "Misfortune Cookie" as delectable parables of caution that when we come to our desserts, they might well be *just*! For if sweets are symbolic of transcendence, they are also symbols of mortality. Dessert is the course that heralds the approach of the end.

Yet who can resist the champagne truffle or the final probe among the dwindling milky squares in search of the caramel cream? How this collection ends, what lies at the bottom of the box, we leave to you to discover and enjoy to the very last morsel.

—JOAN DIGBY
Oyster Bay, New York 1986

Food

And I went unto the angel, and said unto him, Give me the little book. And he said unto me, Take it, and eat it up; and it shall make thy belly bitter, but it shall be in thy mouth sweet as honey.

—REVELATION

John Updike

(American, 1932–)

Food

It is always there,
Man's *real* best friend.
It never bites back;
it is already dead.
It never tells us we are lousy lovers
or asks us for an interview.
It simply begs, *Take me;*
it cries out, *I'm yours.*
Mush me all up, it says;
Whatever is you, is pure.

From the Mahabharata

The giving of food to the best of your ability, forgiveness,
sincerity, mildness, and honour to whom honour is due,—
these make a weapon which is not made of steel.

From the Upanishads

CHĀNDOGYA UPANISHAD

VI, vi (1–5)

"My dear boy, when curds are churned, the finest part rises upwards and turns into butter. So too, dear boy, when food is eaten, the finest part rises upwards and becomes mind. When water is drunk, dear boy, the finest part rises upwards and becomes breath. When light-and-heat is absorbed, dear boy, the finest part rises upwards and becomes the voice.

"For, my dear child, the mind is composed of food, breath is composed of water, while the voice is composed of light-and-heat."

"Good sir, will you kindly instruct me further?"

"I will, my dear child," said he.

TAITTIRĪYA UPANISHAD

2.

From food indeed do creatures come to birth,
Whatever [creatures] dwell on earth.
Then again by food they live,
And again pass into it in the end.
For food is the chief of beings,
Hence is it called the elixir of all.
All food most certainly do they attain
Who reverence Brahman as food.
For food is the chief of beings,
Hence is it called the elixir of all.
From food do beings come to birth,
When born, by food they grow.
Eaten, it eats [all] beings;
Hence it is known as food (an-na, "eatable").

*   *   *

(7–10)

Food should not be despised. That is the sacred rule
(vrata).

Breath is food indeed; the body eats food and is itself dependent (pratiṣṭhita) on breath, [while] breath [in turn] depends on the body. Food, then, depends on food.

He who knows that food depends [and is firmly based] on
food, has [himself] a firm basis; he becomes an owner of food,
an eater of food, rich in offspring, cattle and the vital force of
Brahman, rich in fame.

Food should not be set at naught. That is the sacred rule.

The waters are food indeed; light eats food and is itself
dependent on the waters, [while] the waters [in turn] depend
on light. Food, then, depends on food.

He who knows that food depends [and is firmly based] on
food, has [himself] a firm basis; he becomes an owner of food,
an eater of food, rich in offspring, cattle and the vital force of
Brahman, rich in fame.

Food should be multiplied. That is the sacred rule.

The earth is food indeed; space eats food and is itself dependent on the earth, [while] the earth [in turn] depends on
space. Food, then, depends on food.

He who knows that food depends [and is firmly based] on
food, has [himself] a firm basis; he becomes an owner of food,
an eater of food, rich in offspring, cattle and the vital force of
Brahman, rich in fame.

One should not refuse anyone in [one's own] home. That
is the sacred rule.

And so one should accumulate a large store of food by
every possible means. Of such a man people say: "He has
been fortunate in his food [supply]. If this food has been prepared in an exemplary way [for others, it is as if] it has been
prepared in an exemplary way for himself; if prepared in a
middling way [for others], then it is [as if] prepared in a mid-

dling way for himself; if prepared in a wretched way [for others], then it is [as if] prepared in a wretched way for himself, [that is,] for the man who knows this."

Ease of speech, acquisition and preservation of the in-breath and the out-breath, action *(karma)* with the hands, movement with the feet, excretion by the anus, these are signs in human beings [of the effects of food].

And now [the signs] in natural phenomena *(deva)*: satisfaction in rain, force in the lightning, splendour *(yaśas)* in cattle, light in the constellations, procreative power, immortality and bliss *(ānanda)* in the sexual organs, the All in space.

If one reveres it as the firm foundation *(pratiṣṭhā)*, then one becomes firmly founded [oneself]. If one reveres it as great, one becomes great (oneself). If one reveres it as mind, one becomes mindful (oneself). If one reveres it as homage, [all] desires will do him homage. If one reveres it as Brahman, one becomes possessed of Brahman [oneself]. If one reveres it as what dies around Brahman [while Brahman lives on], his enemies and rivals, ill-wishers and false friends will die round about him.

This one that is here in a man *(puruṣa)* and that one [up] there in the sun,—He is One.

The man who knows this, on departing from this world, draws near to the self that consists of food, draws near to the self that consists of breath, draws near to the self that consists of mind, draws near to the self that consists of understanding, draws near to the self that consists of bliss; then he roams [at will] throughout these worlds, eating what he will, changing his form at will: and, sitting down, he sings this song:

Bravo! Bravo! Bravo!
I am food! I am food! I am food!
I am an eater of food! I am an eater of food! I am an eater of
    food!
I am a maker of verses! I am a maker of verses! I am a maker
    of verses!
I am the first-born of the universal order *(ṛta)*,
Earlier than the gods, in the navel of immortality!

Whoso gives me away, he, verily, has succoured me!
I who am food eat the eater of food!
I have overcome the whole world!

He who knows this shines with a golden light.

—Translated by R. C. Zaehner

Leviticus, Chapters 1–2, 11

And the Lord called unto Moses, and spoke unto him out of the tent of meeting, saying: Speak unto the children of Israel, and say unto them:

When any man of you bringeth an offering unto the Lord, ye shall bring your offering of the cattle, even of the herd or of the flock.

If his offering be a burnt-offering of the herd, he shall offer it a male without blemish; he shall bring it to the door of the tent of meeting, that he may be accepted before the Lord. And he shall lay his hand upon the head of the burnt-offering; and it shall be accepted for him to make atonement for him. And he shall kill the bullock before the Lord; and Aaron's sons, the priests, shall present the blood, and dash the blood round about against the altar that is at the door of the tent of meeting. And he shall flay the burnt-offering, and cut it into its pieces. And the sons of Aaron the priest shall put fire upon the altar, and lay wood in order upon the fire. And Aaron's sons, the priests, shall lay the pieces, and the head, and the suet, in order upon the wood that is on the fire which is upon the altar; but its inwards and its legs shall he wash with water; and the priest shall make the whole smoke on the altar, for a burnt-offering, an offering made by fire, of a sweet savour unto the Lord.

And if his offering to the Lord be a burnt-offering of fowls, then he shall bring his offering of turtle-doves, or of young pigeons. And the priest shall bring it unto the altar, and pinch off its head, and make it smoke on the altar; and the blood thereof shall be drained out on the side of the altar. And he shall take away its crop with the feathers thereof, and cast it beside the altar on the east part, in the place of the ashes. And he shall rend it by the wings thereof, but shall not divide it asunder; and the priest shall make it smoke upon the altar, upon the wood that is upon the fire; it is a burnt-offering, an offering made by fire, of a sweet savour unto the Lord.

And when any one bringeth a meal-offering unto the Lord, his offering shall be of fine flour; and he shall pour oil upon it, and put frankincense thereon. And he shall bring it to Aaron's sons the priests; and he shall take thereout his handful of the fine flour thereof, and of the oil thereof, together with all the frankincense thereof; and the priest shall make the memorial-part thereof smoke upon the altar, an offering made by fire, of a sweet savour unto the Lord. But that which is left of the meal-offering shall be Aaron's and his sons'; it is a thing most holy of the offerings of the Lord made by fire.

And when thou bringest a meal-offering baked in the oven, it shall be unleavened cakes of fine flour mingled with oil, or unleavened wafers spread with oil.

And if thy offering be a meal-offering baked on a griddle, it shall be of fine flour unleavened, mingled with oil. Thou shalt break it in pieces, and pour oil thereon; it is a meal-offering. . . . And every meal-offering of thine shalt thou season with salt; neither shalt thou suffer the salt of the covenant of thy God to be lacking from thy meal-offering; with all thine offerings thou shalt offer salt.

*   *   *

. . . And the Lord spoke unto Moses and to Aaron, saying unto them, Speak unto the children of Israel, saying:

These are the living things which ye may eat among all the beasts that are on the earth. Whatsoever parteth the hoof, and is wholly cloven-footed, and cheweth the cud, among the beasts, that may ye eat. Nevertheless these shall ye not eat of them that only chew the cud, or of them that only part the hoof: the camel, because he cheweth the cud but parteth not the hoof, he is unclean unto you. And the rock-badger, because he cheweth the cud but parteth not the hoof, he is unclean unto you. And the hare, because she cheweth the cud but parteth not the hoof, she is unclean unto you. And the swine, because he parteth the hoof, and is cloven-footed, but cheweth not the cud, he is unclean unto you. Of their flesh ye shall not eat, and their carcasses ye shall not touch; they are unclean unto you.

These may ye eat of all that are in the waters: whatsoever hath fins and scales in the waters, in the seas, and in the rivers, them may ye eat. And all that have not fins and scales in the seas, and in the rivers, of all that swarm in the waters, and of all the living creatures that are in the waters, they are a detestable thing unto you, and they shall be a detestable thing unto you; ye shall not eat of their flesh, and their carcasses ye shall have in detestation. Whatsoever hath no fins nor scales in the waters, that is a detestable thing unto you.

And these ye shall have in detestation among the fowls; they shall not be eaten, they are a detestable thing: the great vulture, and the bearded vulture, and the ospray; and the kite, and the falcon after its kinds; every raven after its kinds; and the ostrich, and the night-hawk and the sea-mew and the hawk after its kinds; and the little owl, and the cormorant, and the great owl; and the horned owl, and the pelican, and the carrion-vulture; and the stork, and the heron after its kinds, and the hoopoe, and the bat.

All winged swarming things that go upon all fours are a detestable thing unto you. Yet these may ye eat of all winged swarming things that go upon all fours, which have jointed legs above their feet, wherewith to leap upon the earth; even these of them ye may eat: the locust after its kinds, and the bald locust after its kinds, and the cricket after its kinds, and the grasshopper after its kinds. But all winged swarming things, which have four feet, are a detestable thing unto you.

And by these ye shall become unclean; whosoever toucheth the carcass of them shall be unclean until the even. And
whosoever beareth aught of the carcass of them shall wash his
clothes, and be unclean until the even. Every beast which
parteth the hoof, but is not cloven-footed, nor cheweth the
cud, is unclean unto you; every one that toucheth them shall
be unclean. And whatsoever goeth upon its paws, among all
beasts that go on all fours, they are unclean unto you; whoso
toucheth their carcass shall be unclean until the even. And he
that beareth the carcass of them shall wash his clothes, and be
unclean until the even; they are unclean unto you.

And these are they which are unclean unto you among
the swarming things that swarm upon the earth: the weasel,
and the mouse, and the great lizard after its kinds, and the
gecko, and the land-crocodile, and the lizard, and the sand-
lizard, and the chameleon. . . . Ye shall not make yourselves
detestable with any swarming thing that swarmeth, neither
shall ye make yourselves unclean with them, that ye should
be defiled thereby. For I am the Lord your God; sanctify
yourselves therefore, and be ye holy; for I am holy; neither
shall ye defile yourselves with any manner of swarming thing
that moveth upon the earth. For I am the Lord that brought
you up out of the land of Egypt, to be your God; ye shall
therefore be holy, for I am holy.

This is the law of the beast, and of the fowl, and of every
living creature that moveth in the waters, and of every creature that swarmeth upon the earth; to make a difference between the unclean and the clean, and between the living thing
that may be eaten and the living thing that may not be eaten.

John Gilgun

(American, 1935–)

The Cosmos Has Teeth

"Queequeg no care what god made him shark," said the sav-
age, agonizingly lifting his hand up and down; "wedder Fejee
god or Nantucket God; but de god wat made shark must be
one dam Ingin."

—HERMAN MELVILLE, *Moby Dick*

We have come together as we do every Sunday at 7:30,
At Dooley's farm, to discuss the Bible,
Specifically, the Book of Hosea,
Prophecies uttered around 740 B.C.
Many meals ago.
"Like grapes in the desert, I found Israel;
Like the first fruits of the fig tree
In its prime," Kevin reads.
Mary brings in food—cheese, crackers,
apple slices, peanuts.
The reading stops as Kevin, in his Big Smith overalls,
leans forward. He eats.
We all lean forward. We eat.
Outside, in the barn, the chickens lean forward
And their blood red combs, the reddest combs in Missouri,
Dooley claims, lean forward with them, of course,
And the chickens eat.
And Dooley's collie leans forward. She eats.
Her pups lean forward, nuzzling. They eat.
In the yard, the elms lean forward.

They are eating the earth.
And the earth, which has been eating the sun all day,
Leans forward toward the moon.
It would devour it if it could.
"Your belly is your God," Dooley says,
Leaning forward in an attitude of reverence
Over the God called Wisconsin Cheddar.
It seems obvious to me that the Creator had large, perfect
     teeth,
That the Big Bang was in fact the Big Belch,
And that the galaxies are in reality plates of steaming roast
     beef.
But I don't say this.
For one thing, I won't risk offending someone's religious
sensibilities,
And for another, I have been taught that it is impolite
To express profound philosophical truths
With my mouth full.

Sir John Davies

(English, 1569–1626)

From *The Immortality of the Soul*

SECTION XVI

Taste

The body's life with meats and air is fed,
   Therefore the soul doth use the tasting pow'r
In veins, which through the tongue and palate spread,
   Distinguish ev'ry relish, sweet and sour.

This is the body's nurse; but since man's wit
  Found th' art of cook'ry to delight his sense,
More bodies are consum'd and kill'd with it,
  Than with the sword, famine, or pestilence.

William King

(English, 1663–1712)

From *The Art of Cookery; in imitation of Horace's Art of Poetry*

You, that from pliant paste would fabrics raise,
Expecting thence to gain immortal praise,
Your knuckles try, and let your sinews know
Their power to knead, and give the form to dough;
Choose your materials right, your seasoning fix,
And with your fruit resplendent sugar mix:
From thence of course the figure will arise,
And elegance adorn the surface of your pies.
    Beauty from order springs; the judging eye
Will tell you if one single plate's awry.
The cook must still regard the present time:
T'omit what's just in season is a crime.
Your infant pease t' asparagus prefer,
Which to the supper you may best defer.
    Be cautious how you change old bills of fare,
Such alterations should at least be rare;
Yet credit to the artist will accrue,
Who in known things still makes th' appearance new.

*   *   *

The things we eat by various juice control
The narrowness or largeness of our soul.
Onions will make ev'n heirs or widows weep;
The tender lettuce brings on softer sleep;
Eat beef or pye-crust if you'd serious be;
Your shell-fish raises Venus from the sea;
For Nature, that inclines to ill or good,
Still nourishes our passions by our food.
    Happy the man that has each fortune tried,
To whom she much has given, and much denied:
With abstinence all delicates he sees,
And can regale himself with toast and cheese:
    Your betters will despise you, if they see
Things that are far suppassing your degree;
Therefore beyond your substance never treat;
'Tis plenty, in small fortune, to be neat.
'Tis certain that a steward can't afford
An entertainment equal with his lord.
Old age is frugal; gay youth will abound
With heat, and see the flowing cup go round.
A widow has cold pye; nurse gives you cake;
From generous merchants ham or sturgeon take.
The farmer has brown bread as fresh as day,
And butter fragrant as the dew of May.
Cornwall squab-pye, and Devon white-pot brings;
And Leicester beans and bacon, food of kings!
    At Christmas-time, be careful of your fame,
See the old tenants' table be the same;
Then, if you would send up the brawner's head,*
Sweet rosemary and bays around it spread:
His foaming tusks let some large pippin grace,
Or midst those thundering spears an orange place;
Sauce like himself, offensive to its foes,
The roguish mustard, dangerous to the nose.

*Boar's head.

Sack and the well-spic'd hippocras the wine,
Wassail the bowl with ancient ribbands fine,
Porridge with plums, and turkeys with the chine.*
If you perhaps would try some dish unknown,
Which more peculiarly you'd make your own,
Like ancient sailors still regard the coast,
By venturing out too far you may be lost.
By roasting that which your forefathers boil'd,
And boiling what they roasted, much is spoil'd.
That cook to British palates is complete,
Whose savoury hand gives turns to common meat.

                              *   *   *

But now the cook must pass through all degrees,
And by his art discordant tempers please,
And minister to health and to disease.
        Far from the parlour have your kitchen plac'd,
Dainties may in their working be disgrac'd.
In private draw your poultry, clean your tripe,
And from your eels their slimy substance wipe.
Let cruel offices be done by night,
For they who like the thing abhor the sight.
        Next, let discretion moderate your cost,
And, when you treat, three courses be the most.
Let never fresh machines your pastry try,
Unless grandees or magistrates are by:
Then you may put a dwarf into a pie.
Or, if you'd fright an alderman and mayor,
Within a pasty lodge a living hare;
Then midst their gravest furs shall mirth arise,
And all the Guild pursue with joyful cries.
        Crowd not your table: let your number be
Not more than seven, and never less than three,
        'Tis the dessert that graces all the feast,
For an ill end disparages the rest:

---

* Backbone with adjoining meat.

A thousand things well done, and one forgot,
Defaces obligation by that blot.
Make your transparent sweet-meats truly nice,
With Indian sugar and Arabian spice:
And let your various creams encircled be
With swelling fruit just ravish'd from the tree.
Let plates and dishes be from China brought,
With lively paint and earth transparent wrought.
The feast now done, discourses are renew'd,
And witty arguments with mirth pursued.
The cheerful master, 'midst his jovial friends,
His glass "to their best wishes" recommends.
The grace-cup follows to his sovereign's health,
And to his country, "plenty, peace, and wealth."
Performing then the piety of *grace*,
Each man that pleases re-assumes his place;
While at his gate, from such abundant store,
He showers his god-like blessings on the poor.

*　*　*

Tables should be like pictures to the sight,
Some dishes cast in shade, some spread in light,
Some at a distance brighten, some near hand,
Where ease may all their *delicace* command:
Some should be mov'd when broken; others last
Through the whole treat, incentive to the taste.

Henry Fielding

(English, 1707–1754)

From *Tom Jones*, Book I, Chapter 1

CONTAINING AS MUCH OF THE BIRTH OF THE FOUNDLING AS IS NECESSARY OR PROPER TO ACQUAINT THE READER WITH IN THE BEGINNING OF THIS HISTORY

I: The Introduction to the Work, or Bill of Fare to the Feast

An author ought to consider himself, not as a gentleman who gives a private or eleemosynary treat, but rather as one who keeps a public ordinary,* at which all persons are welcome for their money. In the former case, it is well known that the entertainer provides what fare he pleases; and though this should be very indifferent, and utterly disagreeable to the taste of his company, they must not find any fault; nay, on the contrary, good-breeding forces them outwardly to approve and to commend whatever is set before them. Now the contrary of this happens to the master of an ordinary. Men who pay for what they eat will insist on gratifying their palates however nice and whimsical these may prove; and if everything is not agreeable to their taste, will challenge a right to censure, to abuse, and to d—n their dinner without control.

To prevent, therefore, giving offence to their customers by any such disappointment, it hath been usual with the honest and well-meaning host to provide a bill of fare which all persons may peruse at their first entrance into the house; and

---
*Eating house or inn.

having thence acquainted themselves with the entertainment which they may expect, may either stay and regale with what is provided for them, or may depart to some other ordinary better accommodated to their taste.

As we do not disdain to borrow wit or wisdom from any man who is capable of lending us either, we have condescended to take a hint from these honest victuallers, and shall prefix not only a general bill of fare to our whole entertainment, but shall likewise give the reader particular bills to every course which is to be served up in this and the ensuing volumes.

The provision, then, which we have here made is no other than *Human Nature*. Nor do I fear that my sensible reader, though most luxurious in his taste, will start, cavil, or be offended, because I have named but one article. The tortoise—as the alderman of Bristol, well learned in eating, knows by much experience—besides the delicious calipash and calipee, contains many different kinds of food; nor can the learned reader be ignorant, that in Human Nature, though here collected under one general name, is such prodigious variety, that a cook will have sooner gone through all the several species of animal and vegetable food in the world, than an author will be able to exhaust so extensive a subject.

An objection may perhaps be apprehended from the more delicate, that this dish is too common and vulgar; for what else is the subject of all the romances, novels, plays, and poems, with which the stalls abound? Many exquisite viands might be rejected by the epicure, if it was a sufficient cause for his contemning of them as common and vulgar, that something was to be found in the most paltry alleys under the same name. In reality, true nature is as difficult to be met with in authors as the Bayonne ham, or Bologna sausage, is to be found in the shops.

But the whole, to continue the same metaphor, consists in the cookery of the author; for, as Mr. Pope tells us—

> True wit is nature to advantage drest;
> What oft was thought, but ne'er so well exprest.

The same animal which hath the honour to have some part of his flesh eaten at the table of a duke, may perhaps be degraded in another part, and some of his limbs gibbeted, as it were, in the vilest stall in town. Where, then, lies the difference between the food of the nobleman and the porter, if both are at dinner on the same ox or calf, but in the seasoning, the dressing, the garnishing, and the setting forth? Hence the one provokes and incites the most languid appetite, and the other turns and palls that which is the sharpest and keenest.

In like manner, the excellence of the mental entertainment consists less in the subject than in the author's skill in well dressing it up. How pleased, therefore, will the reader be to find that we have, in the following work, adhered closely to one of the highest principles of the best cook which the present age, or perhaps that of Heliogabalus,* hath produced. This great man, as is well known to all lovers of polite eating, begins at first by setting plain things before his hungry guests, rising afterwards by degrees as their stomachs may be supposed to decrease, to the very quintessence of sauce and spices. In like manner, we shall represent Human Nature at first to the keen appetite of our reader in that more plain and simple manner in which it is found in the country, and shall hereafter hash and ragout it with all the high French and Italian seasoning of affectation and vice which courts and cities afford. By these means, we doubt not but our reader may be rendered desirous to read on for ever, as the great person just above-mentioned is supposed to have made some persons eat.

*Marcus Aurelius Antonius Heliogabalus, A.D. 204–222, emperor of Rome and a notorious glutton.

Anthelme Brillat-Savarin

(French, 1755–1826)

From *The Physiology of Taste*

APHORISMS OF THE PROFESSOR

*To Serve as Prolegomena to His Work, and as an
Eternal Basis to Science*

I

The world would have been merely nothing except for
life. All that lives, feeds.

II

Animals feed, man eats; wise men alone know how to eat.

III

The destiny of nations depends on the manner wherein
they take their food.

IV

Tell me what thou eatest, and I will tell thee what thou art.

V

The Creator, though condemning man to eat to live, in-
vites him to do so by appetite, and rewards him by enjoyment.

VI

Good living is an act of our judgment by which we grant a preference to those things which are agreeable to the taste above those that have not that quality.

VII

The joys of the table belong equally to all ages, conditions, countries, and times; they mix with all other pleasures, and remain the last to console us for their loss.

VIII

The table is the sole locality where no one during the first hour feels himself tired.

IX

The discovery of a new dish is more beneficial to humanity than the discovery of a new star.

Günter Grass

(German, 1927–)

From *The Flounder*

"Fellow workers!" she shouted at the cooks. "Your cooking lacks historical awareness. Because you refuse to recognize that for centuries the male cook was a product of the monasteries and courts, in other words of the ruling class. We female cooks, on the other hand, have always served the

people. In those days we were anonymous. We had no time
to work up fancy sauces. In our ranks there are no Prince
Pücklers,* no Brillat-Savarins, no famous chefs. In times of
famine we stretched flour with acorns. It was up to us to find
ways of varying the oatmeal porridge. It was a distant relative
of mine, the farm cook Amanda Woyke, and not Ole Fritz, as
you might think, who introduced the potato into Prussia.
While you men—all your ideas have been extravagances:
boned partridge Diplomat-style with truffled *farce*, accompanied by goose-liver dumplings. No, fellow workers! I'm for
pigs' feet with black bread and dill pickles. I'm for cheap pork
kidneys with mustard sauce. If you haven't got the historical
taste of millet and manna grits on your tongue, you have no
business coming here and shooting off your mouth about
grilling and sautéing!"

—Translated by Ralph Manheim

Thomas Hood

(English, 1799–1845)

From "A Recipe for Civilisation"

Surely, those sages err who teach
That man is known from brutes by speech,
Which hardly severs man from woman,
But not th' inhuman from the human,—
Or else might parrots claim affinity,

*Probably Prince Hermann von Pückler-Muskau (1785–1871), Austrian connois-
seur and travel writer, whose name is associated with an elegant ice-cream dessert,
Fürst-Pückler Eis.

And dogs be doctors by latinity,—
Not t' insist (as might be shown),
That beasts have gibberish of their own,
Which once was no dead tongue, though we
Since Æsop's days have lost the key;
Nor yet to hint dumb men,—and, still, not
Beasts that could gossip though they will not,
But play at dummy like the monkeys,
For fear mankind should make them flunkeys.
Neither can man be known by feature
Or form, because so like a creature,
That some grave men could never shape
Which is the aped and which the ape;
Nor by his gait, nor by his height,
Nor yet because he's black or white,
But *rational*,—for so we call
The only COOKING ANIMAL!
The only one who brings his bit
Of dinner to the pot or spit,
For where's the lion e'er was hasty
To put his venison in a pasty?
Ergo, by logic, we repute,
That he who cooks is not a brute,—
But Equus brutum est, which means,
If a horse had sense he'd boil his beans;
Nay, no one but a horse would forage
On naked oats instead of porridge,
Which proves, if brutes and Scotchmen vary,
The difference is culinary.
Further, as man is known by feeding
From brutes,—so men from men, in breeding,
Are still distinguish'd as they eat,
And raw in manner's raw in meat,—
Look at the polish'd nations, hight
The civilized—the most polite
Is that which bears the praise of nations
For dressing eggs two hundred fashions;

Whereas, at savage feeders look;—
The less refined the less they cook;
From Tartar grooms, that merely straddle
Across a steak and warm their saddle,
Down to the Abyssinian squaw,
That bolts her chops and collops raw,
And, like a wild beast, cares as little
To dress her person as her victual,—
For gowns, and gloves, and caps, and tippets,
Are beauty's sauces, spice, and sippets,
And not by shamble bodies put on,
But those who roast and boil their mutton;
So Eve and Adam wore no dresses
Because they lived on water-cresses,
And till they learn'd to cook their crudities,
Went blind as beetles to their nudities.

Nathaniel Tarn

(American, 1928–)

Food

for Lucien Biton

From a thousand years back
        he talks of the grass
which must be covered with salt
        from sea-spray
to make good lamb,
                        the elements
of food-philosophy—

talks of the time before
which is always better of course,
                the art of life
passage of life thru life
                and its digestion
coming together, blending of substances
                in their proper order

                taste of the world
being nothing else than taste of world
                you have under your nose
        odor of blood
        rare / medium / well
        odor of green beans
        odor of goat
the lining of the stomach
                jewelled with wine:
        civilization

and a geography:
        of the city
                of the appropriate places
in which to purchase the ingredients:
                (black-legged pullet of Nantes
blue-skinned, difficult to pluck,
small one of Bresse, made
to be worked on, to be simmered
in cream—well into Normandy
                par exemple)

a demography:
        But no cooking in OUR country
        no working of the food / only for paupers
        the complications of soup: & nothing, ever, boiled
        except for once a year to please the kids
        & the tail-end of peasant in our souls you see . . .

a memorial:
>in my country, when kids left the house,
>*O Loire de Ronsard et la chair attendrie,*
>the individual soup-dish left as well
>& here is my dish & here is my wife's
>—charming little objects, complex, covered,—
>>how shall they come again ever

the good times
>before she died?

>Brief burst of tears
into the wine, the dilution,
>memory of a hard time
the breast gone, the dug, and still needed
>even at seventy
(I cry daily he says everyday)

IN THE CAPITAL, he begins again,
>everything is dying,
you can't find the right ingredients
>any more
yes, well, I'm sure of *my* cheeses
but the strawberries are made by engineers,
I'm sure of the string beans
but the cutlets are doubtful
>(elsewhere than in *my* shop
>the very CUT
>the structure of the piece of meat
>*O Lévi-Strauss!**
>gone out of memory of living men . . .)
Then the flood
>the encyclopaedic memorandum
>>the perfection of wisdom
the brain, three times the speed of anyone I know

*French anthropologist, author of *The Raw and the Cooked.*

in the skull
    oiled by wine and cognac
        self-owned beyond all else:

    THE INTELLECT!

    and now go tell
    those who take food
    and freeze it to death
    before it ever
    reaches the right store
        the right street in the city
            the correct degree of the oven
                the erotic mind . . .

Hilaire Belloc

(English, 1870–1953)

On Food

Alas! What various tastes in food,
Divide the human brotherhood!

Birds in their little nests agree
With Chinamen, but not with me.
Colonials like their oysters hot,
Their omelettes heavy.—I do not.
The French are fond of slugs and frogs,
The Siamese eat puppy-dogs.
The nobles at the brilliant Court

Of Muscovy, consumed a sort
Of candles held and eaten thus
As though they were asparagus.
The Spaniard, I have heard it said,
Eats garlic, by itself, on bread:
Now just suppose a friend or dun
Dropped in to lunch at half-past one
And you were jovially to say,
"Here's bread and garlic! Peg away!"
I doubt if you would gain your end
Or soothe the dun, or please the friend.
In Italy the traveller notes
With great disgust the flesh of goats
Appearing on the table d'hôtes;
And even this the natives spoil
By frying it in rancid oil.
In Maryland they charge like sin
For nasty stuff called terrapin;
And when they ask you out to dine
At Washington, instead of wine,
They give you water from the spring
With lumps of ice for flavouring,
That sometimes kill and always freeze
The high plenipotentiaries.
In Massachusetts all the way
From Boston down to Buzzards Bay
They feed you till you want to die
On rhubarb pie and pumpkin pie,
And horrible huckleberry pie,
And when you summon strength to cry,
"What is there else that I can try?"
They stare at you in mild surprise
And serve you other kinds of pies.
And I with these mine eyes have seen
A dreadful stuff called Margarine
Consumed by men in Bethnal Green.
But I myself that here complain

Confess restriction quite in vain.
I feel my native courage fail
To see a Gascon eat a snail;
I dare not ask abroad for tea;
No cannibal can dine with me;
And all the world is torn and rent
By varying views on nutriment.
And yet upon the other hand,
De gustibus non disputand

—*Um.*

Guy Davenport

(American, 1927–)

The Anthropology of Table Manners from Geophagy Onward

A businessman now risen to a vice-presidency tells me that in his apprentice days he used to cross deepest Arkansas as a mere traveling salesman, and that there were certain farms at which men from his company put up overnight, meals being included in the deal. Once, on a new route, he appeared at breakfast after a refreshing sleep in a feather bed to face a hardy array of buttery eggs, biscuits, apple pie, coffee, and fatback.

This latter item was unfamiliar to him and from the looks of it he was damned if he would eat it. He knew his manners, however, and in passing over the fatback chatted with the lady of the house about how eating habits tend to be local,

individual, and a matter of how one has been raised. He
hoped she wouldn't take it wrong that he, unused to consuming fatback, left it untouched on his plate.

The genial Arkansas matron nodded to this politely,
agreeing that food is different all over the world.

She then excused herself, flapped her copious apron, and
retired from the kitchen. She returned with a double-barreled
shotgun which she trained on the traveling salesman, with
the grim remark, "Eat hit."

And eat hit he did.

Our traveler's offense was to reject what he had been
served, an insult in practically every code of table manners.
Snug in an igloo, the Eskimo scrapes gunk from between his
toes and politely offers it as garnish for your blubber. Among
the Penan of the upper Baram in Sarawak you eat your
friend's snot as a sign of your esteem. There are dinner parties in Africa where the butter for your stewed calabash will
be milked from your hostess's hair. And you dare not refuse.

Eating is always at least two activities: consuming food
and obeying a code of manners. And in the manners is concealed a program of taboos as rigid as Deuteronomy. We rational, advanced, and liberated Americans may not, as in the
Amazon, serve the bride's mother as the wedding feast; we
may not, as in Japan, burp our appreciation, or as in Arabia,
eat with our fingers. Every child has suffered initiation into
the mysteries of table manners: keep your elbows off the
table, ask for things to be passed rather than reach, don't cut
your bread with a knife, keep your mouth closed while chewing, don't talk with food in your mouth, and on and on, and
all of it witchcraft and another notch upward in the rise of the
middle class.

Our escapes from civilization are symptomatic: the first
rule we break is that of table manners. Liberty wears her
reddest cap; all is permitted. I remember a weekend away
from paratrooper barracks when we dined on eggs scrambled
in Jack Daniel's, potato chips and peanut brittle, while the
Sergeant Major, a family man of bankerish decorum in ordi-

nary times, sang falsetto "There Will be Peace in the Valley" stark naked except for cowboy boots and hat.

But to children, hardest pressed by gentility at the table, a little bending of the rules is Cockayne itself. One of my great culinary moments was being taken as a tot to my black nurse's house to eat clay. "What this child needs," she had muttered one day while we were out, "is a bait of clay." Everybody in South Carolina knew that blacks, for reasons unknown, fancied clay. Not until I came to read Toynbee's *A Study of History* years later did I learn that eating clay, or geophagy, is a prehistoric habit (it fills the stomach until you can bring down another aurochs) surviving only in West Africa and South Carolina. I even had the opportunity, when I met Toynbee at a scholarly do, to say that I had been in my day geophagus. He gave me a strange, British look.

The eating took place in a bedroom, for the galvanized bucket of clay was kept under the bed, for the cool. It was blue clay from a creek, the consistency of slightly gritty ice cream. It lay smooth and delicious-looking in its pail of clear water. You scooped it out and ate it from your hand. The taste was wholesome, mineral, and emphatic. I have since eaten many things in respectable restaurants with far more trepidation.

The technical names have yet to be invented for some of the submissions to courtly behavior laid upon me by table manners. At dinners cooked by brides in the early days of their apprenticeship I have forced down boiled potatoes as crunchy as water chestnuts, bleeding pork, gravy in which you could have pickled a kettle of herring, and a *purée* of raw chicken livers.

I have had reports of women with skimpy attention to labels who have made biscuits with plaster of Paris and chicken feed that had to be downed by timid husbands and polite guests; and my venturesome Aunt Mae once prepared a salad with witch hazel, and once, in a moment of abandoned creativity, served a banana pudding that had hard-boiled eggs hidden in it here and there.

Raphael Pumpelly tells in his memoirs of the West in the good old days about a two-gunned, bearded type who rolled into a Colorado hotel with a viand wrapped in a bandana. This he requested the cook to prepare, and seated at a table, nap-kined, wielding knife and fork with manners passably Eastern, consulting the salt and pepper shakers with a nicety, gave a fair imitation of a gentleman eating. And then, with a gleam in his eye and a great burp, he sang out at the end, "Thar, by God, I swore I'd eat that man's liver and I've done it!"

The meaning of this account for those of us who are great scientists is that this hero of the West chose to eat his en-emy's liver in the dining room of a hotel, with manners. Eat-ing as mere consumption went out thousands of years ago; we have forgotten what it is. Chaplin boning the nails from his stewed shoe in *The Gold Rush* is thus an incomparable moment of satire, epitomizing all that we have heard of Brit-ish gentlemen dressing for dinner in the Congo (like Livingstone, who made Stanley wait before the famous en-counter until he could dig his formal wear out of his kit).

Ruskin and Turner never dined together, though an invi-tation was once sent. Turner knew that his manners weren't up to those of the refined Ruskins, and said so, explaining graphically that, being toothless, he sucked his meat. Pro-priety being propriety, there was nothing to be done, and the great painter and his great explicator and defender were damned to dine apart.

Nor could Wittgenstein eat with his fellow dons at a Cam-bridge high table. One wishes that the reason were more straightforward than it is. Wittgenstein, for one thing, wore a leather jacket, with zipper, and dons at high table must wear academic gowns and a tie. For another, Wittgenstein thought it undemocratic to eat on a level fourteen inches higher than the students (at, does one say, low table?).

The code of Cambridge manners could not insist that the philosopher change his leather jacket for more formal gear, nor could it interfere with his conscience. At the same time it could in no wise permit him to dine at high table improperly dressed. The compromise was that the dons sat at high table, the students at their humbler tables, and Wittgenstein ate between, at a card table, separate but equal, and with English decorum unfractured.

Maxim's declined to serve a meal to Lyndon Baines Johnson, at the time President of the United States, on the grounds that its staff did not have a recipe for Texas barbecue, though what they meant was that they did not know how to serve it or how to criticize *Monsieur le Président's* manners in eating it.

The best display of manners on the part of a restaurant I have witnessed was at the Imperial Ramada Inn in Lexington, Kentucky, into the Middle Lawrence Welk Baroque dining room of which I once went with the photographer Ralph Eugene Meatyard (disguised as a businessman), the Trappist Thomas Merton (in mufti, dressed as a tobacco farmer with a tonsure), and an editor of *Fortune* who had wrecked his Hertz car coming from the airport and was covered in spattered blood from head to toe. Hollywood is used to such things (Linda Darnell having a milk shake with Frankenstein's monster between takes), and Rome and New York, but not Lexington, Kentucky. Our meal was served with no comment whatever from the waitresses, despite Merton's downing six martinis and the *Fortune* editor stanching his wounds with all the napkins.

Posterity is always grateful for notes on the table manners of the famous, if only because this information is wholly gratuitous and unenlightening. What does it tell us that Montaigne gulped his food? I have eaten with Allen Tate, whose sole gesture toward the meal was to stub out his cigarette in an otherwise untouched chef's salad, with Isak Dinesen when she toyed with but did not eat an oyster, with Louis Zukofsky who was dining on a half piece of toast, crumb by crumb.

Manners survive the test of adversity. Gertrude Ely, the Philadelphia hostess and patron of the arts, was once inspired on the spur of the moment to invite home Leopold Stokowski and his orchestra, together with a few friends. Hailing her butler, she said breezily that here were some people for pot luck.

"Madam," said the butler with considerable frost, "I was given to understand that you were dining alone this evening; please accept my resignation. Good night to you all."

"Quite," said Miss Ely, who then, with a graciousness unflummoxed and absolute, set every table in the house and distributed splinters of the one baked hen at her disposal, pinches of lettuce, and drops of mayonnaise, not quite with the success of the loaves and fishes of scripture, but at least a speck of something for everybody.

I, who live almost exclusively off fried baloney, Campbell's soup, and Snickers bars, would not find table manners of any particular interest if they had not, even in a life as reclusive and uneventful as mine, involved so many brushes with death. That great woman Katherine Gilbert, the philosopher and aesthetician, once insisted that I eat some Florentine butter that Benedetto Croce had given her. I had downed several portions of muffins smeared with this important butter before I gathered from her ongoing conversation that the butter had been given her months before, somewhere in the Tuscan hills in the month of August, and that it had crossed the Atlantic, by boat, packed with her books, Italian wild flowers, prosciutto, and other mementos of Italian culture.

Fever and double vision set in some hours later, together with a delirium in which I remembered Pico della Mirandola's last meal, served him by Lucrezia and Cesare Borgia. I have been *in extremis* in Crete (octopus and what tasted like shellacked rice, with P. Adams Sitney), in Yugoslavia (a most innocent-looking melon), Genoa (calf's brains), England (a blackish stew that seemed to have been cooked in kerosene), France (an *andouillette*, Maigret's favorite feed, the point being, as I now understand, that you have to be born in Auvergne to stomach it).

Are there no counter-manners to save one's life in these unfair martyrdoms to politeness? I have heard that Edward

Dahlberg had the manliness to refuse dishes at table, but he lost his friends thereby and became a misanthrope. Lord Byron once refused every course of a meal served him by Breakfast Rogers. Manet, who found Spanish food revolting but was determined to study the paintings in the Prado, spent two weeks in Madrid without eating anything at all. Some *Privatdozent* with time on his hands should compile a eulogy to those culinary stoics who, like Marc Antony, drank from yellow pools men did die to look upon. Not the starving and destitute who in wars and sieges have eaten the glue in bookbindings and corn that had passed through horses, wallpaper, bark, and animals in the zoo; but prisoners of civilization who have swallowed gristle on the twentieth attempt while keeping up a brave chitchat with the author of a novel about three generations of a passionately alive family.

Who has manners anymore, anyhow? Nobody, to be sure; everybody, if you have the scientific eye. Even the most oafish teen-ager who mainly eats from the refrigerator at home and at the Burger King in society will eventually find himself at a table where he is under the eye of his father-in-law to be, or his coach, and will make the effort to wolf his roll in two bites rather than one, and even to leave some for the next person when he is passed a bowl of potatoes. He will, naturally, still charge his whole plate with six glops of catsup, knock over his water, and eat his cake from the palm of his hand; but a wife, the country club, and the Rotarians will get him, and before he's twenty-five, he'll be eating fruit salad with extended pinky, tapping his lips with the napkin before sipping his sauterne Almaden, and talking woks and fondues with the boys at the office.

Archaeologists have recently decided that we can designate the beginning of civilization in the concept of sharing the same kill, in which simple idea we can see the inception of the family, the community, the state. Of disintegrating marriages we note that Jack and Jill are no longer sleeping together when the real break is when they are no longer eating together. The table is the last unassailed rite. No culture has worn the *bonnet rouge* there, always excepting the Germans, who have never had any manners at all, of any sort.

The tyranny of manners may therefore be the pressure placed on us of surviving in hostile territories. Eating is the most intimate and at the same time the most public of biological functions. Going from dinner table to dinner table is the equivalent of going from one culture to another, even within the same family. One of my grandmothers served butter and molasses with her biscuits, the other would have fainted to see molasses on any table. One gave you coffee with the meal, the other after. One cooked greens with fatback, the other with hamhock. One put ice cubes in your tea, the other ice from the ice house. My father used to complain that he hadn't had any cold iced tea since the invention of the refrigerator. He was right.

Could either of my grandmothers, the one with English country manners, the other with French, have eaten on an airplane? What would the Roi Soleil have done with that square foot of space? My family, always shy, did not venture into restaurants until well after the Second World War. Aunt Mae drank back the tiny juglet of milk which they used to give you for coffee, and commented to Uncle Buzzie that the portions of things in these cafés are certainly stingy.

I was raised to believe that eating other people's cooking was a major accomplishment, like learning a language or how to pilot a plane. I thought for the longest time that Greeks lived exclusively off garlic and dandelions, and that Jews were so picky about their food that they seldom ate at all. Uncles who had been to France with the AEF reported that the French existed on roast rat and snails. The Chinese, I learned from a book, begin their meals with dessert. Happy people!

Manners, like any set of signals, constitute a language. It is possible to learn to speak Italian; to eat Italian, never. In times of good breeding, the rebel against custom always has table manners to violate. Diogenes assumed the polish of Daniel Boone, while Plato ate with a correctness Emily Post could have studied with profit. Thoreau, Tolstoy, and Gandhi

all ate with pointed reservation, sparely, and in elemental
simplicity. Calvin dined but once a day, on plain fare, and
doubtless imagined the pope gorging himself on pheasant,
nightingale, and minced boar in macaroni.

Honest John Adams, eating in France for the first time,
found the food delicious if unidentifiable, but blushed at the
conversation (a lady asked him if his family had invented
sex); and Emerson once had to rap the water glass at his table
when two guests, Thoreau and Agassiz, introduced the mat-
ing of turtles into the talk. Much Greek philosophy, Dr.
Johnson's best one-liners, and the inauguration of the Christian religion happened at supper tables. Hitler's table-talk was
so boring that Eva Braun and a field marshal once fell asleep
in his face. He was in a snit for a month. Generalissimo
Franco fell asleep while Nixon was talking to him at dinner. It
may be that conversation over a shared haunch of emu is
indeed the beginning of civilization.

To eat in silence, like the Egyptians, seems peculiarly
dreadful, and stiff. Sir Walter Scott ate with a bagpipe dron-
ing in his ear and all his animals around him, and yards of
babbling guests. Only the truly mad eat alone, like Howard
Hughes and Stalin.

Eccentricity in table manners—one has heard of rich uncles who wear oilcloth aviator caps at table—lingers in the
memory longer than other foibles. My spine tingles anew
whenever I remember going into a Toddle House to find all
the tables and the counter set; not only set, but served. One
seat only was occupied, and that by a very eccentric man,
easily a millionaire. He was, the waitress explained some days
later, giving a dinner party there, but no one came. He waited
and waited. He had done it several times before; no one had
ever come. It was the waitress's opinion that he always forgot
to send the invitations; it was mine that his guests could not
bring themselves to believe them.

And there was the professor at Oxford who liked to sit
under his tea table, hidden by the tablecloth, and hand up
cups of tea and slices of cake from beneath. He carried on a

lively conversation all the while, and most of his friends were used to this. There was always the occasional student who came to tea unaware, sat goggling the whole time, and tended to break into cold sweats and fits of stammering.

I was telling about this professor one summer evening in South Carolina, to amuse my audience with English manners. A remote cousin, a girl in her teens, who hailed from the country and had rarely considered the ways of foreigners, listened to my anecdote in grave horror, went home and had a fit.

"It took us half the night to quiet down Effie Mae," we were told sometime later. "She screamed for hours that all she could see was that buggerman under that table, with just his arm risin' up with a cup and saucer. She says she never expects to get over it."

Marvin Cohen

(American, 1931–)

A Daring Experiment in Defiance of Gravity

To test the law of gravity (which I'm always suspicious of, being a lawbreaker), I applied it in reverse to a commonplace act: eating. Here's how. I lay down on a table on my stomach, it was a high table; then I wriggled forward till my whole torso was dangling down, head bottom, to the very floor. Flat *on* the table stretched out was that half of me from feet to groin, at the horizontal. From groin to head (bottommost) made a vertical from the edge of the table. That was my experimental position.

On the floor along with my head was a bowl of food, and a plate of more food. I fed morsels of food with my dangling hands into my dangling mouth. Here was gravity's real test.

Most people eat upright so that the food that enters their mouth can travel down through the neck into the stomach, where digestion and assimilation wait to put their processes to work.

But I was defying the law of gravity by daring the food to travel upward from mouth to neck to stomach. My whole body would know the result, soon.

The result was that the food had nowhere to go, it never moved from settling in the mouth: it *refused* to travel upward—a refusal prompted and instructed by the orthodox dictates of the law of gravity.

My mouth was *bursting* with an accumulation of food that never left the mouth. That wouldn't do, it was intolerable. Gravity would *have* to be obeyed. Starvation, with its deficiency of nourishment, would follow upon the breaking of the law.

So I righted myself upright from my right-angles position, and became a normal man. I was left with a lot of swallowing to do, and I did it. Regularity welcomed me back to my commonplace.

I placed the unfinished bowl and plate on the table, which I sat on, with this time my *feet* dangling down, instead of my head. I easily ate the remainder of both bowl and plate. It all went down well. My body and gravity had come to an understanding.

Ben Jonson

(English, 1572–1637)

Inviting a Friend to Supper

To night, grave sir, both my poore house, and I
Doe equally desire your companie:
Not that we thinke us worthy such a ghest,
But that your worth will dignifie our feast,
With those that come; whose grace may make that seeme
Something, which, else, could hope for no esteeme.
It is the faire acceptance, Sir, creates
The entertaynment perfect: not the cates.
Yet shall you have, to rectifie your palate,
An olive, capers, or some better sallade
Ushring the mutton; with a short-leg'd hen,
If we can get her, full of egs, and then,
Limons, and wine for sauce: to these, a coney
Is not to be despair'd of, for our money;
And, though fowle, now, be scarce, yet there are clarkes,
The skie not falling, thinke we may have larkes.
Ile tell you more, and lye, so you will come:
Of partrich, pheasant, wood-cock, of which some
May yet be there; and godwit, if we can:
Knat, raile, and ruffe too. How so ere, my man
Shall reade a piece of Virgil, Tacitus,
Livie, or of some better booke to us,
Of which wee'll speake our minds, amidst our meate;
And Ile professe no verses to repeate:
To this, if ought appeare, which I not know of,

That will the pastrie, not my paper, show of.
Digestive cheese, and fruit there sure will bee;
But that, which most doth take my Muse, and mee,
Is a pure cup of rich Canary-wine,
Which is the Mermaids, now, but shall be mine:
Of which had Horace, or Anacreon tasted,
Their lives, as doe their lines, till now had lasted.
Tabacco, Nectar, or the Thespian spring,
Are all but Luthers beere, to this I sing.
Of this we will sup free, but moderately,
And we will have no Pooly', or Parrot by;
Nor shall our cups make any guiltie men:
But, at our parting, we will be, as when
We innocently met. No simple word,
That shall be utter'd at our mirthfull boord,
Shall make us sad next morning: or affright
The libertie, that wee'll enjoy to night.

Elaine Osio

(American, 1942–)

I'm Easy

(*Jennie and Sid, Elaine and Tony, are seated at a table.*)

SID (*Looking at his watch*): We should probably start thinking about dinner. Where'd you like to go?

ELAINE: I don't know. I'm easy.

JEN: Me, too.

TONY: No problem.

SID: Whatever.

(A brief pause.)

JEN: I'm easy, but I could live without Mexican. They serve everything in those tortillas. I don't trust food that comes prewrapped.

TONY: I'm easy, too, but no Indian. If I wanted to swallow fire, I'd have joined Circus Vargas.

SID: Whatever everyone wants, but a steakhouse is out. There's so much cholesterol in a porterhouse, you might as well let the cow kick you straight in the heart.

ELAINE: You know I'm not fussy, but let's forget seafood, okay? Living with the cholesterol paranoid that's all we have. I've eaten so many swimming things that Jaws is making me his pen pal.

SID: Okay. Then how about Chinese?

JEN: MSG.

TONY: Korean?

ELAINE: Hot peppers.

JEN: Thai?

SID: They changed the name of their country; God knows what they'll do to their food.

TONY: Greek?

ELAINE: Lamb? You'll run to save whales, but you'll eat little lambs?

TONY: Cajun?

JEN: Too in.

SID: Pasta?

JEN: That's out.

SID: Mideast?

ELAINE: And support Arafat?

TONY: Deli?

SID: Cholesterol with coleslaw.

TONY: French?

JEN: They eat what I spray with Raid.

ELAINE: English?

SID: Doesn't exist.

JEN: Polynesian?

TONY: Too sweet.

JEN: Russian?

SID: Too sour.

ELAINE: Scandinavian?

TONY: Too salty.

SID: Organic?

JEN: Too green.

SID: South American?

ELAINE: God knows what they lace it with.

TONY: Sushi?

SID: If God had intended us to eat things raw, he wouldn't have given us charcoal briquettes.

(There is a long pause.)

TONY: Why don't we just stay here and drink?

ELAINE: Fine. I'm easy.

JEN: Me, too.

TONY: No problem.

SID: Whatever. *(Brief pause.)* But we need some nourishment.

ELAINE: How about some pretzels?

SID: Salt.

JEN: Nuts?

TONY: Oil.

ELAINE: Hot hors d'oeuvres?

SID: Cholesterol.

JEN: Popcorn . . . ?

Marge Piercy

(American, 1936–)

What's That Smell in the Kitchen?

All over America women are burning dinners.
It's lambchops in Peoria; it's haddock
in Providence; it's steak in Chicago;
tofu delight in Big Sur; red
rice and beans in Dallas.
All over America women are burning
food they're supposed to bring with calico
smile on platters glittering like wax.

Anger sputters in her brainpan, confined
but spewing out missiles of hot fat.
Carbonized despair presses like a clinker
from a barbecue against the back of her eyes.
If she wants to grill anything, it's
her husband spitted over a slow fire.
If she wants to serve him anything
it's a dead rat with a bomb in its belly
ticking like the heart of an insomniac.
Her life is cooked and digested,
nothing but leftovers in Tupperware.
Look, she says, once I was roast duck
on your platter with parsley but now I am Spam.
Burning dinner is not incompetence but war.

Starters and Soups

Clarence Day

(American, 1874–1935)

The Egg

Oh who that ever lived and loved
Can look upon an egg unmoved?
The egg it is the source of all.
'Tis everyone's ancestral hall.
The bravest chief that ever fought,
The lowest thief that e'er was caught,
The harlot's lip, the maiden's leg,
They each and all came from an egg.

The rocks that once by ocean's surge
Beheld the first of eggs emerge—
Obscure, defenseless, small and cold—
They little knew what eggs could hold.
The gifts the reverent Magi gave,
Pandora's box, Aladdin's cave,
Wars, loves, and kingdoms, heaven and hell
All lay within that tiny shell.

Oh, join me gentlemen, I beg,
In honoring our friend, the egg.

Tomás de Iriarte y Oropesa

(Spanish, 1750–1791)

The Eggs

Beyond the sunny Philippines
An island lies, whose name I do not know;
But that's of little consequence, if so
You understand that there they had no hens;
Till, by a happy chance, a traveler,
After a while, carried some poultry there.
Fast they increased as any one could wish;
Until fresh eggs became the common dish.
But all the natives ate them boiled—they say—
Because the stranger taught no other way.
At last the experiment by one was tried—
Sagacious man!—of having his eggs fried.
And, O! what boundless honors, for his pains,
His fruitful and inventive fancy gains!
Another, now, to have them baked devised—
Most happy thought!—and still another, spiced.
Who ever thought eggs were so delicate!
Next, some one gave his friends an omelette:
"Ah!" all exclaimed, "what an ingenious feat!"
But scarce a year went by, an artiste shouts,
"I have it now—ye're all a pack of louts!—
With nice tomatoes all my eggs are stewed.
And the whole island thought the mode so good,
That they would so have cooked them to this day,
But that a stranger, wandering out that way,

Another dish the gaping natives taught,
And showed them eggs cooked *à la Huguenot*.

Successive cooks thus proved their skill diverse;
But how shall I be able to rehearse
All of the new, delicious condiments
That luxury, from time to time invents?
Soft, hard, and dropped: and now with sugar sweet,
And now boiled up with milk, the eggs they eat;
In sherbet, in preserves; at last they tickle
Their palates fanciful with eggs in pickle.
All had their day—the last was still the best.
But a grave senior thus, one day, addressed
The epicures: "Boast, ninnies, if you will,
These countless prodigies of gastric skill—
But blessings on the man *who brought the hens!*"

Beyond the sunny Philippines
Our crowd of modern authors need not go
New-fangled modes of cooking eggs to show.

—Translated by G. H. Devereux

Erica Jong

(American, 1942–)

Cheese

Spelunking through the blue caves of the Roquefort
under a golden Gouda moon,
we thought of the breasts of the Virgin

which are also blue. Very few
cheeses are,
and Mary does not belong
in a poem on cheese.
                    Or does She?
We are mice in this wedge
of cheesy poetry, we are about
to be trapped.
                    How peaceful (on the other hand) to be a
                                        cheese!
To merge with the Great Eater
as every mystic (or mouse)
has some time wished.

Goudas whirl in the sky,
shedding their rinds like prayer wheels;
already the Brie is soft with ecstasy.
Look for that Bel Paese which saints speak of
where the holes dream the Swiss cheese,
where plate and knife exist only in visions,
where milk and cream
are merely memories,
like history,
like Mary.

Marvin Cohen

(1931–)

The Shrimp Served at the Party Were Gigantic! Here's an Embarrassing Yarn About It

At the swanky party, the hors d'oeuvres included enormously large shrimp, brought around by uniformed maids on a tray that also had an enormous bowl of catsup sauce in which guests, via toothpick, may dip their gigantic shrimp. But the shrimp was so large that instead of the toothpicks sticking enough out of them to afford handy grips, they got buried and lost within the vasty depths of such broad-bellied shrimp. So it became necessary for each guest manually— with the fingers unassisted—to dip the groaningly heavy shrimp into the silver catsup sauce bowl. But the heaviness of the shrimp, when reinforced by the weightiness of the catsup sauce, and coupled with the slimy slipperiness of the glossy sheen of the outside surfaces of the shrimp, caused people's holds to be dragged down; and heavily laden hands would be involuntarily sunk into the bottomless depths of the bowl; and fingertip holds on the shrimp would be loosened; the shrimp would plunge lost to the bottom; and whole hands up to wrists and including soaking sleeves, cuffs, rings, bracelets, and wristwatches, would be thickly laden with the red, syrupy catsup sauce. Oh, the official social embarrassment! O unsightly redness! O laundry bills to come! O wristwatches clogged! O mess, unholy!

Yet, the party was an unqualified success. The drinks were generously intoxicating. People gushed in a stagger of confusion. The shrimp episode was forgotten, or brought down to reduced proportions, or portions, that had caught the guests red-handed. A party is a party. That's the right perspective to take. It's a social event. Every guest, and the grand hostess herself, is merely only mortal. That shrinks the shrimp, to shrimplike size.

Jonathan Swift

(Anglo-Irish, 1667–1745)

Herrings

Be not sparing,
Leave off swearing.
Buy my herring
Fresh from Malahide*
Better never was try'd.
Come, eat them with pure fresh butter and mustard,
Their bellies are soft, and as white as a custard.
Come, sixpence a dozen to get me some bread,
Or, like my own herrings, I soon shall be dead.

*A fishing port northeast of Dublin.

Oysters

Charming oysters I cry:
My masters, come buy.
So plump and so fresh,
So sweet is their flesh,
No Colchester* oyster
Is sweeter and moister:
Your stomach they settle,
And rouse up your mettle;
They'll make you a dad
Of a lass or a lad;
And madam your wife
They'll please to the life;
Be she barren, be she old,
Be she slut, or be she scold,
Eat my oysters, and lie near her,
She'll be fruitful, never fear her.

Lewis Carroll

(English, 1832–1898)

The Walrus and the Carpenter

'The sun was shining on the sea,
Shining with all his might:
He did his very best to make

*Essex, the first Roman colony in Britain, famous for its oysters.

The billows smooth and bright—
And this was odd, because it was
The middle of the night.

The moon was shining sulkily,
    Because she thought the sun
Had got no business to be there
    After the day was done—
"It's very rude of him," she said,
    "To come and spoil the fun!"

The sea was wet as wet could be,
    The sands were dry as dry.
You could not see a cloud, because
    No cloud was in the sky:
No birds were flying overhead—
    There were no birds to fly.

The Walrus and the Carpenter
    Were walking close at hand;
They wept like anything to see
    Such quantities of sand:
"If this were only cleared away,"
    They said, "it *would* be grand!"

"If seven maids with seven mops
    Swept it for half a year,
Do you suppose," the Walrus said,
    "That they could get it clear?"
"I doubt it," said the Carpenter,
    And shed a bitter tear.

"O Oysters, come and walk with us!"
    The Walrus did beseech.
"A pleasant walk, a pleasant talk,
    Along the briny beach:
We cannot do with more than four,
    To give a hand to each."

The eldest Oyster looked at him.
  But never a word he said:
The eldest Oyster winked his eye,
  And shook his heavy head—
Meaning to say he did not choose
  To leave the oyster-bed.

But four young oysters hurried up,
  All eager for the treat:
Their coats were brushed, their faces washed,
  Their shoes were clean and neat—
And this was odd, because, you know,
  They hadn't any feet.

Four other Oysters followed them,
  And yet another four;
And thick and fast they came at last,
  And more, and more, and more—
All hopping through the frothy waves,
  And scrambling to the shore.

The Walrus and the Carpenter
  Walked on a mile or so,
And then they rested on a rock
  Conveniently low:
And all the little Oysters stood
  And waited in a row.

"The time has come," the Walrus said,
  "To talk of many things:
Of shoes—and ships—and sealing-wax—
  Of cabbages—and kings—
And why the sea is boiling hot—
  And whether pigs have wings."

"But wait a bit," the Oysters cried,
  "Before we have our chat;
For some of us are out of breath,

And all of us are fat!"
"No hurry!" said the Carpenter.
    They thanked him much for that.

"A loaf of bread," the Walrus said,
    "Is what we chiefly need:
Pepper and vinegar besides
    Are very good indeed—
Now if you're ready, Oysters dear,
    We can begin to feed."

"But not on us!" the Oysters cried,
    Turning a little blue,
"After such kindness, that would be
    A dismal thing to do!"
"The night is fine," the Walrus said.
    "Do you admire the view?

"It was so kind of you to come!
    And you are very nice!"
The Carpenter said nothing but
    "Cut us another slice:
I wish you were not quite so deaf—
    I've had to ask you twice!"

"It seems a shame," the Walrus said,
    "To play them such a trick
After we've brought them out so far,
    And made them trot so quick!"
The Carpenter said nothing but
    "The butter's spread too thick!"

"I weep for you," the Walrus said,
    "I deeply sympathize."
With sobs and tears he sorted out
    Those of the largest size,
Holding his pocket-handkerchief
    Before his streaming eyes.

"O Oysters," said the Carpenter.
"You've had a pleasant run!
Shall we be trotting home again?"
But answer came there none—
And this was scarcely odd, because
They'd eaten every one.'

Anton Pavlovich Chekhov

(Russian, 1860–1904)

Oysters

It needs no straining of memory to recall the rainy twilight
autumn evening when I stood with my father in a crowded
Moscow street and felt overtaken by a strange illness. I suffered no pain, but my legs gave way, my head hung helplessly on one side, and words stuck in my throat. I felt that I
should soon fall on the pavement and swoon away.

Had I been taken to hospital at the moment, the doctor
would have written above my bed the word: *Fames*
[Hunger]—a complaint not usually dealt with in medical
text-books.

Beside me on the pavement stood my father in a thread-
bare summer overcoat and a check cap from which projected a
piece of white cotton-wool. On his feet were big, clumsy
goloshes. The vain man, fearing that people might see that
the big goloshes covered neither boots nor stockings, had
cased his legs in old gaiters.

This poor, unintelligent man, whom I loved all the more,
the more tattered and dirty became his once smart summer
overcoat, had come to the capital five months before to seek

work as a clerk. Five months he had tramped the city, seeking employment; only to-day for the first time he had screwed up his courage to beg for alms in the street.

In front of us rose a big, three-storied house with a blue signboard "Restaurant." My head hung helplessly back, and on one side. Involuntarily I looked upward at the bright restaurant windows. Behind them glimmered human figures. To the right were an orchestrion, two oleographs,* and hanging lamps. While trying to pierce the obscurity my eyes fell on a white patch. The patch was motionless; its rectangular contour stood out sharply against the universal background of dark brown. When I strained my eyes I could see that the patch was a notice on the wall, and it was plain that something was printed upon it, but what that something was I could not see.

I must have kept my eyes on the notice at least half an hour. Its whiteness beckoned to me, and, it seemed, almost hypnotised my brain. I tried to read it, and my attempts were fruitless.

But at last the strange sickness entered into its rights.

The roar of the traffic rose to thunder; in the smell of the street I could distinguish a thousand smells; and the restaurant lights and street lamps seemed to flash like lightning. And I began to make out things that I could not make out before.

"Oysters," I read on the notice.

A strange word. I had lived in the world already eight years and three months, and had never heard this word. What did it mean? Was it the proprietor's surname? No, for signboards with innkeepers' names hang outside the doors, and not on the walls inside.

"Father, what are oysters?" I asked hoarsely, trying to turn my face towards his.

My father did not hear me. He was looking at the flow of the crowd, and following every passer-by with his eyes. From

---

*An accordion and two pictures printed in oil colors to imitate paintings.

his face I judged that he dearly longed to speak to the passers, but the fatal, leaden words hung on his trembling lips, and would not tear themselves off. One passer-by he even stopped and touched on the sleeve, but when the man turned to him my father stammered, "I beg your pardon," and fell back in confusion.

"Papa, what does 'oysters' mean?" I repeated.

"It is a kind of animal. . . . It lives in the sea. . . ."

And in a wink I visualised this mysterious animal. Something between a fish and a crab, it must be, I concluded; and as it came from the sea, of course it made up into delightful dishes, hot *bouillabaisse* with fragrant peppercorns and bay leaves, or sour *solianka* [fish stew] with gristle, crab-sauce, or cold with horseradish. . . . I vividly pictured to myself how this fish is brought from the market, cleaned, and thrust quickly into a pot . . . quickly, quickly, because every one is hungry . . . frightfully hungry. From the restaurant kitchen came the smell of boiled fish and crab soup.

This smell began to tickle my palate and nostrils; I felt it permeating my whole body. The restaurant, my father, the white notice, my sleeve, all exhaled it so strongly that I began to chew. I chewed and swallowed as if my mouth were really full of the strange animal that lives in the sea. . . .

The pleasure was too much for my strength, and to prevent myself falling I caught my father's cuff, and leaned against his wet summer overcoat. My father shuddered. He was cold. . . .

"Father, can you eat oysters on fast days?" I asked.

"You eat them alive . . ." he answered. "They are in shells . . . like tortoises, only in double shells."

The seductive smell suddenly ceased to tickle my nostrils, and the illusion faded. Now I understood!

"How horrible!" I exclaimed. "How hideous!"

So that was the meaning of oysters! However, hideous as they were, my imagination could paint them. I imagined an animal like a frog. The frog sat in the shell, looked out with big, bright eyes, and moved its disgusting jaws. What on

earth could be more horrible to a boy who had lived in the
world just eight years and three months? Frenchmen, they
said, ate frogs. But children—never! And I saw this fish
being carried from market in its shell, with claws, bright eyes,
and shiny tail. . . . The children all hide themselves, and the
cook, blinking squeamishly, takes the animal by the claws,
puts it on a dish, and carries it to the dining-room. The
grown-ups take it, and eat . . . eat it alive, eyes, teeth, claws.
And it hisses, and tries to bite their lips.

I frowned disgustedly. But why did my teeth begin to
chew? An animal, disgusting, detestable, frightful, but still I
ate it, ate it greedily, fearing to notice its taste and smell. I ate
in imagination, and my nerves seemed braced, and my heart
beat stronger. . . . One animal was finished, already I saw the
bright eyes of a second, a third . . . I ate these also. At last I ate
the table-napkin, the plate, my father's goloshes, the white
notice. . . . I ate everything before me, because I felt that only
eating would cure my complaint. The oysters glared frightfully from their bright eyes, they made me sick, I shuddered at
the thought of them, but I wanted to eat. To eat!

"Give me some oysters! Give me some oysters." The cry
burst from my lips, and I stretched out my hands.

"Give me a kopeck, gentlemen!" I heard suddenly my
father's dulled, choked voice. "I am ashamed to ask, but, my
God, I can bear it no longer!"

"Give me some oysters!" I cried, seizing my father's coat-
tails.

"And so you eat oysters! Such a little whipper-snapper!"
I heard a voice beside me.

Before me stood two men in silk hats, and looked at me
with a laugh.

"Do you mean to say that this little manikin eats oysters?
Really! This is too delightful! How does he eat them?"

I remember a strong hand dragged me into the glaring
restaurant. In a minute a crowd had gathered, and looked at
me with curiosity and amusement. I sat at a table, and ate
something slippy, damp, and mouldy. I ate greedily, not

chewing, not daring to look, not even knowing what I ate. It seemed to me that if I opened my eyes, I should see at once the bright eyes, the claws, the sharp teeth.

I began to chew something hard. There was a crunching sound.

"Good heavens, he's eating the shells!" laughed the crowd. "Donkey, who ever heard of eating oyster shells?"

After this, I remember only my terrible thirst. I lay on my bed, kept awake by repletion, and by a strange taste in my hot mouth. My father walked up and down the room and gesticulated.

"I have caught cold, I think!" he said. "I feel something queer in my head. . . . As if there is something inside it. . . . But perhaps it is only . . . because I had no food to-day. I have been strange altogether . . . stupid. I saw those gentlemen paying ten roubles for oysters; why didn't I go and ask them for something . . . in loan? I am sure they would have given it."

Towards morning I fell asleep, and dreamed of a frog sitting in a shell and twitching its eyes. At midday thirst awoke me. I sought my father; he still walked up and down the room and gesticulated.

—Translated by R.E.C. Long

John Digby

(English, 1938–)

Thirteen Ways of Cooking a Snail

1
Among the flowering rhododendrons
The only moving thing
The horn of a snail.

2
I was in three minds
How to cook my snail,
To roast, fry, or grill it.

3
It waved its little silvery horn at me.
Ugh. It left a trail of slime on my flowers.

4
A snail and a chef
Are one.
A snail and a chef and a pot
Are one.

5
I did not know how to cook my snail,
The beauty of roasting it
Or the beauty of frying it,
The rich garlic juices running down
My freshly shaven cheeks.

6
The hot water filled my French pot.
I picked up my snail,
I am lucky I am not a snail,
It hissed in the water,
It bubbled and bobbed.
It was cooked.

7
O thin men of Connecticut
Why imagine raw snails?
Do you not see how philosophical
It is to cook them?
It's a sign of French culture.

8
I know the noble roasts
And other juicy meats:
But I also know
The sweet aromas of cooked snails
Served on delicate plates.

9
When I ate my snail
I looked down at my plate
And found it empty!

10
At the sight of a snail
Moving among my rhododendrons
I howl with delight
And my stomach turns somersaults.

11
My snail rode over all
My flowering bushes
Inside his little shell.

He looked at me with fear,
He mistook the shadow of my hand
For the eye of a blackbird.

12
The water is boiling.
My snail is cooking.

13
It was evening. I was still hungry.
It was snowing
Or about to snow.
I was grubbing about in my bushes,
Looking for another snail to cook.

Elio Vittorini

(Italian, 1908–1966)

From *In Sicily*

12

The herring was tidied up, put on a plate, sprinkled with oil, and I and my mother sat at table—in the kitchen, I mean. My mother sat with her glistening chestnut hair and the red blanket about her shoulders, turned away from the sun that was streaming through the window. The table stood against the wall, and I and my mother sat facing each other; on the floor was the brazier and on top of it the plate of herring almost overflowing with oil. My mother flung me a napkin, handed me a little plate and fork, and drew a half-eaten loaf out of a drawer.

"You don't mind my not laying a tablecloth?" she asked.

"Oh, no," said I.

And she said: "I can't every day . . . I'm old now."

But Sundays and feast days apart, I remembered, we had always eaten without a tablecloth in my childhood, and my mother always said she couldn't wash every day. I began to eat the herring and bread, and asked: "Why is there no soup?"

My mother looked at me and said: "How was I to know you were going to turn up?"

I looked at her and said: "But I'm thinking of you. Don't you make soup for yourself?"

"Thinking of me?" said my mother. "I've hardly ever eaten soup in my life . . . I used to make soup for you boys and your father, but as for me, this is what I used to eat: herrings in winter, roast capsicums in summer, lots of oil and lots of bread. . . ."

"Always that?" I asked.

"Always. Why not?" said my mother. "Of course with olives, too, and sometimes pork sausages, when we had pork. . . ."

"Did we keep a pig?" I asked.

"Yes, don't you remember?" said my mother. "We used to keep a pig some years, in those line-keepers' huts. We'd feed it on prickly pears, and then we'd kill it. . . ."

I recalled what the countryside was like around a line-keeper's hut along the railway track, with the prickly pear trees and the shrieks of the pig. We were happy then, I thought to myself, in those line-keepers' huts. All the countryside to roam about in, without having to cultivate it, no peasants, only an occasional sheep, and the men from the sulfur mines returning from work at night, when we were already in bed. We were happy then, I thought to myself. . . .

"Didn't we keep chickens, too?" I asked.

"Yes, we kept a few, of course," said my mother.

"We used to make mustard," said I.

"We used to make all sorts of things . . ." said my mother. "Tomatoes dried in the sun. . . . Prickly pear cakes."

"We were happy," I said, and thought it too, recalling the tomatoes drying in the sun during the summer afternoons, without a living soul about throughout the vast countryside. It was dry, sulfur-colored country, and I remembered the great humming in the summertime and the engulfing silences, and once more I thought how happy we were. "We were happy," I said. "We used to have wire netting."

"Those places," said my mother, "were infested with malaria."

"The terrible malaria," said I.

"Terrible, certainly!"

"And the crickets . . ." said I. Beyond the wire netting that covered the windows and the veranda, I remembered, was a wood teeming with crickets in the sunlit solitude. "I thought it was the crickets, the malaria!" I added.

My mother laughed. "Perhaps that's why you caught so many?"

"Did I catch them?" I said. "But it's their chirping I thought was called 'malaria,' not they. Did I catch them?"

"You certainly did!" said my mother. "Twenty or thirty at a time!"

I said: "I think I caught them because I thought they were grasshoppers. What did I do with them?"

My mother laughed again. "I have an idea you ate them."

"Ate them?" I exclaimed.

"Yes," said my mother. "You and your brothers."

She laughed. I was put out. "Could it be possible?" I asked.

"Perhaps you were hungry," said my mother.

"We were hungry?"

"Perhaps."

"But we were so contented at home," I protested.

My mother looked at me. "Yes," she said. "Your father got his money at the end of every month, and then for ten days we were all right, we were the envy of every peasant and sulphur miner. . . . But after those ten days we were like them. They'd be eating snails."

"Snails?" said I.

"Yes, and wild endives," said my mother.

"Did they only have snails to eat?" I asked.

"Yes, as a rule, the poor people only had snails to eat," said my mother. "And we were poor the last twenty days of the month."

"Would we be eating snails for twenty days?"

"Snails . . . and wild endives," said my mother.

I pondered over it, smiled, and then said: "Anyhow, I expect they were pretty good."

"Excellent. . . . You could cook them in so many different ways," said my mother.

"How, in so many ways?"

"Just boiled, for instance. Or with garlic and tomatoes. Or dipped in flour and fried."

"What an idea!" I said. "Shell and all?"

"Of course!" said my mother. "We ate them by sucking them out of their shells. Don't you remember?"

"I remember, I remember . . ." I said. "You got the flavor in sucking the shells."

"We used to spend hours sucking . . ." said my mother.

—Translated by Wilfrid David

Giuseppi Tomasi di Lampedusa

(Italian, 1896–1957)

From *The Leopard*

The Prince was too experienced to offer Sicilian guests, in a town of the interior, a dinner beginning with soup, and he infringed the rules of *haute cuisine* all the more readily as he disliked it himself. But rumors of the barbaric foreign usage of serving insipid liquid as first course had reached the major citizens of Donnafugata too insistently for them not to quiver with a slight residue of alarm at the start of a solemn dinner like this. So when three lackeys in green, gold, and powder entered, each holding a great silver dish containing a towering mound of macaroni, only four of the twenty at table avoided showing their pleased surprise: the Prince and Princess from foreknowledge, Angelica from affectation, and Concetta from lack of appetite. All the others, including Tancredi, showed their relief in varying ways, from the fluty and ecstatic grunts of the notary to the sharp squeak of Francesco Paolo. But a threatening circular stare from the host soon stifled these improper demonstrations.

Good manners apart, though, the appearance of those monumental dishes of macaroni was worthy of the quivers of admiration they evoked. The burnished gold of the crusts, the fragrance of sugar and cinnamon they exuded, were but preludes to the delights released from the interior when the knife broke the crust; first came a smoke laden with aromas, then chicken livers, hard-boiled eggs, sliced ham, chicken, and truffles in masses of piping-hot, glistening macaroni, to which the meat juice gave an exquisite hue of suède.

The beginning of the meal, as happens in the provinces, was quiet. The Archpriest made the sign of the Cross, and plunged in head-first without a word. The organist absorbed the succulent dish with closed eyes; he was grateful to the Creator that his ability to shoot hare and woodcock could bring him ecstatic pleasures like this, and the thought came to him that he and Teresina could exist for a month on the cost of one of these dishes. Angelica, the lovely Angelica, forgot her Tuscan affectations and part of her good manners and devoured her food with the appetite of her seventeen years and the vigor derived from grasping her fork halfway up the handle. Tancredi, in an attempt to link gallantry and greed, tried to imagine himself tasting, in the aromatic forkfuls, the kisses of his neighbor Angelica, but he realized at once that the experiment was disgusting and suspended it, with a mental reservation about reviving this fantasy with the pudding. The Prince, although rapt in the contemplation of Angelica sitting opposite him, was the only one able to note that the *demi-glace* was too rich, and made a mental note to tell the cook so next day; the others ate without thinking of anything, and without realizing that the food seemed so delicious because a whiff of sensuality had wafted into the house.

—Translated by Archibald Colquhoun

Cheryl Pallant

(American, 1960–)

The Pizza

A regular-size pizza lounged in its tin tray on a counter. Since the pie's removal from the oven, the cheese had bulged up, away from the crust, and then burst apart, oil trickling around its side like lava.

The lunch hour had ended. Customers no longer rushed in. A few sauntered in, prepared to linger at booths in the corner furthest from the counter.

The pizza cooled to room temperature.

A man stepped up to the counter and ordered a soda. Then a boy entered the restaurant requesting lemonade. Not a slice was wanted from the pie.

Close to the oregano, the pizza observed the items beside him. A ladle sat near a pot of simmering tomato sauce. A mound of dough waited to be kneaded and shaped. Grated cheese crowded in a bowl unprotected and helpless to a squadron of invading flies.

The pizza, too long idle, began to wonder, "Why am I here?"

Another customer, this time a woman, ordered a calzone and a large soda. Her fingers tapped the Lucite until receiving her food.

The pizza, conscious of its contents, wondered further, "Is it cheese that makes me what I am or is it my sauce? If I had no sauce, would I still be pizza? Should I accept hot peppers or rely on my standard ingredients for flavor?"

As the pizza pondered these questions, he got colder. His

surface gleam faded. Oil soaked through the hardening cheese into the crust. Spices lodged tightly into crevices once moist. He looked at the stack of uniform napkins, complacent even when blown by the wind bursting in through the opening and closing of the door.

Another woman came in. He watched as a pepperoni pizza was placed into a flimsy cardboard box, the lid closed upon it shutting out light and obstructing all views. Shortly after, a mushroom-and-onion pie met with a similar fate.

Seeing these occurrences did not please him. Instead, dread and anxiety filled him up to his circumference, more turmoil than is healthy for any pizza. Without legs, he could neither flee nor jog, nor take Valium, for that matter. He wanted to talk with another pie. "Surely, an Extra Large would be able to answer my questions and ease my fears," he thought. But before the opportunity arose, a woman and her son came in and ordered.

"That one will be fine. Warmed up," she said, pointing. He was shoved back into the oven.

Once in its warmth, he stretched out, relaxing, enjoying the torrid atmosphere. His cheese softened. The oil and sauce began to bubble again. Spices regained mobility, moving millimeters from their former dwellings.

So comfortable was he in his metal womb, he decided he preferred this site to that of the counter. Stay he did. What was left besides his charred remains had to be scraped off the oven shelf with a knife.

Louis Simpson

(American, 1923–)

Caviare at the Funeral

*This was the village where the deacon ate all the caviare at
the funeral.*

CHEKHOV, "IN THE RAVINE"

On the way back from the cemetery
they discussed the funeral arrangements
and the sermon, "such a comfort to the family."

They crowded into the parlor.
It was hot, and voices were beginning to rise.
The deacon found himself beside a plate
heaped with caviare. He helped himself
to a spoonful. Then another.

Suddenly he became aware
that everyone's eyes were upon him,
ruin staring him in the face.
He turned pale. Then tried to carry it off—
one may as well be hanged for a sheep
as a lamb, et cetera.

Meeting their eyes with a stern expression
he took another spoonful,
and another. He finished the plate.

Next morning he was seen at the station
buying a ticket for Kurovskoye,*
a village much like ours, only smaller.

Ivan Turgenev

(Russian, 1818–1883)

Cabbage-Soup

The son of a widowed peasant-woman died—a young fellow
aged twenty, the best labourer in the village.

The lady-proprietor of that village, on learning of the
peasant-woman's affliction, went to call upon her on the very
day of the funeral.

She found her at home.

Standing in the middle of her cottage, in front of the
table, she was ladling out [meatless] cabbage-soup from the
bottom of a smoke-begrimed pot, in a leisurely way, with her
right hand (her left hung limply by her side), and swallowing
spoonful after spoonful.

The woman's face had grown sunken and dark; her eyes
were red and swollen . . . . but she carried herself indepen-
dently and uprightly, as in church.

"O Lord!" thought the lady; "she can eat at such a moment . . . . but what coarse feelings they have!"

And then the lady-mistress recalled how, when she had
lost her own little daughter, aged nine months, a few years
before, she had refused, out of grief, to hire a very beautiful

* A town about fifty miles southeast of Moscow.

villa in the vicinity of Petersburg, and had passed the entire summer in town!—But the peasant-woman continued to sip her cabbage-soup.

At last the lady could endure it no longer—"Tatyána!" said she. . . . "Good gracious!—I am amazed! Is it possible that thou didst not love thy son? How is it that thy appetite has not disappeared?—How canst thou eat that cabbage-soup?"

"My Vásya is dead," replied the woman softly, and tears of suffering again began to stream down her sunken cheeks,—"and, of course, my own end has come also: my head has been taken away from me while I am still alive. But the cabbage-soup must not go to waste; for it is salted."

The lady-mistress merely shrugged her shoulders and went away. She got salt cheaply.

—Translated by Isabel F. Hapgood

Wang Chien

(Chinese, eighth century A.D.)

A Bride

On the third day, taking my place to cook,
Washing my hands to make the bridal soup,
I decide that not my mother-in-law
But my husband's young sister shall have the first taste.

—Translated by Witter Bynner

Alphonse Daudet

(French, 1840–1897)

Cheese-Soup

It was a little chamber in the fifth story, one of those attics where the rain beats straight upon the skylight; at the present hour, when night has come, such rooms seem to be lost, roof and all, in gloom and storm. And yet this chamber is pleasant, cozy, and upon entering it, one feels an indescribable sensation of comfort, which the gusts of wind without, and the torrents of rain dripping from the gutters only increase. You might almost believe yourself to be in a warm nest at the top of some tall tree. For the moment the nest is empty; its occupant is not there, but you feel sure he will soon return. Everything within seems to await his coming. Upon a smothered fire a little soup-kettle is boiling tranquilly with a murmur of satisfaction. It keeps rather a late vigil, and although accustomed to that, judging by its sides browned through frequent contact with the flames, it becomes impatient now and then, and its cover rises, stirred by the steam; then a warm, appetizing whiff ascends, and permeates the whole chamber.

Oh! the delicious odor of cheese-soup!

At times too the fire clears itself of cinders, which come tumbling down through the logs, while a tiny flame darts out its tongue from beneath, lighting the lower part of the room, as if making a tour of inspection to be assured that everything is in order. Ah, yes, order itself reigns there, and the master may return any moment he chooses. The Algerian curtains are drawn in front of the windows, and draped comfortably about the bed. There is the big arm-chair spreading itself at full length in front of the fire; the table stands in one corner, the cloth spread, dishes set for one solitary diner, the lamp ready to be lighted, and beside the plate is a book, the companion of that lonely repast. And not only is the soup-pot worn through frequent contact with the fire, but the flowers upon each dish are also faded, through repeated washings, and the book is worn at the edges. Age and long use have softened the appearance of all these well-worn things. One feels too that this lodger is obliged to return very late each evening, and that it pleases him, when he enters, to find that little supper simmering away, perfuming and warming the chamber to which he returns.

Oh! the savory odor of cheese-soup!

Observing the neatness of that bachelor apartment, I imagine that its tenant must be some employé, one of those beings whose devotion to the minutest details compels them to regulate all their living with the same punctuality with which they dispose of things official, and as methodically as they label each portfolio.

The extreme lateness of his return would seem to indicate that he is one of the night force in the postal or telegraph service. I fancy I see him, seated behind a grating, his half-sleeves of lustrine drawn up to the elbow, his velvet calotte upon his head, while he sorts and stamps letters, winds the blue banderoles of despatches, preparing for Paris asleep, or awake in pursuit of pleasure, the affairs of to-morrow.

But no—this is not his business. For, as it penetrates each recess of the chamber, the tiny flame of the hearth gleams upon large photographs hanging on the walls. Emerging from the shadow, framed in gold and magnificently draped, may be seen the Emperor Augustus, Mahomet, Félix, Roman knight, Armenian governor, crowns, helmets, tiaras, and turbans, while beneath all these different head-dresses there is always the same head, erect and solemn, the head of the master of the place, the fortunate and lordly personage for whom that fragrant soup simmers away, bubbling gently upon the warm cinders.

Oh! the delicious odor of that cheese-soup!

Ah, no! this is no employé of the post-office. This is some emperor, a world-master, one of those providential beings who on those evenings when the repertoire is given causes the roof of the Odéon to tremble, one who has merely to command, "Seize him, guards!" and the guards obey on the instant. At this present moment he is there in his palace, across the water. With buskined heels, his chlamys* upon his shoulder, he wanders beneath porticos, declaiming with portentous frown, wearing a wearied air through all his tragic tirades. And indeed it is dispiriting to play to empty benches. And the auditorium of the Odéon seems so vast, so cold, on the evening of a tragedy! Suddenly the emperor, half-frozen beneath his purple, feels a warm thrill run through his body. His eye kindles, his nostrils dilate. For he is dreaming of the warm room to which he will return, the table set, the lamp ready to light, all his little belongings arranged in order, with that homely attention to trifles shown by the actor who in private life makes amends for stage extravagances and irregularities. He fancies himself uncovering that soup-pot and filling his flowered plate.

Oh, the savory odor of that cheese-soup!

From that moment he is no longer the same man. The stiff folds of his chlamys, the marble stairs, the coldness of the porticos, these things vex him no longer. He becomes animated, hastens the play, precipitates the action. For what if his fire should go out! As the evening advances, the vision grows nearer, and puts new life into him. Miraculous! the Odéon itself seems to be thawing. The old habitués of the orchestra, aroused from their torpor, find this Marancourt truly magnificent, especially in the last scenes. And indeed, as the *dénoûement* approaches the decisive hour when the traitors are to be poniarded, and princesses to be married, the face of the emperor wears a beatific expression, an air of singular serenity. His stomach hollow with hunger after so many emotions and tirades, he fancies he is at home again, seated at his little table, and his glance wanders from Cinna to

---

*A short mantle worn in ancient Greece, here in acting a classical role.

Maximus with a kindly and tender smile, as though already
he saw those charming white threads which lengthen on the
end of a spoon when cheese-soup, after simmering properly,
is just cooked, and poured out piping-hot.

Bouillabaisse

We were sailing along the Sardinian coast towards La
Madeleine Island. It was an early morning excursion. Our
oarsmen pulled slowly; leaning over the side of our boat, I
looked at the sea, transparent as some spring, the sunlight
diving to the very bottom. Medusæ and starfish sprawled
among the seaweed. Big lobsters lay motionless, their long
claws buried in the fine sand. All these might be seen at a
depth of from eighteen to twenty feet, in a sort of aquarium,
clear as crystal. At the bow of the boat a fisherman, standing
with a long cleft reed in his hand, made a sign to the
oarsmen, "Softly, softly!" and suddenly between the points
of his fork he held a beautiful lobster suspended, spreading
out its claws with a terrified movement, though still asleep.
At my side another sailor let his line drop upon the water's
surface in the wake of the boat, and brought in a haul of
marvellous little fishes, which as they died were colored with
a thousand bright and changing tints—a death-agony beheld
through a prism.

The fishing ended, we landed among the high, gray rocks.
A fire was quickly kindled, which burned with a pale light in
the bright sunshine; bread cut in big slices was placed upon
small plates of red earthen-ware, and we sat about the soup-
kettle, plates held out and nostrils distended. Was it because
of the landscape, the sunshine, or that horizon of sea and
sky? I have never eaten anything that tasted better than that
lobster bouillabaisse. And afterwards that delightful siesta
upon the sand,—a slumber filled with the lulling murmurs of
the sea, while the wavelets, as if covered with innumerable
shining scales, flash and glitter, even although the eyes are
closed.

Herman Melville

(American, 1819–1891)

From *Moby Dick*

CHAPTER XV
Chowder

It was quite late in the evening when the little Moss came snugly to anchor, and Queequeg and I went ashore; so we could attend to no business that day, at least none but a supper and a bed. The landlord of the Spouter-Inn had recommended us to his cousin Hosea Hussey of the Try Pots, whom he asserted to be the proprietor of one of the best kept hotels in all Nantucket, and moreover he had assured us that cousin Hosea, as he called him, was famous for his chowders. In short, he plainly hinted that we could not possibly do better than try pot-luck at the Try Pots. But the directions he had given us about keeping a yellow warehouse on our starboard hand till we opened a white church to the larboard, and then keeping that on the larboard hand till we made a corner three points to the starboard, and that done, then ask the first man we met where the place was: these crooked directions of his very much puzzled us at first, especially as, at the outset, Queequeg insisted that the yellow warehouse—our first point of departure—must be left on the larboard hand, whereas I had understood Peter Coffin to say it was on the starboard. However, by dint of beating about a little in the dark, and now and then knocking up a peaceable inhabitant to inquire the way, we at last came to something which there was no mistaking.

Two enormous wooden pots painted black, and suspended by asses' ears, swung from the cross-trees of an old top-mast, planted in front of an old doorway. The horns of the cross-trees were sawed off on the other side, so that this old top-mast looked not a little like a gallows. Perhaps I was over sensitive to such impressions at the time, but I could not help staring at this gallows with a vague misgiving. A sort of crick was in my neck as I gazed up to the two remaining horns; yes, *two* of them, one for Queequeg, and one for me. It's ominous, thinks I. A Coffin my Innkeeper upon landing in my first whaling port; tombstones staring at me in the whale-men's chapel; and here a gallows! and a pair of prodigious black pots too! Are these last throwing out oblique hints touching Tophet?

I was called from these reflections by the sight of a freck-led woman with yellow hair and a yellow gown, standing in the porch of the inn, under a dull red lamp swinging there, that looked much like an injured eye, and carrying on a brisk scolding with a man in a purple woollen shirt.

"Get along with ye," said she to the man, "or I'll be combing ye!"

"Come on, Queequeg," said I, "all right. There's Mrs. Hussey."

And so it turned out; Mr. Hosea Hussey being from home, but leaving Mrs. Hussey entirely competent to attend to all his affairs. Upon making known our desires for a supper and a bed, Mrs. Hussey, postponing further scolding for the present, ushered us into a little room, and seating us at a table spread with the relics of a recently concluded repast, turned round to us and said—"Clam or Cod?"

"What's that about Cods, ma'am?" said I, with much po-liteness.

"Clam or Cod?" she repeated.

"A clam for supper? a cold clam; is *that* what you mean, Mrs. Hussey?" says I; "but that's a rather cold and clammy reception in the winter time, ain't it, Mrs. Hussey?"

But being in a great hurry to resume scolding the man in the purple shirt, who was waiting for it in the entry, and seeming to hear nothing but the word "clam," Mrs. Hussey hurried towards an open door leading to the kitchen, and bawling out "clam for two," disappeared.

"Queequeg," said I, "do you think that we can make out a supper for us both on one clam?"

However, a warm savory steam from the kitchen served to belie the apparently cheerless prospect before us. But when that smoking chowder came in, the mystery was delightfully explained. Oh, sweet friends! hearken to me. It was made of small juicy clams, scarcely bigger than hazel nuts, mixed with pounded ship biscuit, and salted pork cut up into little flakes; the whole enriched with butter, and plentifully seasoned with pepper and salt. Our appetites being sharpened by the frosty voyage, and in particular, Queequeg seeing his favorite fishing food before him, and the chowder being surpassingly excellent, we despatched it with great expedition: when leaning back a moment and bethinking me of Mrs. Hussey's clam and cod announcement, I thought I would try a little experiment. Stepping to the kitchen door, I uttered the word "cod" with great emphasis, and resumed my seat. In a few moments the savory steam came forth again, but with a different flavor, and in good time a fine cod-chowder was placed before us.

We resumed business; and while plying our spoons in the bowl, thinks I to myself, I wonder now if this here has any effect on the head? What's that stultifying saying about chowder-headed people? "But look, Queequeg, ain't that a live eel in your bowl? Where's your harpoon?"

Fishiest of all fishy places was the Try Pots, which well deserved its name; for the pots there were always boiling chowders. Chowder for breakfast, and chowder for dinner, and chowder for supper, till you began to look for fish-bones coming through your clothes. The area before the house was paved with clamshells. Mrs. Hussey wore a polished necklace of codfish vertebra; and Hosea Hussey had his account books bound in superior old shark-skin. There was a fishy flavor to the milk, too, which I could not at all account for, till one morning happening to take a stroll along the beach among some fishermen's boats, I saw Hosea's brindled cow feeding on fish remnants, and marching along the sand with each foot in a cod's decapitated head, looking very slip-shod, I assure ye.

Supper concluded, we received a lamp, and directions from Mrs. Hussey concerning the nearest way to bed; but, as Queequeg was about to precede me up the stairs, the lady reached forth her arm, and demanded his harpoon; she allowed no harpoon in her chambers. "Why not?" said I; "every true whaleman sleeps with his harpoon—but why not?" "Because it's dangerous," says she. "Ever since young Stiggs coming from that unfort'nt v'y'ge of his, when he was gone four years and a half, with only three barrels of *ile*, was found dead in my first floor back, with his harpoon in his side; ever since then I allow no boarders to take sich dangerous weepons in their rooms at night. So, Mr. Queequeg" (for she had learned his name), "I will just take this here iron, and keep it for you till morning. But the chowder; clam or cod to-morrow for breakfast, men?"

"Both," says I; "and let's have a couple of smoked herring by way of variety."

Charles Simic

(American, 1938–)

Soup

Take a little backache
Melt some snow from the year of your birth
Add the lump in your throat
And the fear of the dark

Instead of oil a pinch of chill
But let it be northern
Instead of parsley
Swear loudly into it

Then stir it with the night
Until its fins and penny-nails
Are blended.

*   *   *

On what shall we cook it?

On something like a cough
On the morning star about to fade
On the whisker of a black cat
On an oval locket with a picture of Jesus
On the nipple of a sleeping woman

Let's cook it until we raise
That heavy autumnal cloud
From its bowels
Even if it takes a hundred years.

*   *   *

What do you think it will taste like?

Like barbed wire, like burglar's tools
Like a word you'd rather forget
The way the book tastes to the goat
Who is chewing and spitting its pages
Also like the ear of a girl you are about to undress
Also like the rim of a smile

In the twentieth century
We arouse the sun's curiosity
By whistling for the soup
To be served.

*   *   *

What in the world shall we eat it with?

With a shoe that left last night
To baptize itself in the rain
With two eyes that quarrel in the same head
With a finger which is the divining-rod
Searching for its clearest streak
With a hat in which the thoughts
Grind each other into black pepper

We'll dive into the soup
With a grain of salt between our teeth
And won't come up
Until we learn its song.

*   *   *

And this is what we'll have on the side:

Lust on halfshells with lemon wedges
Mushrooms stuffed with death and almonds
The bread of memory, a black bread
Blood sausages of yes and no

A hiccup in aspic with paprika
Cold wind fried in onions
A roast of darkest thoughts
Young burp with fish ears
Green apples glazed with envy

We'll wash it all down
With the ale brewed from the foam
Gathered at the mouths
Of our old pursuers:
The mad, god-sent, bloodhounds.

Tony Curtis

(Welsh, 1946–)

Soup

One night our block leader set a competition:
two bowls of soup to the best teller of a tale.
That whole evening the hut filled with words—
tales from the old countries
of wolves and children
potions and love-sick herders
stupid woodsmen and crafty villagers.
Apple-blossom snowed from blue skies,
orphans discovered themselves royal.
Tales of greed and heroes and cunning survival,
soldiers of the Empires, the Church, the Reich.

And when they turned to me
I could not speak,
sunk in the horror of that place,
my throat a corridor of bones, my eyes
and nostrils clogged with self-pity.
"Speak," they said, "everyone has a story to tell."
And so I closed my eyes and said:
I have no hunger for your bowls of soup, you see
I have just risen from the Shabbat meal—
my father has filled our glasses with wine,
bread has been broken, the maid has served fish.
Grandfather has sung, tears in his eyes, the old songs.
My mother holds her glass by the stem, lifts
it to her mouth, the red glow reflecting on her throat.
I go to her side and she kisses me for bed.

My grandfather's kiss is rough and soft like an apricot.
The sheets on my bed are crisp and flat
like the leaves of a book . . .

I carried my prizes back to my bunk: one bowl
I hid, the other I stirred
and smelt a long time, so long
that it filled the cauldron of my head,
drowning a family of memories.

M.F.K. Fisher

(American, 1908–)

The Brothers

Once there were two brothers. They were twins, but their
nine closed months were all they had in common.

One brother, the elder by some minutes, was a big fellow,
red-faced and hairy. He spent all his days afield and swiftly
grew into a great hunter, and at night he made into savoury
stews the day's killing. His father loved the stews and his
elder son who made them.

The younger brother was his mother's love. In him she
admired her own sly, clever ways. He stayed by her side and
learned from her to make lentil pottage which he could sell
each day, and profitably, to the workers.

One day the hunting was very bad, and the sun too hot.
Then chill came suddenly into the darkening air, and the
older brother, still far afield and very tired, turned empty-
handed homeward. No fine stew tonight to cheer him and to
warm his old man's innards! Afterwards no rest by the fire

for the two of them! He sighed and longed to be home, full and warm.

The younger brother sat by a great pot of his steaming soup, with hard sour bread in a pile beside him. The day was almost over, with no more labourers to buy food from him. But he sat on, quiet and sure, waiting for what he knew must happen sometime, and perhaps today.

Suddenly his toes curled under him with scorn and fear, for he saw his elder brother. The great lazy spendthrift lout! He smiled and waited.

And you know what happened. Jacob was the little crafty fellow who sold lentil soup, and Esau was the hungry man who gave his birthright for a bowl of it. And Jacob's mother Rebekah was, like many women, a good cook and a good teacher of cookery for one purpose or another, but never for pleasure. She taught her dear son to be the father of all (almost all) *restaurateurs*.

Her other son she never understood, nor his father Isaac neither, for they would spend all day catching a deer, simply that they might cook it and eat it and then lie by the fire and talk about it. They may have been the first gastronomers.

Meats

George Gordon, Lord Byron
(English, 1788–1824)

From *Don Juan*

But man is a carnivorous production,
 And must have meals, at least one meal a day;
He cannot live, like woodcocks, upon suction,
 But, like the shark and tiger, must have prey;
Although his anatomical construction
 Bears vegetables, in a grumbling way,
Your labouring people think beyond all question
Beef, veal, and mutton, better for digestion.

Walter de la Mare
(English, 1873–1956)

Meat

From out his red and sawdust shop
This butcher, born to chepe and chop,
Surveys without a trace of grief
Perambulating tombs of beef.

From an unmoved and pale-blue eye,
He gloats on these sarcophagi—
Whether they're walking or riding in 'busses
He gloats on these sarcophaguses,
And as he gloats (with greedy eye)
He says, 'Buy! Buy! Buy! Buy! Buy! Buy!'

It's probable we never shall
Convince him that an animal
Is not mere layers of lean and fat;
He may have butched too much for that.
But still; some day we may be able
To wean him to the vegetable.
Turnip, potato, parsnip, swede—
If only upon these he'd feed,
One beast the fewer then might bleed
He'd be less butcherous than of yore
And help the greengrocer next door.

Thomas Hood

(1799–1845)

A Butcher!

Whoe'er has gone thro' London Street,
Has seen a Butcher gazing at his meat,
        And how he keeps
        Gloating upon a sheep's
Or bullock's personals, as if his own;
        How he admires his halves

And quarters—and his calves,
As if, in truth, upon his own legs grown;—
        His fat! *his* suet!
His kidneys peeping elegantly thro' it!
            His thick flank!
            And *his* thin!
            His shank!
            His shin!
Skin of his skin, and bone too of his bone!

        With what an air
He stands aloof, across the thoroughfare
Gazing—and will not let a body by,
Tho' buy! buy! buy! be constantly his cry.
Meanwhile, with arms akimbo, and a pair
Of Rhodian legs, he revels in a stare
At his Joint Stock—for one may call it so,
        Howbeit without a *Co.*
The dotage of self-love was never fonder
Than he of his brute bodies all a-row;
Narcissus in the wave did never ponder
        With love so strong,
        On his "portrait charmant,"
As our vain Butcher on his carcase yonder.

        Look at his sleek round skull!
How bright his cheek, how rubicund his nose is!
        His visage seems to be
        Ripe for beef-tea;
Of brutal juices the whole man is full.
In fact, fulfilling the metempsychosis,
The Butcher is already half a Bull.

Günter Grass

(1927–)

From *The Flounder*

MEAT

Raw rotten deep-frozen boiled.
Supposedly the Wolf (elsewhere the Vulture)
was the first custodian of fire.
In all the myths the she-cook was crafty:
while the Wolves slept (the Vultures
were deep in cloud) she hid
the coals in her moist pouch.
She stole the fire from the sky.

No longer cutting sinews with long teeth.
No longer foretasting the aftertaste of carrion.
Softly the dead wood called, wanting to burn.
Once we had assembled (for fire is an assembler)
plans kindled, thoughts crackled,
sparks rose up and names for raw and cooked.

When liver shriveled over the fire,
boars' heads were baked in clay,
when fish were lined up on a green branch
or stuffed guts were bedded in ashes,
when bacon sizzled on hot stones
and stirred blood turned to pudding,
then fire triumphed over rawness,
then we men among ourselves discussed taste.
The smoke betrayed us,
we dreamed of metal,
and that was the (foreshadowed) beginning of history.

*   *   *

Who will join me in a dish of tripe? It soothes, appeases the anger of the outraged, stills the fear of death, and reminds us of tripe eaten in former days, when there was always a half-filled pot of it on the stove. A chunk of the fat paunch and the limp, honeycombed walls of the second stomach—four pounds for three fifty. It's the widespread distaste for innards that makes beef heart and pork kidneys, calf's lung and tripe cheap.

She took her time. She pounded the pieces and brushed them inside and out, as though some beggar's sweaty rags had found their way to her washboard. She removed the wrinkled skin, but she spared the belly fat, for tripe fat has a special quality—instead of hardening into tallow, it dissolves like soap.

When a last meal was prepared for blacksmith Rusch and his guests, seven quarts of water seasoned with salt, caraway seed, cloves, ginger root, bay leaf, and coarsely pounded peppercorns were set over an open fire. The limp pieces, cut into finger-long strips, were added until the pot was full, and when the water came to a boil the scum was skimmed off. Then the daughter covered her father's favorite dish and let it boil for four hours. At the end she added garlic, freshly grated nutmeg, and more pepper.

The time it takes. Those are the best hours. When the tough has to be made tender, but can't be hurried. How often Mother Rusch and I, while the billowing tripe kept the kitchen stable-warm, sat at the table pushing checkers over the board, discovering the sea route to India, or catching flies on the smooth-polished table top, and telling each other about the tripe of olden times, when we were Pomorshian* and still heathen. And about older than olden times, when elk cows were the only source of meat.

---

*From the Polish province of Pomorze. The other place names in this section all refer to North Sea mercantile trade routes.

Later on, after the daughter had cooked her father's last dish of tripe, she cooked for rich coopers at guild banquets, for Hanseatic merchants who cared about nothing but Öresund tolls, for fat abbots and King Stephen Batory, who wanted his tripe sour and Polish. Still later Amanda Woyke, in her farm kitchen, cooked up tripe with turnips and potatoes into a soup that she seasoned with lovage. And still later Lena Stubbe taught the patrons of the Danzig-Ohra soup kitchen to enjoy proletarian cabbage soups made with (cut-rate) tripe. And to this very day Maria Kuczorra, canteen cook at the Lenin Shipyard in Gdańsk, makes a thick soup once a week out of *kaldauny* (tripe).

When you are feeling cold inside—try the walls of the cow's second stomach. When you are sad, cast out by all nature, sad unto death, try tripe, which cheers us and gives meaning to life. Or in the company of witty friends, godless enough to sit in the seat of the scornful, spoon up caraway-seasoned tripe out of deep dishes. Or cooked with tomatoes, Andalusian-style with chickpeas, or à la Portugaise with kidney beans and bacon. Or if love needs an appetizer, pre-cook tripe in white wine, then steam it with diced celery root. On cold, dry days, when the east wind is banging at the windowpanes and driving your Ilsebill up the wall, tripe thickened with sour cream and served with potatoes in their jackets will help. Or if we must part, briefly or forever, like the time I was a prisoner in the Stockturm and my daughter served me a last meal of peppered tripe.

—Translated by Ralph Manheim

François Rabelais

(French, 1483-95?–1553)

From *Gargantua and Pantagruel*

IV

How Gargamelle, Bigswoln With Gargantua, Ate an Abundance of Tripe

The occasion and manner of Gargamelle's delivery were as I am about to relate; if you do not believe me, may your vent-peg slip, may your stopper fail your (rectal) organ, your fundament fall and your flue pipe collapse!

This is exactly what happened to Gargamelle, on February third, after dinner. And why? Because she had eaten too abundantly of tripe . . . of that tripe which comes from beeves [beef] . . . from beeves which are fatted in their stalls and put to graze in meadows . . . in meadows which bear two crops of grass each year. . . .

Three hundred and sixty-seven thousand and fourteen of these fat beeves had been slaughtered. They were to be salted on Shrove Tuesday so that there would be pressed beef aplenty that spring for the invocation of thirst and its subsequent exorcization by wine.

There was abundance of tripe, as you may imagine, such succulent tripe, too, that every one licked his fingers with glee. But there was a rub—and a four-devil power rub at that! Alas, the tripe could not be kept on hand long or it would spoil—a most disagreeable thought! They therefore decided to guzzle it all down to the last scrap. For fear of leaving any, they summoned all the citizenry of Sinais, Seuilly, La Roche Clermault and Vaugaudry, without forgetting their friends from Coudray-Montpensier and Gué de

Vède* and other neighbors, all accomplished tosspots, debonair fellows and ha! fine cuedrivers, skilled tailpushers, all!

That dear man Grangousier, mightily pleased at their company, ordered meat by the ton, wine by the thousand gallons. No pains were spared to honor his guests. But he *did* caution his wife to eat sparingly, since she was near her time, and in her condition tripe was not exactly the most suitable diet.

"Whoever eats the skins of these chitterlings," he announced, "is an unparalleled turdchewer!"

Despite his warnings, Gargamelle consumed sixteen quarters, two bushels and six pecks; in cases, barrels and pots. La! the sweet fecality that must have swelled up within her!

After dinner, they all made helter-skelter for La Saussaie, a meadow planted with willow trees. Here, on the soft greensward, they danced so gleefully to the tune of airy flutes and melodious bagpipes that to watch them was a most heavenly pastime.

—Translated by Jacques Le Clercq

Alberto Moravia

(Italian, 1907–)

From *Two Women*

The goat, a black and white one, was tied to a stake, and the evacuees, for lack of anything better to do, were examining it and calculating how much it weighed and how much meat it would produce once it had been skinned and cleaned. While

*Villages around Chinon in Touraine, Rabelais's native region.

we were standing thus in the fine rain, our shoes deep in mud, Rosetta said to me in a low voice: "Mum, I'm sorry for that poor goat. It's alive now, and in a few minutes they're going to kill it. If I had any say in the matter, I shouldn't kill it." "What would you eat, then?" I said. "Bread and vegetables," she replied. "What need is there to eat meat? After all I'm made of flesh too and the flesh I'm made of isn't so very different from the flesh of that she-goat. What fault is it of hers that she's an animal and can't reason and defend herself?" I quote these words of Rosetta's to give an idea of how

she still argued and thought at that time, in the midst of war
and famine. Her words may perhaps sound oversimple and
even foolish, but they bear witness to her own particular sort
of perfection which made it impossible to attribute any kind
of defect to her.

In the meantime the butcher, a man called Ignazio who
looked like anything but a butcher—a melancholy, listless
kind of person with a riotous mop of greying hair above his
forehead, long side whiskers and deep-set blue eyes—had
taken off his coat and stood there in his waistcoat. A couple of
knives and a small basin had been placed on a little table near
the stake to which the goat was tied, just as in a hospital
before an operation. Ignazio took up one of the knives, tested
its edge on the palm of his hand, then went up to the goat
and seized it by the horns, throwing its head back. The goat
rolled its eyes, which seemed to be starting out of its head
with fright, and you could see it had understood; it gave a
bleat that sounded just like a moan, as much as to say:
"Don't kill me, have pity." But Ignazio caught his lower lip
with his teeth and with one blow drove the knife up to the
handle into the goat's throat, still keeping hold of it by the
horns. Filippo, who was acting as his assistant, was quick to
put the basin under the goat's throat; and the blood flowed
out of the wound like a little fountain, black and thick and
smoking hot in the cold air. The goat shuddered, then half-
closed its eyes which were already grown dim, as though as
the blood flowed into the basin so its life ebbed away, and
with its life, the sight of its eyes. Finally it bent its knees
and—still trustingly, you might say—let itself slowly fall
into the hands of the man who had slaughtered it. Rosetta
had walked away in the rain which was still falling and I
should have liked to go and join her, but I had to stay where I
was because there was not much meat and I did not wish to
lose my share; besides, Filippo had promised me the entrails,
which are so very good when roasted on a gridiron over a fire
of wood and soft charcoal. Ignazio, meanwhile, had lifted the
goat by its hind legs and dragged it off through the mud to

hang it up on two posts, head downward and feet outspread. We watched him as he worked.

First of all he took hold of one of the forelegs and made a cut just above the hoof, as you might cut a hand at the wrist. Then he selected a thin but tough stick and inserted it between the wooly hide and the flesh of the foot: the skin of a goat is only lightly joined to its flesh, and is very easily detached, like a leaf that is ready to fall. Having inserted the stick, he twisted it in such a way as to make a hole and then, throwing it away, put the foot into his mouth like a whistle, and blew hard into it until the veins in his neck stood out and his face turned purple. He blew and blew, and the goat began to swell out more and more as Ignazio's breath penetrated steadily into it and circulated between the hide and the flesh. Ignazio still went on blowing and blowing, and finally the goat, blown up tight like a wine skin, was dangling between the two posts, almost twice as large as before. Then he dropped the foot, wiped his blood-soiled mouth, and with his knife made an incision in the hide throughout the whole length of the belly, from the groin right up to the neck. Then he started detaching the hide from the flesh with his hands. It was a truly strange thing to see how easily the hide came away—just like taking off a glove—as he pulled steadily at it and now and then used his knife to cut the filaments which still remained attached to it. Gradually he took off the whole skin and then threw it on the ground, hairy and bloodstained, like a cast-off garment; and now the goat was naked, and all red with a few white or bluish patches here and there. It was still drizzling but no one had moved. Ignazio took his knife again, opened up the belly of the goat lengthwise, thrust in his hands and immediately shouted to me: "Cesira, hold out your arm!" I ran forward and he pulled out the whole mass of the entrails, unwinding them one by one, in an orderly fashion, as though they had been a skein of wool. At intervals he cut them and put them over my arm, still warm and stinking unbelievably and dirtying me with dung. And meanwhile he kept saying, as if to himself: "This is a dish fit for kings,

or rather, as it's for you women, I should say for queens.
Clean them well and roast them over a slow fire."

—*Translated by Angus Davidson*

Nikos Kazantzakis

(Greek, 1883–1957)

From *The Odyssey, A Modern Sequel*

BOOK X

The butcher stuck the young boar cleanly through the throat
till blood, like water from a watermill's cascade,
splattered the granite calves of the great dragon-god.
They placed huge caldrons on the hearthstones, lit a fire,
and cast the boar in boiling water to scald him quickly.
Then a young slave jeered at the lack-brain votarist:
"He'd have no need of God if only he'd eat his boar!
Whang! After nine months' time his wife would bear twin
sons!"
The butcher slyly laughed and threw his eyes toward heaven:
"The guy's got brains, my lad. He wants to be dead sure!
When these fat chattering priests have eaten well, by God,
if he should want *ten* sons, they'll all slink out one night,
filled with the boar-god's strength, and make him rows of
sons!"
While the slaves gossiped thus, on the high terraces
the freshly shaven, triple-chinned old high priest sat
and boomed out thunderous praises to his bestial god.
The night before, after he'd eaten and drunk well,
his crocodile god with all its grace so moved his heart
that he had snatched his waxen plaque, and all night long

adorned his scaly master with a flattering hymn:
"O Lord Manure, bottomless belly, all swallowing sewer,
you eat and drink to bursting, sprawl your limbs in slush,
then slowly shut your eyes, groggy with rich repast.
The whole world hangs between your teeth like rotted meat,
and then your harbingers, the blowflies, come and lug
the imagination's dappled filth for appetizers!
And you, a eunuch now without love's joys or frenzies,
nestle in muck with swollen belly, and softly fart
until your greasy, godly stench oils all the air.
You're good, you love the world, you give us dregs and slops,
small scraps of meat and drops of grease hang from your
lips—
permit me, God, to pick and poke at your rich teeth!
Though you're a mighty crocodile, I but a worm.
I'm still flesh of your flesh, breath of your stinking breath.
Ah, help your tiny worm to be like you one day!"
The high priest dabbed the dripping sweat from his fat chins
and threw dark glances at the sluggish holy men
who on their swollen bellies crossed plump hands and sighed:
"Your psalm is good, my brother, and your skill is great;
when we have eaten the boar tonight, we'll praise him, too."
They stooped, half-shut their eyes, and watched the slaves
below
who had laid out the lustrous boar and plucked its hair
until its white skin gleamed amid the gathering dusk.
They ripped his entrails out, and to the milling boys
threw the great scrotum, to be rolled in ashes first
then filled with dry corn seed and made a noisy rattle.
On the hot flaming hearth, to tease the appetite,
they roasted the fat testes, penis, the throat's apple.
while high above them the priests licked their lips with greed.
Then an obscene coarse priest with a hawk's nose spoke first:
"The boar's delicious, brothers; our blessings should bear
fruit;
and may the stoutest here soon bring the bride God's grace!"
They were still laughing when a boy, a widow's son,

brought them the steaming tidbits in a warm clay pot
then stood among them watching, pale with hunger pangs.
The priests fell on the meat like vultures, gulped it down,
and the frail lad stood trembling, sniffing the fragrant meat,
until his empty entrails sagged and his heart fainted.
Then all at once he fell down dead at the god's feet.
As the slaves scooped him up and brought him to his mother,
the ancient high priest shook his solemn head with scorn:
"A slave's soul has no worth, my brothers; it lacks strength
to tread on this great earth with gallantry and freedom.
I pity the poor slaves, they're nought but airy mist,
a light breeze scatters them, a fragrance knocks them down;
it's only just they crawl on earth on hands and knees.
Today I'll write a hymn to God and pray for this great
grace."

—Translated by Kimon Farir

John Digby

(1938–)

Invocation to Drive Out Evil Spirits
Through the Pig

Mr. Pig, this is the night of the feast in the long-house. This
is the night when we cleanse the long-house of all evil spirits.
This is the night when we gather together. This is the night
when enemies put aside their clubs. This is the night when
old wars are forgotten.

Mr. Pig, this is the night when the spirits dance wildly in

the flames of the fire in the long-house. This is the night when evil spirits wake in the long-house. This is the night when evil spirits lurk in the corners of the long-house. This is the night when evil spirits attempt to snatch away our souls in the long-house. This is the night when evil spirits steal our children away from the long-house.

Mr. Pig, we have fed you well. We have nursed you at our mothers' breasts. We have given you our young wives' milk. It has flowed like rivers among the mountains. We have let you to play in our gardens. We have given you snatches of paradise. We have tended you like a child of our own. We have given you a name. We have nursed you well. We have never scolded you.

Mr. Pig, now we truss you with strong vines. This is the night we release your spirit. This is the night when we sprinkle your blood at the four corners of the long-house. This is the night when we offer your spirit to the waking evil. This is the night when we ask you to pacify the evil ones. This is the night when we beg your spirit to devour evil. This is the night when we quarter your flesh.

Mr. Pig, this is the night when we offer you to the evil spirits. This is the night when we send you to paradise. Mr. Pig, this is the knife.

Charles Lamb

(English, 1775–1834)

A Dissertation Upon Roast Pig

Mankind, says a Chinese manuscript, which my friend M. was obliging enough to read and explain to me, for the first seventy thousand ages ate their meat raw, clawing or biting it from the living animal, just as they do in Abyssinia to this day. This period is not obscurely hinted at by their great Confucius in the second chapter of his *Mundane Mutations,* where he designates a kind of golden age by the term Cho-fang, literally the Cooks' Holiday. The manuscript goes on to say, that the art of roasting, or rather broiling (which I take to be the elder brother) was accidentally discovered in the manner following. The swineherd, Ho-ti, having gone out into the woods one morning, as his manner was, to collect mast [nuts] for his hogs, left his cottage in the care of his eldest son Bo-bo, a great lubberly boy, who being fond of playing with fire, as younkers of his age commonly are, let some sparks escape into a bundle of straw, which kindling quickly, spread the conflagration over every part of their poor mansion till it was reduced to ashes. Together with the cottage (a sorry antediluvian make-shift of a building, you may think it), what was of much more importance, a fine litter of new-farrowed pigs, no less than nine in number, perished. China pigs have been esteemed a luxury all over the East from the remotest periods that we read of. Bo-bo was in the utmost consternation, as you may think, not so much for the sake of the tenement, which his father and he could easily build up again with a few dry branches, and the labor of an hour or two, at any time, as for the loss of the pigs. While he was thinking what he should say to his father, and wringing his hands over the smoking remnants of one of those untimely sufferers, an odor assailed his nostrils, unlike any scent which he had before experienced. What could it proceed from?—not from the burnt cottage—he had smelt that smell before—indeed this was by no means the first accident of the kind which had occurred through the negligence of this unlucky young fire-brand. Much less did it resemble that of any known herb, weed, or flowers. A premonitory moistening at the same time overflowed his nether lip. He knew not what to think. He next stooped down to feel the pig, if there were any signs of life in it. He burnt his fingers, and to cool them he applied them in his booby fashion to his mouth. Some of the crumbs of the scorched skin had come away with his fingers, and for the first time in his life (in the world's life indeed, for before him no man had known it) he tasted—*crackling*! Again he felt and fumbled at the pig. It did not burn him so much now, still he licked his fingers from a sort of habit. The truth at length broke into his slow understanding, that it was the pig that smelt so, and the pig that tasted so delicious; and, surrendering himself up to the new-born pleasure, he fell to tearing up whole handfuls of the scorched skin with the flesh next it, and was cramming it down his throat in his beastly fashion, when his sire entered amid the smoking rafters, armed with retributory cudgel, and finding how affairs stood, began to rain blows upon the young rogue's shoulders, as thick as hail-stones, which Bo-bo heeded not any more than if they had been flies. The tickling pleasure, which he experienced in his lower regions, had rendered him quite callous to any inconveniences he might feel in those remote quarters. His father might lay on, but he could not beat him from his pig, till he had fairly made an end of it, when, becoming a little more sensible of his situation, something like the following dialogue ensued.

"You graceless whelp, what have you got there devouring? Is it not enough that you have burnt me down three houses with your dog's tricks, and be hanged to you, but you must be eating fire, and I know not what—what have you got there, I say?"

"O father, the pig, the pig, do come and taste how nice the burnt pig eats."

The ears of Ho-ti tingled with terror. He cursed his son, and he cursed himself that ever he should beget a son that should eat burnt pig.

Bo-bo, whose scent was wonderfully sharpened since morning, soon raked out another pig, and fairly rending it asunder, thrust the lesser half by main force into the fists of Ho-ti, still shouting out "Eat, eat, eat the burning pig, father, only taste—O Lord,"—with such-like barbarous ejaculations, cramming all the while as if he would choke.

Ho-ti trembled in every joint while he grasped the abominable thing, wavering whether he should not put his son to death for an unnatural young monster, when the crackling scorching his fingers, as it had done his son's, and applying the same remedy to them, he in his turn tasted some of its flavor, which, make what sour mouths he would for a pretence, proved not altogether displeasing to him. In conclusion (for the manuscript here is a little tedious) both father and son fairly sat down to the mess, and never left off till they had despatched all that remained of the litter.

Bo-bo was strictly enjoined not to let the secret escape, for the neighbors would certainly have stoned them for a couple of abominable wretches, who could think of improving upon the good meat which God had sent them. Nevertheless, strange stories got about. It was observed that Ho-ti's cottage was burnt down now more frequently than ever. Nothing but fires from this time forward. Some would break out in broad day, others in the night-time. As often as the sow farrowed, so sure was the house of Ho-ti to be in a blaze; and Ho-ti himself, which was the more remarkable, instead of chastising his son, seemed to grow more indulgent to him than ever. At length they were watched, the terrible mystery discovered, and father and son summoned to take their trial at Pekin, then an inconsiderable assize town. Evidence was given, the obnoxious food itself produced in court, and verdict about to be pronounced, when the foreman of the jury begged that some of the burnt pig, of which the culprits stood accused, might be handed into the box. He handled it, and they all handled it, and burning their fingers, as Bo-bo and his father had done before them, and nature prompting to each of them the same remedy, against the face of all the facts, and the clearest charge which judge had ever given—to the surprise of the whole court, townsfolk, strangers, reporters, and all present—without leaving the box, or any manner of consultation whatever, they brought in a simultaneous verdict of Not Guilty.

The judge, who was a shrewd fellow, winked at the manifest iniquity of the decision: and, when the court was dismissed, went privily, and bought up all the pigs that could be had for love or money. In a few days his Lordship's town house was observed to be on fire. The thing took wing, and now there was nothing to be seen but fires in every direction. Fuel and pigs grew enormously dear all over the district. The insurance offices one and all shut up shop. People built slighter and slighter every day, until it was feared that the very science of architecture would in no long time be lost to the world. Thus this custom of firing houses continued, till in process of time, says my manuscript, a sage arose, like our Locke, who made a discovery, that the flesh of swine, or indeed of any other animal, might be cooked (*burnt*, as they called it) without the necessity of consuming a whole house to dress it. Then first began the rude form of a gridiron. Roasting by the string, or spit, came in a century or two later; I forget in whose dynasty. By such slow degrees, concludes the manuscript, do the most useful and seemingly the most obvious arts, make their way among mankind.

Without placing too implicit faith in the account above given, it must be agreed, that if a worthy pretext for so dangerous an experiment as setting houses on fire (especially in these days) could be assigned in favor of any culinary object, that pretext and excuse might be found in ROAST PIG.

Of all the delicacies in the whole *mundus edibilis* [edible world], I will maintain it to be the most delicate—*princeps obsoniorum* [prince of delicacies].

I speak not of your grown porkers—things between pig and pork—those hobbydchoys—but a young and tender suckling—under a moon old—guiltless as yet of the sty—with no original speck of the *amor immunditiæ* [love of filth], the hereditary failing of the first parent, yet manifest—his voice as yet not broken, but something between a childish treble, and a grumble—the mild forerunner, or *præludium*, of a grunt.

He must be roasted. I am not ignorant that our ancestors ate them seethed, or boiled—but what a sacrifice of the exterior tegument!

There is no flavor comparable, I will contend, to that of the crisp, tawny, well-watched, not over-roasted, *crackling*, as it is well called—the very teeth are invited to their share of the pleasure at this banquet in overcoming the coy, brittle resistance—with the adhesive oleaginous—O call it not fat—but an indefinable sweetness growing up to it—the tender blossoming of fat—fat cropped in the bud—taken in the shoot—in the first innocence—the cream and quintessence of the child-pig's yet pure food—the lean, no lean, but a kind of animal manna—or, rather, fat and lean (if it must be so) blended and running into each other, that both together make but one ambrosian result, or common substance.

Behold him, while he is doing—it seemeth rather a refreshing warmth, than a scorching heat, that he is so passive to. How equably he twirleth round the string!—Now he is just done. To see the extreme sensibility of that tender age, he hath wept out his pretty eyes—radiant jellies—shooting stars—

See him in the dish, his second cradle, how meek he lieth!—wouldst thou have had this innocent grow up to the grossness and indocility which too often accompany maturer swinehood? Ten to one he would have proved a glutton, a

sloven, an obstinate, disagreeable animal—wallowing in all
manner of filthy conversation—from these sins he is happily
snatched away—

> Ere sin could blight, or sorrow fade,
> Death came with timely care—
>   [S. T. Coleridge, "Epitaph on an Infant"]

his memory is odoriferous—no clown curseth, while his
stomach half rejecteth, the rank bacon—no coal-heaver
bolteth him in reeking sausages—he hath a fair sepulchre in
the grateful stomach of the judicious epicure—and for such a
tomb might be content to die.

He is the best of sapors. Pine-apple is great. She is indeed
almost too transcendent—a delight, if not sinful, yet so like
to sinning, that really a tender-conscienced person would do
well to pause—too ravishing for mortal taste, she woundeth
and excoriateth the lips that approach her—like lovers' kisses,
she biteth—she is a pleasure bordering on pain from the
fierceness and insanity of her relish—but she stoppeth at the
palate—she meddleth not with the appetite—and the coarsest
hunger might barter her consistently for a mutton chop.

Pig—let me speak his praise—is no less provocative of the
appetite, than he is satisfactory to the criticalness of the cen-
sorious palate. The strong man may batten on him, and the
weakling refuseth not his mild juice.

Unlike to mankind's mixed characters, a bundle of virtues
and vices, inexplicably intertwisted, and not to be unravelled
without hazard, he is—good throughout. No part of him is
better or worse than another. He helpeth, as far as his little
means extend, all around. He is the least envious of banquets.
He is all neighbors' fare.

I am one of those who freely and ungrudgingly impart a
share of the good things of this life which fall to their lot (few
as mine are in this kind), to a friend. I protest I take as great
an interest in my friend's pleasures, his relishes, and proper
satisfactions, as in mine own. "Presents," I often say, "en-
dear Absents." Hares, pheasants, partridges, snipes, barn-

door chicken (those "tame villatic fowl" [John Milton, *Samson Agonistes*]), capons, plovers, brawn, barrels of oysters, I dispense as freely as I receive them. I love to taste them, as it were, upon the tongue of my friend. But a stop must be put somewhere. One would not, like Lear, "give everything." I make my stand upon pig. Methinks it is an ingratitude to the Giver of all good flavors, to extra-domiciliate, or send out of the house, slightingly, (under pretext of friendship, or I know not what) a blessing so particularly adapted, predestined, I may say, to my individual taste.—It argues an insensibility.

I remember a touch of conscience in this kind at school. My good old aunt, who never parted from me at the end of a holiday without stuffing a sweet-meat, or some nice thing, into my pocket, had dismissed me one evening with a smoking plum-cake, fresh from the oven. In my way to school (it was over London bridge) a gray-headed old beggar saluted me (I have no doubt at this time of day that he was a counterfeit). I had no pence to console him with, and in the vanity of self-denial, and the very coxcombry of charity, school-boy-like, I made him a present of—the whole cake! I walked on a little, buoyed up, as one is on such occasions, with a sweet soothing of self-satisfaction; but before I had got to the end of the bridge, my better feelings returned, and I burst into tears, thinking how ungrateful I had been to my good aunt, to go and give her good gift away to a stranger, that I had never seen before, and who might be a bad man for aught I knew; and then I thought of the pleasure my aunt would be taking in thinking that I—I myself, and not another—would eat her nice cake—and what should I say to her the next time I saw her—how naughty I was to part with her pretty present—and the odor of that spicy cake came back upon my recollection, and the pleasure and the curiosity I had taken in seeing her make it, and her joy when she sent it to the oven, and how disappointed she would feel that I had never had a bit of it in my mouth at last—and I blamed my impertinent spirit of alms-giving, and out-of-place hypocrisy of goodness, and above all I wished never to see the face again of that insidious, good-for-nothing, old gray impostor.

Our ancestors were nice in their methods of sacrificing these tender victims. We read of pigs whipt to death with something of a shock, as we hear of any other obsolete custom. The age of discipline is gone by, or it would be curious to inquire (in a philosophical light merely) what effect this process might have towards intenerating and dulcifying a substance, naturally so mild and dulcet as the flesh of young pigs. It looks like refining a violet. Yet we should be cautious, while we condemn the inhumanity, how we censure the wisdom of the practice. It might impart a gusto—

I remember an hypothesis, argued upon by the young students, when I was at St. Omer's, and maintained with much learning and pleasantry on both sides, "Whether, supposing that the flavor of a pig who obtained his death by whipping *(per flagellationem extremam)* [by extreme flagellation] superadded a pleasure upon the palate of a man more intense than any possible suffering we can conceive in the animal, is man justified in using that method of putting the animal to death?" I forget the decision.

His sauce should be considered. Decidedly, a few bread crumbs, done up with his liver and brains, and a dash of mild sage. But, banish, dear Mrs. Cook, I beseech you, the whole onion tribe. Barbecue your whole hogs to your palate, steep them in shalots, stuff them out with plantations of the rank and guilty garlic; you cannot poison them, or make them stronger than they are—but consider, he is a weakling—a flower.

Dick Gregory

(American, 1932–)

If You Had to Kill Your Own Hog

My momma could never understand how white folks could twist the words of the Bible around to justify racial segregation. Yet she could read the Ten Commandments, which clearly say, "Thou shalt not kill," and still justify eating meat. Momma couldn't read the newspaper very well, but she sure could interpret the Word of God. "God meant you shouldn't kill people," she used to say. But I insisted, "Momma, He didn't say that. He said, 'Thou shalt not kill.' If you leave that statement alone, a whole lot of things would be safe from killing. But if you are going to twist the words about killing to mean what you want them to mean, then let white folks do the same thing with justifying racial segregation."

"You can't live without eating meat," Momma would persist. "You'd starve." I couldn't buy that either. You get milk from a cow without killing it. You do not have to kill an animal to get what you need from it. You get wool from the sheep without killing it. Two of the strongest animals in the jungle are vegetarians—the elephant and the gorilla. The first two years are the most important years of a man's life, and during that period he is not involved with eating meat. If you suddenly become very ill, there is a good chance you will be taken off a meat diet. So it is a myth that killing is necessary for survival. The day I decide that I must have a piece of steak to nourish my body, I will also give the cow the same right to nourish herself on human beings.

There is so little basic difference between animals and humans. The process of reproduction is the same for chickens, cattle, and humans. If suddenly the air stopped circulating on the earth, or the sun collided with the earth, animals and humans would die alike. A nuclear holocaust will wipe out all life. Life in the created order is basically the same and should be respected as such. It seems to me the Bible says it is wrong to kill—period.

If we can justify *any* kind of killing in the name of religion, the door is opened for all kinds of other justifications. The fact of killing animals is not as frightening as our human tendency to justify it—to kill and not even be aware that we are taking life. It is sobering to realize that when you misuse one of the least of Nature's creatures, like the chicken, you are sowing the seed for misusing the highest of Nature's creatures, man.

Animals and humans suffer and die alike. If you had to kill your own hog before you ate it, most likely you would not be able to do it. To hear the hog scream, to see the blood spill, to see the baby being taken away from its momma, and to see the look of death in the animal's eye would turn your stomach. So you get the man at the packing house to do the killing for you. In like manner, if the wealthy aristocrats who are perpetrating conditions in the ghetto actually heard the screams of ghetto suffering, or saw the slow death of hungry little kids, or witnessed the strangulation of manhood and dignity, they could not continue the killing. But the wealthy are protected from such horror. They have people to do the killing for them. The wealthy profit from the daily murders of ghetto life but they do not see them. Those who immerse themselves in the daily life of the ghetto see the suffering— the social workers, the police, the local merchants, and the bill collectors. But the people on top never really see.

By the time you see a piece of meat in the butcher shop window, all the blood and suffering have been washed away. When you order a steak in a restaurant, the misery has been forgotten and you see the finished product. You see a steak with butter and parsley on it. It looks appetizing and appealing and you are pleased enough to eat it. You never even consider the suffering which produced your meal or the other animals killed that day in the slaughterhouse. In the same way, all the wealthy aristocrats ever see of the black community is the finished product, the window dressing, the steak on the platter—Ralph Bunche and Thurgood Marshall. The United Nations or the Supreme Court bench is the restaurant and the ghetto street corner is the slaughterhouse.

Life under ghetto conditions cuts short life expectancy. The Negro's life expectancy is shorter than the white man's. The oppressor benefits from continued oppression financially; he makes more money so that he can eat a little better. I see no difference between a man killing a chicken and a man killing a human being, by overwork and forcing ghetto conditions upon him, both so that he can eat a little better. If you can justify killing to eat meat, you can justify the conditions of the ghetto. I cannot justify either one.

Every time the white folks made my momma mad, she would grab the Bible and find something bitter in it. She would come home from the rich white folks' house, after they had just called her "nigger" or patted her on the rump or caught her stealing some steaks, open her Bible and read aloud, "It is easier for a camel to pass through the eye of a needle than for a rich man to get into Heaven." When you get involved with distorting the words of the Bible, you don't have to be bitter. The same tongue can be used to bless and curse men.

Upton Sinclair

(American, 1878–1968)

From *The Jungle*

So, as the wheel turned, a hog was suddenly jerked off his feet and borne aloft.

At the same instant the ear was assailed by a most terrifying shriek; the visitors started in alarm, the women turned pale and shrank back. The shriek was followed by another, louder and yet more agonizing—for once started upon that journey, the hog never came back; at the top of the wheel he was shunted off upon a trolley, and went sailing down the room. And meantime another was swung up, and then another, and another, until there was a double line of them, each dangling by a foot and kicking in frenzy—and squealing. The uproar was appalling, perilous to the ear-drums; one feared there was too much sound for the room to hold—that the walls must give way or the ceiling crack. There were high squeals and low squeals, grunts, and wails of agony; there would come a momentary lull, and then a fresh outburst, louder than ever, surging up to a deafening climax. It was too much for some of the visitors—the men would look at each other, laughing nervously, and the women would stand with hands clenched, and the blood rushing to their faces, and the tears starting in their eyes.

Meantime, heedless of all these things, the men upon the floor were going about their work. Neither squeals of hogs nor tears of visitors made any difference to them; one by one they hooked up the hogs, and one by one with a swift stroke they slit their throats. There was a long line of hogs, with squeals and life-blood ebbing away together; until at last each started again, and vanished with a splash into a huge vat of boiling water.

It was all so very businesslike that one watched it fascinated. It was pork-making by machinery, pork-making by applied mathematics. And yet somehow the most matter-of-fact person could not help thinking of the hogs; they were so innocent, they came so very trustingly; and they were so very human in their protests—and so perfectly within their rights! They had done nothing to deserve it; and it was adding insult to injury, as the thing was done here, swinging them up in this cold-blooded, impersonal way, without a pretence at apology, without the homage of a tear. Now and then a visitor wept, to be sure; but this slaughtering-machine ran on, visitors or no visitors. It was like some horrible crime committed in a dungeon, all unseen and unheeded, buried out of sight and of memory.

One could not stand and watch very long without becoming philosophical, without beginning to deal in symbols and similes, and to hear the hog-squeal of the universe. Was it permitted to believe that there was nowhere upon the earth, or above the earth, a heaven for hogs, where they were requited for all this suffering? Each one of these hogs was a separate creature. Some were white hogs, some were black; some were brown, some were spotted; some were old, some were young; some were long and lean, some were monstrous. And each of them had an individuality of his own, a will of his own, a hope and a heart's desire; each was full of self-confidence, of self-importance, and a sense of dignity. And trusting and strong in faith he had gone about his business, the while a black shadow hung over him and a horrid Fate waited in his pathway. Now suddenly it had swooped upon him, and had seized him by the leg. Relentless, remorseless, it was; all his protests, his screams, were nothing to it—it did its cruel will with him, as if his wishes, his feelings, had simply no existence at all; it cut his throat and watched him gasp out his life. And now was one to believe that there was nowhere a god of hogs, to whom this hog-personality was precious, to whom these hog-squeals and agonies had a meaning? Who would take this hog into his arms and comfort him, reward him for his work well done, and show him the meaning of his sacrifice? Perhaps some glimpse of all this was in the thoughts of our humble-minded Jurgis, as he turned to go on with the rest of the party, and muttered: "Dieve—but I'm glad I'm not a hog!"

The carcass hog was scooped out of the vat by machinery, and then it fell to the second floor, passing on the way through a wonderful machine with numerous scrapers, which adjusted themselves to the size and shape of the animal, and sent it out at the other end with nearly all of its bristles removed. It was then again strung up by machinery, and sent upon another trolley ride; this time passing between two lines of men, who sat upon a raised platform, each doing a certain single thing to the carcass as it came to him. One scraped the outside of a leg; another scraped the inside of the same leg. One with a swift stroke cut the throat; another with two swift strokes severed the head, which fell to the floor and vanished through a hole. Another made a slit down the body; a second opened the body wider; a third with a saw cut the breast-bone; a fourth loosened the entrails; a fifth pulled them out—and they also slid through a hole in the floor. There were men to scrape each side and men to scrape the back; there were men to clean the carcass inside, to trim it and wash it. Looking down this room, one saw, creeping slowly, a line of dangling hogs a hundred yards in length; and for every yard there was a man, working as if a demon were after him. At the end of this hog's progress every inch of the carcass had been gone over several times; and then it was rolled into the chilling-room, where it stayed for twenty-four hours, and where a stranger might lose himself in a forest of freezing hogs.

*   *   *

Then the party went across the street to where they did the killing of beef—where every hour they turned four or five hundred cattle into meat. Unlike the place they had left, all this work was done on one floor; and instead of there being one line of carcasses which moved to the workmen, there were fifteen or twenty lines, and the men moved from one to another of these. This made a scene of intense activity, a picture of human power wonderful to watch. It was all in one great room, like a circus amphitheatre, with a gallery for visitors running over the centre.

Along one side of the room ran a narrow gallery, a few feet from the floor; into which gallery the cattle were driven by men with goads which gave them electric shocks. Once crowded in here, the creatures were prisoned, each in a separate pen, by gates that shut, leaving them no room to turn around; and while they stood bellowing and plunging, over the top of the pen there leaned one of the "knockers," armed with a sledge-hammer, and watching for a chance to deal a blow. The room echoed with the thuds in quick succession, and the stamping and kicking of the steers. The instant the animal had fallen, the "knocker" passed on to another; while a second man raised a lever, and the side of the pen was raised, and the animal, still kicking and struggling, slid out to the "killing-bed." Here a man put shackles about one leg, and pressed another lever, and the body was jerked up into the air. There were fifteen or twenty such pens, and it was a matter of only a couple of minutes to knock fifteen or twenty cattle and roll them out. Then once more the gates were opened, and another lot rushed in; and so out of each pen there rolled a steady stream of carcasses, which the men upon the killing-beds had to get out of the way.

The manner in which they did this was something to be seen and never forgotten. They worked with furious intensity, literally upon the run—at a pace with which there is nothing to be compared except a football game. It was all highly specialized labor, each man having his task to do; generally this would consist of only two or three specific cuts,

and he would pass down the line of fifteen or twenty carcasses, making these cuts upon each. First there came the
"butcher," to bleed them; this meant one swift stroke, so
swift that you could not see it—only the flash of the knife;
and before you could realize it, the man had darted on to the
next line, and a stream of bright red was pouring out upon
the floor. This floor was half an inch deep with blood, in spite
of the best efforts of men who kept shovelling it through
holes; it must have made the floor slippery, but no one could
have guessed this by watching the men at work.

The carcass hung for a few minutes to bleed; there was no
time lost, however, for there were several hanging in each
line, and one was always ready. It was let down to the
ground, and there came the "headsman," whose task it was to
sever the head, with two or three swift strokes. Then came
the "floorsman," to make the first cut in the skin; and then
another to finish ripping the skin down the centre; and then
half a dozen more in swift succession, to finish the skinning.
After they were through, the carcass was again swung up;
and while a man with a stick examined the skin, to make sure
that it had not been cut, and another rolled it up and tumbled
it through one of the inevitable holes in the floor, the beef
proceeded on its journey. There were men to cut it, and men
to split it, and men to gut it and scrape it clean inside. There
were some with hose which threw jets of boiling water upon
it, and others who removed the feet and added the final
touches. In the end, as with the hogs, the finished beef was
run into the chilling-room, to hang its appointed time.

Marvin Cohen

(1931–)

Slabs of Meat on Adjoining Hooks

At the meat market on adjoining hooks hung a pair of slabs of meat. It was closing time, there was no one about. They were sealed shut in a vault-like refrigerator, which took up an enormous space.

They were being preserved by the frozenness. As they hung side by side, those two slabs of meat decided to talk— what could be more natural?

The first slab asked the second slab where he had come from. "A cow," was the answer.

The second slab asked the first slab the same question, and was given the same answer. So their backgrounds were similar! They were friends already.

To push their luck, they tried for the miracle of coincidence: that is, to determine whether they had both derived from the same cow, which would seal their friendship in the sacred status of "brothers." Alas, no. The first slab came from a totally different cow, as different from the second slab's cow as the second slab's cow was different from the first slab's cow. But at least they had in common the same difference that they shared. So, though not brothers, they were equals: and that was enough.

This finding gave their conversation a lull from the tension of inquiry, and so put a break to their first major word exchange. The lull itself was gathering tension and was rapidly speeding toward a displacement of itself by a second speech cluster. Communication would advance and deepen.

They were prepared to understand each other and only needed more information.

How mutually at one were their intervals of instinct! If not *literal* brothers, they were much akin.

"Do you mind if I raise the question of sex?" asked the first slab. "No, I was tending toward the subject myself," the second slab remarked, to keep up the accord, in their harmonious ease.

The first slab went on: "There seems to be a paradox, or else something else, in this fact that . . ."

The second slab interrupted: "May I finish it?" The first slab nodded. The second slab, granted the privilege of a favored friend, took it from there: "You were just saying, or about to, that we're both former parts of cows, and cows are female, but we're male. How can a part of a female be male? For in our case that's what we are."

"Exactly what I was wondering, and in the same words," confirmed the first slab: "Let's jointly meditate (for joints we were, in the cow whole) on solving this sexual problem, if it bears solving, which it may not. It may remain, like everything else, a mystery."

They pondered. Whole eternities went by.

Still no solution. But morning's bustling business had begun. They were auctioned off and removed from their hooks, both sold to the same meat buyer for a restaurant firm. They went silently side by side in the same refrigerated cargo van that delivered them to a restaurant kitchen, where they were cooked according to order by customers during the hungry lunch hour. The first slab went into four or five separate bellies, as likewise the second in other bellies. Their friendship paused, with their unresolved question. Will mentalities elsewhere care to inherit the problem? The problem is all that remains—and may it always remain—of their firm but intellectual friendship.

Henry Fielding

(1707–1754)

The Roast Beef of Old England

When mighty roast Beef was the *Englishman's* Food,
It ennobled our Hearts, and enriched our Blood;
Our Soldiers were brave, and our Courtiers were good.
    Oh the Roast Beef of Old *England*,
    And Old *England's* Roast Beef!

Then, *Britons*, from all nice Dainties refrain,
Which effeminate *Italy*, *France*, and *Spain*;
And mighty Roast Beef shall command on the Main.
    Oh the Roast Beef, &c.

Jonathan Swift

(1667–1745)

From *Directions to Servants*

If you are bringing up a Joint of Meat in a Dish, and it falls
out of your Hand, before you get into the Dining Room, with
the Meat on the Ground, and the Sauce spilled, take up the

Meat gently, wipe it with the Lap of your Coat, then put it
again into the Dish, and serve it up; and when your Lady
misses the Sauce, tell her, it is to be sent up in a Plate by
itself.

When you carry up a Dish of Meat, dip your Fingers in
the Sauce, or lick it with your Tongue, to try whether it be
good, and fit for your Master's Table.

Eugene Field

(American, 1850–1895)

Rare Roast Beef

When the numerous distempers to which all flesh is heir
Torment us till our very souls are reeking with despair;
When that monster fiend, Dyspepsy, rears its spectral hydra
    head,
Filling *bon vivants* and epicures with certain nameless dread;
When *any* ill of body or of intellect abounds,
Be it sickness known to Galen or disease unknown to
    Lowndes,—*
In such a dire emergency it is my firm belief
That there is no diet quite so good as rare roast beef.

And even when the body's in the very prime of health,
When sweet contentment spreads upon the cheeks her rosy
    wealth,

---

*The first is Claudius Galen, a medieval writer *circa* A.D. 130; the second is possibly one of several physicians Field consulted about his perpetual stomach
disorders, jokingly attributed to a fondness for eating pastry and reading in bed.

And when a man devours three meals per day and pines for
    more,
And growls because instead of three square meals there are
    not four,—
Well, even then, though cake and pie do service on the side,
And coffee is a luxury that may not be denied,
Still of the many viands there is one that's hailed as chief,
And that, as you are well aware, is rare roast beef.

Some like the sirloin, but I think the porterhouse is best,—
'T is juicier and tenderer and meatier than the rest;
Put on this roast a dash of salt, and then of water pour
Into the sizzling dripping-pan a cupful, and no more;
The oven being hot, the roast will cook in half an hour;
Then to the juices in the pan you add a little flour,
And so you get a gravy that is called the cap sheaf
Of that glorious *summum bonum*, rare roast beef.

Served on a platter that is hot, and carved with thin, keen
    knife,
How does this savory viand enhance the worth of life!
Give me no thin and shadowy slice, but a thick and steaming
    slab,—
Who would not choose a generous hunk to a bloodless little
    dab?
Upon a nice hot plate how does the juicy morceau steam,
A symphony in scarlet or a red incarnate dream!
Take from me eyes and ears and all, O Time, thou ruthless
    thief!
Except these teeth wherewith to deal with rare roast beef.

Most every kind and rôle of modern victuals have I tried,
Including roasted, fricasseed, broiled, toasted, stewed, and
    fried,
Your canvasbacks and papa-bottes* and mutton-chops
    subese,†

*Plovers.

†*Soubise,* an onion cream sauce.

Your patties *à la Turkey* and your doughnuts *à la* grease;
I've whiled away dyspeptic hours with crabs in marble halls,
And in the lowly cottage I've experienced codfish balls;
But I've never found a viand that could so allay all grief
And soothe the cockles of the heart as rare roast beef.

I honor that sagacious king who, in a grateful mood,
Knighted the savory loin that on the royal table stood;
And as for me I'd ask no better friend than this good roast,
Which is my squeamish stomach's fortress *(feste Burg)* and
    host;
For with this ally with me I can mock Dyspepsy's wrath,
Can I pursue the joy of Wisdom's pleasant, peaceful path.
So I do off my vest and let my waistband out a reef
When I soever set me down to rare roast beef.

Roland Barthes

(French, 1915–1980)

Steak and Chips

Steak is a part of the same sanguine mythology as wine. It is
the heart of meat, it is meat in its pure state; and whoever
partakes of it assimilates a bull-like strength. The prestige of
steak evidently derives from its quasi-rawness. In it, blood is
visible, natural, dense, at once compact and sectile. One can
well imagine the ambrosia of the Ancients as this kind of
heavy substance which dwindles under one's teeth in such a
way as to make one keenly aware at the same time of its
original strength and of its aptitude to flow into the very

blood of man. Full-bloodedness is the raison d'être of steak; the degrees to which it is cooked are expressed not in calorific units but in images of blood; rare steak is said to be *saignant* (when it recalls the arterial flow from the cut in the animal's throat), or *bleu* (and it is now the heavy, plethoric, blood of the veins which is suggested by the purplish colour—the superlative of redness). Its cooking, even moderate, cannot openly find expression; for this unnatural state, a euphemism is needed: one says that steak is *à point*, 'medium', and this in truth is understood more as a limit than as a perfection.

To eat steak rare therefore represents both a nature and a morality. It is supposed to benefit all the temperaments, the sanguine because it is identical, the nervous and lymphatic because it is complementary to them. And just as wine becomes for a good number of intellectuals a mediumistic substance which leads them towards the original strength of nature, steak is for them a redeeming food, thanks to which they bring their intellectualism to the level of prose and exorcize, through blood and soft pulp, the sterile dryness of which they are constantly accused. The craze for steak tartare, for instance, is a magic spell against the romantic association between sensitiveness and sickliness; there are to be found, in this preparation, all the germinating states of matter: the blood mash and the glair of eggs, a whole harmony of soft and life-giving substances, a sort of meaningful compendium of the images of pre-parturition.

Like wine, steak is in France a basic element, nationalized even more than socialized. It figures in all the surroundings of alimentary life: flat, edged with yellow, like the sole of a shoe, in cheap restaurants; thick and juicy in the bistros which specialize in it; cubic, with the core all moist throughout beneath a light charred crust, in haute cuisine. It is a part of all the rhythms, that of the comfortable bourgeois meal and that of the bachelor's bohemian snack. It is a food at once expeditious and dense, it effects the best possible ratio between economy and efficacy, between mythology and its multifarious ways of being consumed.

Moreover, it is a French possession (circumscribed today, it is true, by the invasion of American steaks). As in the case of wine there is no alimentary constraint which does not make the Frenchman dream of steak. Hardly abroad, he feels nostalgia for it. Steak is here adorned with a supplementary virtue of elegance, for among the apparent complexity of exotic cooking, it is a food which unites, one feels, succulence and simplicity. Being part of the nation, it follows the index of patriotic values: it helps them to rise in wartime, it is the very flesh of the French soldier, the inalienable property which cannot go over to the enemy except by treason. In an old film *(Deuxième Bureau contre. Kommandantur)*, the maid of the patriotic *curé* gives food to the Boche* spy disguised as a French underground fighter: *'Ah, it's you, Laurent! I'll give you some steak.'* And then, when the spy is unmasked: *'And when I think I gave him some of my steak!'*—the supreme breach of trust.

Commonly associated with chips, steak communicates its national glamour to them: chips are nostalgic and patriotic like steak. *Match* told us that after the armistice in Indo-China *'General de Castries, for his first meal, asked for chips'*. And the President of the Indo-China Veterans, later commenting on this information added: *'The gesture of General de Castries asking for chips for his first meal has not always been understood.'* What we were meant to understand is that the General's request was certainly not a vulgar materialistic reflex, but an episode in the ritual of appropriating the regained French community. The General understood well our national symbolism; he knew that *la frite,* chips, are the alimentary sign of Frenchness.

—Translated by Annette Lavers

*The French soldiers' slang name for a German.

Bertolt Brecht

(German, 1898–1956)

To Eat of Meat Joyously

To eat of meat joyously, a juicy loin cut
And with the fresh-baked, fragrant rye bread
Chunks from the whole cheese, and to swallow
Cold beer from the jug: such things are held in
Low esteem, but to my mind, to be put into the grave
Without ever enjoying a mouthful of good meat
Is inhuman, and I say that, I who
Am not good at eating.

—*Translated by Lee Baxendall*

Arthur Rimbaud

(French, 1854–1891)

At the Green Cabaret 5 P.M.

For a full week, the soles of my boots had bled
On the cobblestones; I came to Charleroi.
At the Green Cabaret, I called for slices of bread
With butter, and ham which should not be too hot.

Quite happy, I stretched my legs beneath the table's
Green; I considered the artless histories
Of the tapestry. And it was wonderful, like the fables,
When the girl with the great breasts, she of the lively eyes,

—She's not the type that a kiss could frighten away!—
Laughing, she brought me bread and butter that lay
Upon a colored platter with ham half-cold,

Ham rosy and white, and perfumed with a dash
Of garlic, and she filled a great foaming glass
Which a ray of the tardy sun turned into gold.

—Translated by Gerard Previn Meyer

Tony Curtis

(1946–)

Preparations

In the valley there is an order to these things:
Chapel suits and the morning shift called off.
She takes the bus to Pontypridd* to buy black,
But the men alone proceed to the grave,
Neighbours, his butties,† and the funeral regulars.
The women are left in the house; they bustle
Around the widow with a hushed, furious
Energy that keeps grief out of the hour.

*A town near Cardiff where these coal miners shop.

†butties, buddies, workmates.

She holds to the kitchen, concerned with sandwiches.
It is a ham-bone big as a man's arm and the meat
Folds over richly from her knife. A daughter sits
Watching butter swim in its dish before the fire.
The best china laid precisely across the new tablecloth:
They wait. They count the places over and over like a rosary.

Oliver Goldsmith

(Anglo-Irish, 1728–1774)

From "The Haunch of Venison"

Thanks, my lord, for your venison, for finer or fatter
Ne'er rang'd in a forest, or smok'd in a platter;
The haunch was a picture for painters to study,
The fat was so white, and the lean was so ruddy;
Though my stomach was sharp, I could scarce help regretting
To spoil such a delicate picture by eating:
I had thoughts, in my chamber, to place it in view,
To be shown to my friends as a piece of virtû . . .

Robert Burns

(Scottish, 1759–1796)

To a Haggis*

Fair fa' your honest, sonsie face,
Great Chieftan o' the Puddin-race!
Aboon them a' ye tak your place,
              Painch, tripe, or thairm:
Weel are ye wordy of a *grace*
              As lang's my arm.

The groaning trencher there ye fill,
Your hurdies like a distant hill,
Your *pin* wad help to mend a mill
              In time o' need,
While thro' your pores the dews distil
              Like amber bead.

His knife see Rustic-labour dight,
An' cut you up wi' ready slight,
Trenching your gushing entrails bright
              Like onie ditch;
And then, O what a glorious sight,
              Warm-reekin, rich!

*The vocabulary on page 176 will help you to understand the poem. If you read it aloud, the robust sound will convey the sense of Burns's language. In the poem, the haggis—spiced stuffed sheep stomach—is praised as the food of *real men*, not those spindle-legged effete types who feed on French cuisine!

Then, horn for horn they stretch an' strive,
Deil tak the hindmost, on they drive,
Till a' their weel-swall'd kytes belyve
          Are bent like drums;
Then auld Guidman, maist like to rive,
          Bethankit hums.

Is there that owre his French *ragout*,
Or *olio* that wad staw a sow,
Or *fricassee* wad mak her spew
          Wi' perfect sconner,
Looks down wi' sneering, scornfu' view
          On sic a dinner?

Poor devil! see him owre his trash,
As feckless as a wither'd rash,
His spindle shank a guid whip-lash,
          His nieve a nit;
Thro' bluidy flood or field to dash,
          O how unfit!

But mark the Rustic, *haggis-fed*,
The trembling earth resounds his tread,
Clap in his walie nieve a blade,
          He'll mak it whissle;
An' legs, an' arms, an' heads will sned,
          Like taps o' thrissle.

Ye Pow'rs wha mak mankind your care,
And dish them out their bill o' fare,
Auld Scotland wants nae skinking ware
          That jaups in luggies;
But, if ye wish her gratefu' pray'r,
          Gie her a *Haggis*!

Vocabulary

fa'	befall
sonsie	comely
painch	belly
thairm	intestine
hurdies	buttocks
pin	skewer
dight	make ready
horn	spoon
well-swall'd kytes belyve	stuffed bellies soon
maist like to rive	almost ready to burst
bethankit hums	mumbles grace
owre	over
ragout, olio, fricassee	fancy French meat stews
staw	stuff
sconner	disgust
rash	rush
His . . . nit	Legs as thin as a whip lash, fist the size of a nut
walie nieve	good-size fist
sned	lop off
Like tops o' thrissle	as easily as thistle tops
jaupes in luggies	splashes around in a bowl

From *Punch* (circa 1860)

IRISH STEW

Air—"Happy Land"

Irish stew, Irish stew!
 Whatever else my dinner be,
Once again, once again,
 I'd have a dish of thee.

Mutton chops, and onion slice,
  Let the water cover,
With potatoes, fresh and nice;
  Boil, but not quite over,
    Irish stew, Irish stew!
Ne'er from thee, my taste will stray.
      I could eat
      Such a treat
Nearly every day.
              La, la, la, la!

BOILED CHICKEN

Air—"North Creina"

Lesbia hath a fowl to cook;
  But, being anxious not to spoil it,
Searches anxiously our book,
  For how to roast, and how to boil it.
Sweet it is to dine upon—
  Quite alone, when small its size is;—
And, when cleverly 'tis done,
  Its delicacy quite surprises.
        Oh! my tender pullet dear!
My boiled—not roasted—tender Chicken!
      I can wish
      No other dish,
With thee supplied, my tender Chicken!

Lesbia, take some water cold,
  And having on the fire placed it,
And some butter, and be bold—
  When 'tis hot enough—taste it.
Oh! the Chicken meant for me
  Boil before the fire grows dimmer;
Twenty minutes let it be
  In the saucepan left to simmer.

Oh, my tender Chicken dear!
My boil'd, delicious, tender Chicken!
Rub the breast
(To give a zest)
With lemon-juice, my tender Chicken.

Lesbia hath with sauce combined
Broccoli white, without a tarnish;
'Tis hard to tell if 'tis design'd
For vegetable or for garnish.
Pillow'd on a butter'd dish,
My Chicken temptingly reposes,
Making gourmands for it wish,
Should the savor reach their noses.
Oh, my tender pullet dear!
My boiled—not roasted—tender Chicken!
Day or night,
Thy meal is light.
For supper, e'en, my tender Chicken.

Alan Sillitoe

(English, 1928–)

Chicken

One Sunday Dave went to visit a workmate from his foundry who lived in the country near Keyworth. On the way back he pulled up by the laneside to light a fag, wanting some warmth under the leaden and freezing sky. A hen strutted from a gap in the hedge, as proud and unconcerned as if it owned the land for miles around. Dave picked it up without getting off his bike and stuffed it in a sack-like shopping-bag already weighted by a stone of potatoes. He rode off, wobbling slightly, not even time to kill it, preferring in fact the boasting smiles of getting it home alive, in spite of its thumps and noise.

It was nearly teatime. He left his bike by the back door, and walked through the scullery into the kitchen with his struggling sack held high in sudden light. His mother laughed: "What have you done, picked up somebody's best cat?"

He took off his clips. "It's a live chicken."

"Where the hell did you get that?" She was already suspicious.

"Bought it in Keyworth. A couple of quid. All meat, after you slit its gizzard and peel off the feathers. Make you a nice pillow, mam."

"It's probably got fleas," Bert said.

He took it from the sack, held it by both legs with one hand while he swallowed a cup of tea with the other. It was a fine plump bird, a White Leghorn hen feathered from tail to topnotch. Its eyes were hooded, covered, and it clucked as if about to lay eggs.

"Well," she said, "we'll have it for dinner sometime next week"—and told him to kill it in the backyard so that there'd be no mess in her clean scullery, but really because she couldn't bear to see it slaughtered. Bert and Colin followed him out to see what sort of a job he'd make of it.

He set his cap on the window-sill. "Get me a sharp knife, will you, somebody?"

"Can you manage?" Colin asked.

"Who are you talking to? Listen, I did it every day when I was in Germany—me and the lads, anyway—whenever we went through a farm. I was good at it. I once killed a pig with a sledge hammer, crept up behind it through all the muck with my boots around my neck, then let smash. It didn't even know what happened. Brained it, first go." He was so lit up by his own story that the chicken flapped out of his grasp, heading for the gate. Bert, knife in hand, dived from the step and gripped it firm: "Here you are, Dave. Get it out of its misery."

Dave forced the neck on to a half-brick, and cut through neatly, ending a crescendo of noise. Blood swelled over the back of his hand, his nose twitching at the smell of it. Then he looked up, grinning at his pair of brothers: "You thought I'd need some help, did you?" He laughed, head back, grizzled wire hair softening in the atmosphere of slowly descending mist: "You can come out now, mam. It's all done." But she stayed wisely by the fire.

Blood seeped between his fingers, making the whole palm sticky, the back of his hand wet and freezing in bitter air. They wanted to get back inside, to the big fruit pie and tea, and the pale blinding fire that gave you spots before the eyes if you gazed at it too long. Dave looked at the twitching rump, his mouth narrow, grey eyes considering, unable to believe it was over so quickly. A feather, minute and beautiful so that he followed it up as far as possible with his eyes, spun and settled on his nose. He didn't fancy knocking it off with the knife-hand. "Bert, flick it away, for Christ's sake!"

The chicken humped under his sticky palm and hopped its way to a corner of the yard. "Catch it," Dave called, "or it'll fly back home. It's tomorrow's dinner."

"I can't," Bert screamed. He'd done so a minute ago, but it was a different matter now, to catch a hen on the rampage with no head.

It tried to batter a way through the wooden door of the lavatory. Dave's well-studded boots slid along the asphalt, and his bones thumped down hard, laying him flat on his back. Full of strength, spirit and decision, it trotted up his chest and on to his face, scattering geranium petals of blood all over his best white shirt. Bert's quick hands descended, but it launched itself from Dave's forehead and off towards the footscraper near the back door. Colin fell on it, unable to avoid its wings spreading sharply into his eyes before doubling away.

Dave swayed on his feet. "Let's get it quick." But three did not make a circle, and it soared over its own head and the half-brick of its execution, and was off along the pock-marked yard. You never knew which way it would dive or zigzag. It avoided all hands with uncanny skill, fighting harder now for its life than when it still had a head left to fight for and think with: it was as if the head a few feet away was transmitting accurate messages of warning and direction that it never failed to pick up, an unbreakable line of communication while blood still went through its veins and heart. When it ran over a crust of bread Colin almost expected it to bend its neck and peck at it.

"It'll run down in a bit, like an alarm clock," Dave said, blood over his trousers, coat torn at the elbow, "then we'll get the bleeder." As it ran along the yard the grey December day was stricken by an almost soundless clucking, only half-hearted, as if from miles away, yet tangible nevertheless, maybe a diminution of its earlier protests.

The door of the next house but one was open, and when Bert saw the hen go inside he was on his feet and after it. Dave ran too, the sudden thought striking him that maybe it would shoot out of the front door as well and get run over by a trolley-bus on Wilford Road. It seemed still to have a brain and mind of its own, determined to elude them after its un-called-for treatment at their hands. They all entered the house without thinking to knock, hunters in a state of ecstasy at having cornered their prey at last, hardly separated from the tail of the hen.

Kitchen lights were full on, a fire in the contemporary-style grate, with Mr. Grady at that moment panning more coal on to it. He was an upright hardworking man who lived out his life in overtime on the building sites, except for the treat of his Sunday tea. His wife was serving food to their three grown kids and a couple of relations. She dropped the plate of salmon and screamed as the headless chicken flew up on to the table, clearly on a last bound of energy, and began to spin crazily over plates and dishes. She stared at the three brothers in the doorway.

"What is it? Oh dear God, what are you doing? What is it?"

Mr. Grady stood, a heavy poker in his hand, couldn't speak while the animal reigned over his table, continually hopping and taking-off, dropping blood and feathers, its webbed feet scratching silently over butter and trifle, the soundless echo of clucking seeming to come from its gaping and discontinued neck.

Dave, Bert and Colin were unable to move, stared as it stamped circle-wise over bread and jelly, custard and cress. Colin was somehow expecting Mr. Grady to bring down the poker and end this painful and ludicrous situation—in which the hen looked like beating them at last.

It fell dead in the salad, greenery dwarfed by snowing feathers and flecks of blood. The table was wrecked, and the reality of his ruined, hard-earned tea-party reached Mr Grady's sensitive spot. His big face turned red, after the whiteness of shock and superstitious horror. He fixed his wild eyes on Dave, who drew back, treading into his brothers' ankles:

"You bastards," Grady roared, poker still in hand and watched by all. "You bastards, you!"

"I'd like my chicken back," Dave said, as calmly as the sight of Grady's face and shattered table allowed.

Bert and Colin said nothing. Dave's impetuous thieving had never brought them anything but trouble, as far as they could remember—now that things had gone wrong. All this trouble out of one chicken.

Grady girded himself for the just answer: "It's *my* chicken now," he said, trying to smile over it.

"It ain't," Dave said, obstinate.

"You sent it in on purpose," Grady cried half tearful again, his great chest heaving. "I know you lot, by God I do. Anything for devilment."

"I'd like it back."

Grady's eyes narrowed, the poker higher. "Get away from my house."

"I'm not going till I've got my chicken."

"Get out." He saw Dave's mouth about to open in further argument, but Grady was set on the ultimate word—or at least the last one that mattered, under the circumstances. He brought the poker down on the dead chicken, cracking the salad bowl, a gasp from everyone in the room, including the three brothers. "You should keep your animals under control," he raved. "I'm having this. Now put yourselves on the right side of my doorstep or I'll split every single head of you."

That final thump of the poker set the full stop on all of them, as if the deathblow had been Grady's and gave him the last and absolute right over it. They retreated. What else could you do in face of such barbarity? Grady had always had that sort of reputation. It would henceforth stick with him, and he deserved it more than ever. They would treat him accordingly.

Dave couldn't get over his defeat and humiliation—and his loss that was all the more bitter since the hen had come to him so easily. On their way to the back door he was crying: "I'll get that fat bleeding navvy. What a trick to play on somebody who lives in the same yard! I'll get the bastard. He'll pay for that chicken. By God he will. He's robbed a man of his dinner. He won't get away with a thing like that."

But they were really thinking about what they were going to say to their mother, who had stayed in the house, and who would no doubt remind them for the next few weeks that there was some justice left in the world, and that for the time being it was quite rightly on the side of Mr. Grady.

Charles Simic

(1938–)

The Chicken Without a Head

for Ron and Lynn Sukenick

When two times two was three,
The chicken without a head was hatched.
When the earth was still flat,
It fell off its edge, daydreaming.
When there were 13 signs in the zodiac,
It found a dead star for its gizzard.
When the first fox was getting married,
It taught itself to fly with one wing.
When all the eggs were still golden,
The clouds in the sky tasted like sweet corn.
When the rain flooded its coop,
Its wishbone was its arc.
Ah, when the chicken used to roast itself,
The lightning was its skewer,
The thunder its baste and salt!

The chicken without a head made a sigh,
And then a hailstone out of that sigh,
And a window for the hailstone to stike.
Nine lives it made for itself
And nine coats of solitude to dress them in.
It made its own shadow. No, I'm lying.
It only made a bedbug to bite some holes in the shadow.
Made it all out of nothing. Made a needle
To sew back its broken eggshell.
Made a naked woman—God made the others.

Its father made the knife, but it honed the blade
Until it threw back its image like a funhouse mirror.
Made it all a little at a time.
Who's to say it'd be happier if it didn't?

A soldier met the headless chicken
On a lonely street at night
And had his hair turn white.
A preacher met the devil's drumstick
And made the sign of a cross.
A drunk met his guardian angel
And wanted to ride on its back.
A poor widow met her supper
And ran home for a fork and knife.
A birdwatcher met a jailbird
And wrote down the color of its feathers.
A girl met the same trickster
And let it scratch her
Where it didn't itch.
An orphan met the headless one
And hid it under his shirt,
Then in a book,
Then in his pillow.

Hear the song of a chicken without a head
As it goes listening to its own droppings:
A song in which two parallel lines
Meet at infinity, in which God
Makes the last of the little apples,
In which the golden fleece is heard growing
On a little girl's pubis. The song
Of swearwords dreaming of a pure mouth.
The song of a doornail raised from the dead.
Equally, the song of joy because accomplices
Have been found, because the egg's safe
In the cuckoo's nest. The only song
You wade into until your hat floats.

A song of contagious laughter.
A lethal song.
That's right, the song of night-vision.

Punch my judy and I'll punch yours.
The chicken's in love with the invisible.
Asleep, it writes her love letters.
Sleepless, it sends them tied to a feather.
The earth and the heaven send them back:
No road, no door, no address to the invisible.
   A headless chicken in a headless year
Of a headless week of a headless month,
On a headless evening of a headless day.
Searched for an appropriate engagement ring
Saying over and over and over again:
No finger, no teat, no braid on the invisible . . .
   Randy chicken, the stump of its neck
Like a bloody swollen genital, undressed
Until only its death-rattle was left . . .
The invisible, in the meantime,
Close by, in love with itself.

The chicken on fire and the words
Around it like a ring of fabulous beasts.
Each night it threw them a portion of its innards.
The words were hungry. The night, without end.
Whatever our gallows-bird made, the head unmade.
Its long lost, its axed-off head
Yawned in the sky like a winter moon.
Down below the great work went on:
The table that supplies itself with bread,
A saw that cuts a dream in half,
Wings so fast that they won't get wet in heavy rain,
The egg that says to the frying pan:
I swear it by the hair in my yolk,
There's no such thing as a chicken without a head.

The chicken without a head ran home to roost.
Alongside a fleeing spark it ran.
Ran over a puddle the color of its blackest feather,
Over one foot in the grave.
Ran under your sister's skirt;
Wildest hope honing the ticks of its heart;
Armies parting to let it pass . . .
Gobbled shudders driven up its spine as it ran.
Deafening silence rose like dust in its wake.
Ran with dropped drawers after a swift word.
Red ink, black ink trickling from its talons.
Ran, leaving its muddy tracks, its crooked scrawl,
Leaving its squinting head far behind.
Time flying elsewhere—ran through a church door,
Through a prison door headless into the thin air.
Ran, and is still running this Good Friday,
Between raindrops, tripping over its puns,
Hellfoxes on its trail.

Mark Twain

(American, 1835–1910)

Hunting the Deceitful Turkey

When I was a boy my uncle and his big boys hunted with the
rifle, the youngest boy Fred and I with a shotgun—a small
single-barrelled shotgun which was properly suited to our
size and strength; it was not much heavier than a broom. We
carried it turn about, half an hour at a time. I was not able to
hit anything with it, but I liked to try. Fred and I hunted

feathered small game, the others hunted deer, squirrels, wild turkeys, and such things. My uncle and the big boys were good shots. They killed hawks and wild geese and such like on the wing; and they didn't wound or kill squirrels, they *stunned* them. When the dogs treed a squirrel, the squirrel would scamper aloft and run out on a limb and flatten himself along it, hoping to make himself invisible in that way—and not quite succeeding. You could see his wee little ears sticking up. You couldn't see his nose, but you knew where it was. Then the hunter, despising a "rest" for his rifle, stood up and took offhand aim at the limb and sent a bullet into it immediately under the squirrel's nose, and down tumbled the animal, unwounded but unconscious; the dogs gave him a shake and he was dead. Sometimes when the distance was great and the wind not accurately allowed for, the bullet would hit the squirrel's head; the dogs could do as they pleased with that one—the hunter's pride was hurt, and he wouldn't allow it to go into the gamebag.

In the first faint gray of the dawn the stately wild turkeys would be stalking around in great flocks, and ready to be sociable and answer invitations to come and converse with other excursionists of their kind. The hunter concealed himself and imitated the turkey-call by sucking the air through the leg-bone of a turkey which had previously answered a call like that and lived only just long enough to regret it. There is nothing that furnishes a perfect turkey-call except that bone. Another of Nature's treacheries, you see. She is full of them; half the time she doesn't know which she likes best—to betray her child or protect it. In the case of the turkey she is badly mixed: she gives it a bone to be used in getting it into trouble, and she also furnishes it with a trick for getting itself out of the trouble again. When a mamma-turkey answers an invitation and finds she has made a mistake in accepting it, she does as the mamma-partridge does—remembers a previous engagement and goes limping and scrambling away, pretending to be very lame; and at the same time she is saying to her not-visible children, "Lie low, keep still, don't expose yourselves; I shall be back as soon as I have beguiled this shabby swindler out of the country."

When a person is ignorant and confiding, this immoral device can have tiresome results. I followed an ostensibly lame turkey over a considerable part of the United States one morning, because I believed in her and could not think she would deceive a mere boy, and one who was trusting her and considering her honest. I had the single-barrelled shotgun, but my idea was to catch her alive. I often got within rushing distance of her, and then made my rush; but always, just as I made my final plunge and put my hand down where her back had been, it wasn't there; it was only two or three inches from there and I brushed the tail-feathers as I landed on my stomach—a very close call, but still not quite close enough; that is, not close enough for success, but just close enough to convince me that I could do it next time. She always waited for me, a little piece away, and let on to be resting and greatly fatigued; which was a lie, but I believed it, for I still thought her honest long after I ought to have begun to doubt her, suspecting that this was no way for a high-minded bird to be acting. I followed, and followed, and followed, making my periodical rushes, and getting up and brushing the dust off, and resuming the voyage with patient confidence; indeed, with a confidence which grew, for I could see by the change of climate and vegetation that we were getting up into the high latitudes, and as she always looked a little tireder and a little more discouraged after each rush, I judged that I was safe to win, in the end, the competition being purely a matter of staying power and the advantage lying with me from the start because she was lame.

Along in the afternoon I began to feel fatigued myself. Neither of us had had any rest since we first started on the excursion, which was upwards of ten hours before, though latterly we had paused awhile after rushes, I letting on to be thinking about something else; but neither of us sincere, and both of us waiting for the other to call game but in no real hurry about it, for indeed those little evanescent snatches of rest were very grateful to the feelings of us both; it would naturally be so, skirmishing along like that ever since dawn and not a bite in the meantime; at least for me, though sometimes as she lay on her side fanning herself with a wing and praying for strength to get out of this difficulty a grasshopper happened along whose time had come, and that was well for her, and fortunate, but I had nothing—nothing the whole day.

More than once, after I was very tired, I gave up taking her alive, and was going to shoot her, but I never did it, although it was my right, for I did not believe I could hit her; and besides, she always stopped and posed, when I raised the gun, and this made me suspicious that she knew about me and my marksmanship, and so I did not care to expose myself to remarks.

I did not get her, at all. When she got tired of the game at last, she rose from almost under my hand and flew aloft with the rush and whir of a shell and lit on the highest limb of a great tree and sat down and crossed her legs and smiled down at me, and seemed gratified to see me so astonished.

I was ashamed, and also lost; and it was while wandering the woods hunting for myself that I found a deserted log cabin and had one of the best meals there that in my lifedays I have eaten. The weed-grown garden was full of ripe tomatoes, and I ate them ravenously, though I had never liked them before. Not more than two or three times since have I tasted anything that was so delicious as those tomatoes. I surfeited myself with them, and did not taste another one until I was in middle life. I can eat them now, but I do not like the look of them. I suppose we have all experienced a surfeit at one time or another. Once, in stress of circumstances, I ate part of a barrel of sardines, there being nothing else at hand, but since then I have always been able to get along without sardines.

Ambrose Bierce

(American, 1842–1914?)

Thanksgiving Day

There be those whose memories though vexed with a rake would yield no matter for gratitude. With a waistcoat fitted to the occasion, it is easy enough to eat one's allowance of turkey and hide away one's dishonest share of the wine; if this be returning thanks, why, then, gratitude is considerably easier, and vastly more agreeable, than "falling off a log," and may be acquired in one easy lesson. But if more than this be required—if to be grateful is more than merely to be gluttonous, your true philosopher (he of the austere brow upon which logic has stamped its eternal impress, and from whose heart sentiment has been banished along with other vestigial vices) will think twice and again before leveling his serviceable shins in humble observance of the day.

For here is the nut of reason that he is compelled to crack for the kernel of emotion appropriate to the rite. Unless the blessings that we think we enjoy are favors of the Omnipotent, to be grateful is to be absurd. If they are, then, also, the evils with which we are indubitably afflicted have the same origin. Grant this, as you must, and you make an offset of the ill against the good, or are driven either to the untenable position that we should be grateful for both, or the no more defensible one that all evils are blessings in disguise.

Truth is, my fine fellow of the distensible weskit, your annual gratitude is a sorry pretense, a veritable sham, a cloak, dear man, to cover your unhandsome gluttony; and when by

chance you actually do take to your knees on one day in the
year it is for physical relief and readier digestion of your bird.
Nevertheless, there is truly a subtle but significant relation
between the stuffing of the flesh and the gratitude of the
spirit, as you shall see.

I have ever held and taught the identity of Stomach and
Soul—one entity considered under two aspects. Gratitude I
believe to be a kind of imponderable ether evolved, mainly,
from the action of the gastric fluid upon rich provend and
comforting tope. Like other gases it ascends, and so passes out
at mouth, audible, intelligible, gracious. This beautiful theory
has been tested by convincing experiment in the manner scientific, as here related.

Experiment I. A quantity of grass was put into a leathern
bottle and a gill of the gastric fluid of a sheep introduced. In
ten minutes the neck of the bottle emitted a contented bleat.

Experiment II. A pound of beef was substituted for the
grass and the fluid of a dog for that of the sheep. The result
was a cheerful bark, accompanied by agitation of the bottom
of the bottle, as if an attempt were making to wag it.

Experiment III. The bottle was charged with a handful of
chopped turkey, a glass of old port, and four ounces of human
gastric fluid obtained from a coroner. At first nothing escaped
from the neck but a deep sigh of satisfaction, followed by a
grunt like that of a banqueting pig. The proportion of turkey
being increased and the gas confined, the bottle was greatly
distended, appearing to suffer a slight uneasiness. The restriction being removed, the experimenter had the happiness to
hear, distinctly articulated, the words: "Praise God, from
whom all blessings flow—praise Him all bottles here below!"

Against such demonstration as this all theological inter-
pretation of the phenomena of gratitude is of no avail.

Samuel Butler

(English, 1835–1902)

From *Erewhon*, Chapter 26

Some two thousand five hundred years ago the Erewhonians were still uncivilised, and lived by hunting, fishing, a rude system of agriculture, and plundering such few other nations as they had not yet completely conquered. They had no schools or systems of philosophy, but by a kind of dog-knowledge did that which was right in their own eyes and in those of their neighbours; the common sense, therefore, of the public being as yet unvitiated, crime and disease were looked upon much as they are in other countries.

But with the gradual advance of civilisation and increase in material prosperity, people began to ask questions about things that they had hitherto taken as matters of course, and one old gentleman, who had great influence over them by reason of the sanctity of his life, and his supposed inspiration by an unseen power, whose existence was now beginning to be felt, took it into his head to disquiet himself about the rights of animals—a question that so far had disturbed no-body.

All prophets are more or less fussy, and this old gentleman seems to have been one of the more fussy ones. Being maintained at the public expense, he had ample leisure, and not content with limiting his attention to the rights of animals, he wanted to reduce right and wrong to rules, to consider the foundations of duty and of good and evil, and otherwise to put all sorts of matters on a logical basis, which people whose time is money are content to accept on no basis at all.

As a matter of course, the basis on which he decided that duty alone could rest was one that afforded no standing-room for many of the old-established habits of the people. These, he assured them, were all wrong, and whenever any one ventured to differ from him, he referred the matter to the unseen power with which he alone was in direct communication, and the unseen power invariably assured him that he was right. As regards the rights of animals he taught as follows:

"You know," he said, "how wicked it is of you to kill one another. Once upon a time your forefathers made no scruple about not only killing, but also eating their relations. No one would now go back to such detestable practises, for it is notorious that we have lived much more happily since they were abandoned. From this increased prosperity we may confidently deduce the maxim that we should not kill and eat our fellow-creatures. I have consulted the higher power by whom you know that I am inspired, and he has assured me that this conclusion is irrefragable.

"Now it cannot be denied that sheep, cattle, deer, birds, and fishes are our fellow-creatures. They differ from us in some respects, but those in which they differ are few and secondary, while those that they have in common with us are many and essential. My friends, if it was wrong of you to kill and eat your fellow-men, it is wrong also to kill and eat fish, flesh, and fowl. Birds, beasts, and fishes, have as full a right to live as long as they can unmolested by man, as man has to live unmolested by his neighbours. These words, let me again assure you, are not mine, but those of the higher power which inspires me.

"I grant," he continued, "that animals molest one another, and that some of them go so far as to molest man, but I have yet to learn that we should model our conduct on that of the lower animals. We should endeavour, rather, to instruct them, and bring them to a better mind. To kill a tiger, for example, who has lived on the flesh of men and women whom he has killed, is to reduce ourselves to the level of the tiger, and is unworthy of people who seek to be guided by the highest principles in all, both their thoughts and actions.

"The unseen power who has revealed himself to me alone among you, has told me to tell you that you ought by this time to have outgrown the barbarous habits of your ancestors. If, as you believe, you know better than they, you should do better. He commands you, therefore, to refrain from killing any living being for the sake of eating it. The only animal food that you may eat, is the flesh of any birds, beasts, or fishes that you may come upon as having died a natural death, or any that may have been born prematurely, or so deformed that it is a mercy to put them out of their pain; you may also eat all such animals as have committed suicide. As regards vegetables you may eat all those that will let you eat them with impunity."

So wisely and so well did the old prophet argue, and so terrible were the threats he hurled at those who should disobey him, that in the end he carried the more highly educated part of the people with him, and presently the poorer classes followed suit, or professed to do so. Having seen the triumph of his principles, he was gathered to his fathers, and no doubt entered at once into full communion with that unseen power whose favour he had already so pre-eminently enjoyed.

He had not, however, been dead very long, before some of his more ardent disciples took it upon them to better the instruction of their master. The old prophet had allowed the use of eggs and milk, but his disciples decided that to eat a fresh egg was to destroy a potential chicken, and that this came to much the same as murdering a live one. Stale eggs, if it was quite certain that they were too far gone to be able to be hatched, were grudgingly permitted, but all eggs offered for sale had to be submitted to an inspector, who, on being satisfied that they were addled, would label them "Laid not less than three months" from the date, whatever it might happen to be. These eggs, I need hardly say, were only used in puddings, and as a medicine in certain cases where an emetic was urgently required. Milk was forbidden inasmuch as it could not be obtained without robbing some calf of its natural sustenance, and thus endangering its life.

It will be easily believed that at first there were many who gave the new rules outward observance, but embraced every opportunity of indulging secretly in those flesh-pots to which they had been accustomed. It was found that animals were continually dying natural deaths under more or less suspicious circumstances. Suicidal mania, again, which had hitherto been confined exclusively to donkeys, became alarmingly prevalent even among such for the most part self-respecting creatures as sheep and cattle. It was astonishing how some of these unfortunate animals would scent out a butcher's knife if there was one within a mile of them, and run right up against it if the butcher did not get it out of their way in time.

Dogs, again, that had been quite law-abiding as regards domestic poultry, tame rabbits, sucking pigs, or sheep and lambs, suddenly took to breaking beyond the control of their masters, and killing anything that they were told not to touch. It was held that any animal killed by a dog had died a natural death, for it was the dog's nature to kill things, and he had only refrained from molesting farmyard creatures hitherto because his nature had been tampered with. Unfortunately the more these unruly tendencies became developed, the more the common people seemed to delight in breeding the very animals that would put temptation in the dog's way. There is little doubt, in fact, that they were deliberately evading the law; but whether this was so or no they sold or ate everything their dogs had killed.

Evasion was more difficult in the case of the larger animals, for the magistrates could not wink at all the pretended suicides of pigs, sheep, and cattle that were brought before them. Sometimes they had to convict, and a few convictions had a very terrorising effect—whereas in the case of animals killed by a dog, the marks of the dog's teeth could be seen, and it was practically impossible to prove malice on the part of the owner of the dog.

Another fertile source of disobedience to the law was furnished by a decision of one of the judges that raised a great outcry among the more fervent disciples of the old prophet. The judge held that it was lawful to kill any animal in self-defence and that such conduct was so natural on the part of a man who found himself attacked, that the attacking creature should be held to have died a natural death. The High Vegetarians had indeed good reason to be alarmed, for hardly had this decision become generally known before a number of animals, hitherto harmless, took to attacking their owners with such ferocity, that it became necessary to put them to a natural death. Again, it was quite common at that time to see a carcase of a calf, lamb, or kid exposed for sale with a label from the inspector certifying that it had been killed in self-defence. Sometimes even the carcase of a lamb or calf was exposed as "warranted stillborn," when it presented every appearance of having enjoyed at least a month of life.

As for the flesh of animals that had *bona fide* died a natural death, the permission to eat it was nugatory, for it was generally eaten by some other animal before man got hold of it; or failing this it was often poisonous, so that practically people were forced to evade the law by some of the means above spoken of, or to become vegetarians. This last alternative was so little to the taste of the Erewhonians, that the laws against killing animals were falling into desuetude, and would very likely have been repealed, but for the breaking out of a pestilence, which was ascribed by the priests and prophets of the day to the lawlessness of the people in the matter of eating forbidden flesh. On this, there was a reaction; stringent laws were passed, forbidding the use of meat in any form or shape, and permitting no food but grain, fruits, and vegetables to be sold in shops and markets. These laws were enacted about two hundred years after the death of the old prophet who had first unsettled people's minds about the rights of animals; but they had hardly been passed before people again began to break them.

I was told that the most painful consequence of all this

folly did not lie in the fact that law-abiding people had to go
without animal food—many nations do this and seem none
the worse, and even in flesh-eating countries such as Italy,
Spain, and Greece, the poor seldom see meat from year's end
to year's end. The mischief lay in the jar which undue pro-
hibition gave to the consciences of all but those who were
strong enough to know that though conscience as a rule
boons, it can also bane. The awakened conscience of an individual will often lead him to do things in haste that he had
better have left undone, but the conscience of a nation awakened by a respectable old gentleman who has an unseen
power up his sleeve will pave hell with a vengeance.

Young people were told that it was a sin to do what their
fathers had done unhurt for centuries; those, moreover, who
preached to them about the enormity of eating meat, were an
attractive academic folk, and though they overawed all but
the bolder youths, there were few who did not in their hearts
dislike them. However much the young person might be
shielded, he soon got to know that men and women of the
world—often far nicer people than the prophets who
preached abstention—continually spoke sneeringly of the
new doctrinaire laws, and were believed to set them aside in
secret, though they dared not do so openly. Small wonder,
then, that the more human among the student classes were
provoked by the touch-not, taste-not, handle-not precepts of
their rulers, into questioning much that they would otherwise
have unhesitatingly accepted.

One sad story is on record about a young man of promis-
ing amiable disposition, but cursed with more conscience than
brains, who had been told by his doctor (for as I have above
said disease was not yet held to be criminal) that he ought to
eat meat, law or no law. He was as much shocked and for
some time refused to comply with what he deemed the un-
righteous advice given him by his doctor; at last, however,
finding that he grew weaker and weaker, he stole secretly on
a dark night into one of those dens in which meat was surrep-
titiously sold, and bought a pound of prime steak. He took it

home, cooked it in his bedroom when every one in the house had gone to rest, ate it, and though he could hardly sleep for remorse and shame, felt so much better next morning that he hardly knew himself.

Three or four days later, he again found himself irresistibly drawn to this same den. Again he bought a pound of steak, again he cooked and ate it, and again, in spite of much mental torture, on the following morning felt himself a different man. To cut the story short, though he never went beyond the bounds of moderation, it preyed upon his mind that he should be drifting, as he certainly was, into the ranks of the habitual lawbreakers.

All the time his health kept on improving, and though he felt sure that he owed this to the beefsteaks, the better he became in body, the more his conscience gave him no rest; two voices were forever ringing in his ears—the one saying, "I am Common Sense and Nature; heed me, and I will reward you as I rewarded your fathers before you." But the other voice said: "Let not that plausible spirit lure you to your ruin. I am Duty; heed me, and I will reward you as I rewarded your fathers before you."

Sometimes he even seemed to see the faces of the speakers. Common Sense looked so easy, genial, and serene, so frank and fearless, that do what he might he could not mistrust her; but as he was on the point of following her, he would be checked by the austere face of Duty, so grave, but yet so kindly; and it cut him to the heart that from time to time he should see her turn pitying away from him as he followed after her rival.

The poor boy continually thought of the better class of his fellow-students, and tried to model his conduct on what he thought was theirs. "They," he said to himself, "eat a beefsteak? Never." But they most of them ate one now and again, unless it was a mutton chop that tempted them. And they used him for a model much as he did them. "He," they would say to themselves, "eat a mutton chop? Never." One night, however, he was followed by one of the authorities, who was always prowling about in search of law-breakers, and was caught coming out of the den with half a shoulder of mutton concealed about his person. On this, even though he had not been put in prison, he would have been sent away with his prospects in life irretrievably ruined; he therefore hanged himself as soon as he got home.

Lewis Carroll

(1832–1898)

From *Through the Looking Glass*

Alice glanced nervously along the table, as she walked up the large hall, and noticed that there were about fifty guests, of all kinds: some were animals, some birds, and there were even a few flowers among them. "I'm glad they've come without waiting to be asked," she thought: "I should never have known who were the right people to invite!"

There were three chairs at the head of the table; the Red and White Queens had already taken two of them, but the middle one was empty. Alice sat down in it, rather uncomfortable at the silence, and longing for some one to speak.

At last the Red Queen began. "You''ve missed the soup and fish," she said. "Put on the joint!" And the waiters set a leg of mutton before Alice, who looked at it rather anxiously, as she had never had to carve a joint before.

"You look a little shy; let me introduce you to that leg of mutton," said the Red Queen. "Alice—Mutton; Mutton—Alice." The leg of mutton got up in the dish and made a little bow to Alice; and Alice returned the bow, not knowing whether to be frightened or amused.

"May I give you a slice?" she said, taking up the knife and fork, and looking from one Queen to the other.

"Certainly not," the Red Queen said, very decidedly: "it isn't etiquette to cut any one you"ve been introduced to. Remove the joint!"

Charles Dickens

(English, 1812–1870)

From *David Copperfield*

The leg of mutton came up very red within, and very pale without; besides having a foreign substance of a gritty nature sprinkled over it, as if it had had a fall into the ashes of that remarkable kitchen fire-place. But we were not in a condition to judge of this fact from the appearance of the gravy, forasmuch as the "young gal" had dropped it all upon the stairs—where it remained, by-the-by, in a long train, until it was worn out. The pigeon-pie was not bad, but it was a delusive pie; the crust being like a disappointing head, phrenologically speaking—full of lumps and bumps, with nothing particular underneath. In short, the banquet was such a failure that I should have been quite unhappy—about the failure, I mean, for I am always unhappy about Dora—if I had not been relieved by the great good-humour of my company, and by a bright suggestion from Mr. Micawber.

"My dear friend Copperfield," said Mr. Micawber, "accidents will occur in the best-regulated families; and in families not regulated by that pervading influence which sanctifies while it enhances the—a—I would say, in short, by the influence of Woman, in the lofty character of Wife, they may be expected with confidence, and must be borne with philosophy. If you will allow me to take the liberty of remarking that there are few comestibles better, in their way, than a devil, and that I believe, with a little division of labour, we could accomplish a good one if the young person in attendance could produce a gridiron, I would put it to you that this little misfortune may be easily repaired."

There was a gridiron in the pantry, on which my morning rasher of bacon was cooked. We had it in, in a twinkling, and immediately applied ourselves to carrying Mr. Micawber's idea into effect. The division of labour to which he had referred was this: Traddles cut the mutton into slices; Mr. Micawber (who could do anything of this sort to perfection) covered them with pepper, mustard, salt, and cayenne; I put them on the gridiron, turned them with a fork, and took them off, under Mr. Micawber's direction; and Mrs. Micawber heated, and continually stirred, some mushroom ketchup in a little saucepan. When we had slices enough done to begin upon, we fell to, with our sleeves still tucked up at the wrists, more slices sputtering and blazing on the fire, and our attention divided between the mutton on our plates and the mutton then preparing.

What with the novelty of this cookery, the excellence of it, the bustle of it, the frequent starting up to look after it, the frequent sitting down to dispose of it as the crisp slices came off the gridiron hot and hot, the being so busy, so flushed with the fire, so amused, and in the midst of such a tempting noise and savour, we reduced the leg of mutton to the bone.

T. E. Lawrence

(English, 1888–1935)

From *The Seven Pillars of Wisdom*

The bowl was now brim-full, ringed round its edge by white rice in an embankment a foot wide and six inches deep, filled with legs and ribs of mutton till they toppled over. It needed two or three victims to make in the centre a dressed pyramid of meat such as honour prescribed. The centre-pieces were the boiled, upturned heads, propped on their severed stumps of neck, so that the ears, brown like old leaves, flapped out on the rice surface. The jaws gaped emptily upward, pulled open to show the hollow throat with the tongue, still pink, clinging to the lower teeth; and the long incisors whitely crowned the pile, very prominent above the nostrils' pricking hair and the lips which sneered away blackly from them.

This load was set down on the soil of the cleared space between us, where it steamed hotly, while a procession of minor helpers bore small cauldrons and copper vats in which the cooking had been done. From them, with much-bruised bowls of enamelled iron, they ladled out over the main dish all the inside and outside of the sheep; little bits of yellow intestine, the white tail-cushion of fat, brown muscles and meat and bristly skin, all swimming in the liquid butter and grease of the seething. The bystanders watched anxiously, muttering satisfactions when a very juicy scrap plopped out.

The fat was scalding. Every now and then a man would drop his baler with an exclamation, and plunge his burnt fingers, not reluctantly, in his mouth to cool them: but they persevered till at last their scooping rang loudly on the bottoms of the pots; and, with a gesture of triumph, they fished out the intact livers from their hiding place in the gravy and topped the yawning jaws with them.

Two raised each smaller cauldron and tilted it, letting the liquid splash down upon the meat till the rice-crater was full, and the loose grains at the edge swam in the abundance; and yet they poured, till, amid cries of astonishment from us, it was running over, and a little pool congealing in the dust. That was the final touch of splendour, and the host called us to come and eat.

We feigned a deafness, as manners demanded: at last we heard him, and looked surprised at one another, each urging his fellow to move first; till Nasir rose coyly, and after him we all came forward to sink on one knee round the tray, wedging in and cuddling up till the twenty-two for whom there was barely space were grouped around the food. We turned back our sleeves to the elbow, and, taking lead from Nasir with a low "In the name of God the merciful, the loving-kind," we dipped together.

The first dip, for me, at least, was always cautious, since the liquid fat was so hot that my unaccustomed fingers could seldom bear it; and so I would toy with an exposed and cooling lump of meat till others' excavations had drained my rice-segment. We would knead between the fingers (not soiling the palm), neat balls of rice and fat and liver and meat cemented by gentle pressure, and project them by leverage of the thumb from the crooked forefinger into the mouth. With the right trick and the right construction the little lump held together and came clean off the hand; but when surplus butter and odd fragments clung, cooling, to the fingers, they had to be licked carefully to make the next effort slip easier away.

As the meat pile wore down (nobody really cared about rice: flesh was the luxury) one of the chief Howeitat* eating with us would draw his dagger, silver hilted, set with turquoise, a signed masterpiece of Mohammed Ibn Zari, of

*A Bedouin people.

Jauf,*and would cut crisscross from the larger bones long diamonds of meat easily torn up between the fingers; for it was
necessarily boiled very tender, since all had to be disposed of
with the right hand, which alone was honourable.

Our host stood by the circle, encouraging the appetite
with pious ejaculations. At top speed we twisted, tore, cut,
and stuffed: never speaking, since conversation would insult a
meal's quality; though it was proper to smile thanks when an
intimate guest passed a select fragment, or when Mohammed
el Dheilan gravely handed over a huge barren bone with a
blessing. On such occasions I would return the compliment
with some hideous impossible lump of guts, a flippancy which
rejoiced the Howeitat, but which the gracious, aristocratic
Nasir saw with disapproval.

At length some of us were nearly filled, and began to play
and pick; glancing sideways at the rest till they too grew
slow, and at last ceased eating, elbow on knee, the hand hanging down from the wrist over the tray edge to drip, while the
fat, butter, and scattered grains of rice cooled into a stiff
white grease which gummed the fingers together. When all
had stopped, Nasir meaningly cleared his throat, and we rose
up together in haste with an explosive "God requite it you, O
host," to group ourselves outside among the tent-ropes while
the next twenty guests inherited our leaving.

*An oasis in northern Saudi Arabia.

François Marie Arouet de Voltaire

(French, 1694–1778)

From *Zadig, or Destiny*

CHAPTER XII
The Supper

Sétoc could not part with this man in whom wisdom dwelt,
and he took him to the great fair at Bassora,* where the chief
merchants of the inhabited world were accustomed to con-
gregate. For Zadig it was an evident consolation to see so
many men assembled in one place. The universe seemed to
him to be a big family, the members of which gathered together at Bassora.

From the second day he found himself eating with an
Egyptian, an Indian from the Ganges country, an inhabitant
of Cathay, a Greek, a Celt and several other travellers who in
their frequent travels towards the Arabian Gulf had learned
enough Arabic to make themselves understood. The Egyptian
seemed very wroth.

"What an accursed place Bassora is!" he said. "No one
here will lend me a thousand ounces of gold on a parcel of the
finest dry-goods in the world."

"What are the dry-goods," asked Sétoc, "on which you
cannot obtain that amount?"

"My aunt's body," replied the Egyptian. "She was the
finest woman in Egypt. She always used to accompany me,
and now she has died on the road, I've had her made into one
of the finest mummies we have. In my own country I could
pawn her for as much as I liked. It's very strange that here

*Basra, a city in Iraq.

nobody will give me a paltry thousand ounces of gold on such solid security."

Getting angrier and angrier, he set about eating some excellent boiled fowl. The Indian took his hand and stopped him. "What are you going to do?" he cried sorrowfully.

"Eat this chicken," said the man with the mummy.

"Take care," continued the man from the Ganges, "take care! Your dead aunt's soul may have passed into this chicken's body, and you do not wish to expose yourself to the possibility of eating your aunt. To cook a chicken is a manifest outrage on nature."

"What are you talking about with your nature and your chickens?" demanded the choleric Egyptian. "We worship a bull, and many a good meal do we make of beef."

"You worship a bull! Is it possible?" said the man from the Ganges.

"Nothing more possible," answered the other. "We've done so for a hundred and thirty-five thousand years, and none of us find anything amiss in it."

"A hundred and thirty-five thousand years?" returned the Indian. "You exaggerate somewhat. Why, India has only been populated eighty-four thousand, and we're certainly older than you. Brahma forbade us to eat beef before you dreamed of putting the ox on either the altar or the spit."

"A nice booby Brahma to compare with our Apis," sneered the Egyptian. "What did your Brahma do that was so wonderful?"

"It was Brahma taught men to read and write," answered the Brahmin, "and it's to him the world owes the game of chess."

"Not a bit of it," interrupted a Chaldean seated near by; "we owe such great benefits to the fish Oannes, and it is only fair to render unto him the things that are his. Everyone will tell you he was a divine being, that he had a golden tail and a fine human head, and that he came out of the water to preach on earth for three hours each day. He had numerous children who were all kings, as everyone knows. I have his picture at home, and I hold it in veneration, as is my duty. You may eat beef as much as you like, but it is assuredly very great sacrilege to cook fish.

Herman Melville
(1819–1891)

From *Moby Dick*

CHAPTER LXV
The Whale as a Dish

That mortal man should feed upon the creature that feeds his lamp, and, like Stubb, eat him by his own light, as you may say; this seems so outlandish a thing that one must needs go a little into the history and philosophy of it.

It is upon record, that three centuries ago the tongue of the Right Whale was esteemed a great delicacy in France, and commanded large prices there. Also, that in Henry VIIIth's time, a certain cook of the court obtained a handsome reward for inventing an admirable sauce to be eaten with barbacued porpoises, which, you remember, are a species of whale. Porpoises, indeed, are to this day considered fine eating. The meat is made into balls about the size of billiard balls, and being well seasoned and spiced might be taken for turtle balls or veal balls. The old monks of Dumfermline were very fond of them. They had a great porpoise grant from the crown.

The fact is, that among his hunters at least, the whale would by all hands be considered a noble dish, were there not so much of him; but when you come to sit down before a meat-pie nearly one hundred feet long, it takes away your appetite. Only the most unprejudiced of men like Stubb, nowadays partake of cooked whales; but the Esquimaux are

not so fastidious. We all know they live upon whales, and
have rare old vintages of prime old train oil. Zogranda, one of
their most famous doctors, recommends strips of blubber for
infants, as being exceedingly juicy and nourishing. And this
reminds me that certain Englishmen, who long ago were accidentally left in Greenland by a whaling vessel—that these
men actually lived for several months on the mouldy scraps
of whales which had been left ashore after trying out the
blubber. Among the Dutch whalemen these scraps are called
"fritters;" which, indeed, they greatly resemble, being brown
and crisp, and smelling something like old Amsterdam house-
wives' dough-nuts or oly-cooks, when fresh. They have such
an eatable look that the most self-denying stranger can hardly
keep his hands off.

But what further depreciates the whale as a civilized dish,
is his exceeding richness. He is the great prize ox of the sea,
too fat to be delicately good. Look at his hump, which would
be as fine eating as the buffalo's (which is esteemed a rare
dish), were it not such a solid pyramid of fat. But the sper-
maceti itself, how bland and creamy that is; like the transparent, half-jellied, white meat of a cocoanut in the third
month of its growth, yet far too rich to supply a substitute
for butter. Nevertheless, many whalemen have a method of
absorbing it into some other substance, and then partaking of
it. In the long try watches of the night it is a common thing
for the seamen to dip their ship-biscuit into the huge oil-pots
and let them fry there awhile. Many a good supper have I
thus made.

In the case of a small Sperm Whale the brains are ac-
counted a fine dish. The casket of the skull is broken into
with an axe, and the two plump, whitish lobes being with-
drawn (precisely resembling two large puddings), they are
then mixed with flour, and cooked into a most delectable
mess, in flavor somewhat resembling calves' head, which is
quite a dish among some epicures; and every one knows that
some young bucks among the epicures, by continually dining
upon calves' brains, by and by get to have a little brains of

their own, so as to be able to tell a calf's head from their own heads; which, indeed, requires uncommon discrimination. And that is the reason why a young buck with an intelligent looking calf's head before him, is somehow one of the saddest sights you can see. The head looks a sort of reproachfully at him, with an "Et tu Brute!" expression.

It is not, perhaps, entirely because the whale is so excessively unctuous that landsmen seem to regard the eating of him with abhorrence; that appears to result, in some way, from the consideration before mentioned: i.e. that a man should eat a newly murdered thing of the sea, and eat it too by its own light. But no doubt the first man that ever murdered an ox was regarded as a murderer; perhaps he was hung; and if he had been put on his trial by oxen, he certainly would have been; and he certainly deserved it if any murderer does. Go to the meatmarket of a Saturday night and see the crowds of live bipeds staring up at the long rows of dead quadrupeds. Does not that sight take a tooth out of the cannibal's jaw? Cannibals? who is not a cannibal? I tell you it will be more tolerable for the Fejee that salted down a lean missionary in his cellar against a coming famine; it will be more tolerable for that provident Fejee, I say, in the day of judgment, than for thee, civilized and enlightened gourmand, who nailest geese to the ground and feastest on their bloated livers in thy paté-de-foie-gras.

But Stubb, he eats the whale by its own light, does he? and that is adding insult to injury, is it? Look at your knifehandle, there, my civilized and enlightened gourmand dining off that roast beef, what is that handle made of?—what but the bones of the brother of the very ox you are eating? And what do you pick your teeth with, after devouring that fat goose? With a feather of the same fowl. And with what quill did the Secretary of the Society for the Suppression of Cruelty to Ganders formally indite his circulars? It is only within the last month or two that that society passed a resolution to patronize nothing but steel pens.

Fish

Juan Ruiz

(Spanish, 1283?–1351)

About the Battle of the Lord Flesh-Season and the Lady Lent

A holy season dedicated to God was drawing near.
I went back toward my own homeland to take a little rest,
As Lent would be upon us in a week; meanwhile, great fear
And mounting terror penetrated everybody's breast.

While I was in my house with Sir Shrove-Thursday as my
    guest,
Two messages were brought me by a messenger who sped.
I'll tell you what the contents were, but I won't be exact,
As I returned the letters to the messenger when read:

"From me—the servant of our great Creator—Holy Lent,
Who by Almighty God to all his sinners have been sent;
To all archpriests and clerics not involved in love affairs,
Greetings in Jesus' name until High Eastertide is spent.

"Know ye that I have been informed that for almost a year
The Lord of Flesh has acted most intractable, engaged
In laying waste to all my lands, in doing grievous harm,
And spilling lots of blood, because of which I'm much
    enraged.

"And for this cause, by virtue of your true obedience
I give you firm commands, on pain of judgment later on,
That on behalf of me, my Fast and my long Penitence,
You challenge him with this my letter of good reference.

"Tell him straightforwardly that from this time in seven days
I in my very person, with my companies complete,
Shall come to fight against him and against his stubborn
      ways.
I doubt that he would pause for us in slaughtering his meat.

"Return this letter to the messenger when it's been read;
Let him reveal it to the land, not hide it in his sleeve.
Let none of your folk say that it was not to them made
      known.
In Castro Urdiales writ, and in Burgos received."*

Another note he brought, an open letter, with a seal—
A big and lovely seashell hanging from the paper's end—
Which was the official stamp used by the lady I have named,
The message ran like this and to the Lord of Flesh was sent:

"From me, the Lady Lent, who am the magistrate of seas
And constable of all the souls who will be saved if true,
To you, the gluttonous Lord Flesh, who can't be satisfied,
To you I send Sir Fast in my own name, to challenge you.

"In six days from today you and your well-armed company
Must be out on the battlefield to wage a war with me.
And up to Holy Saturday I'll fight you without fail.
You won't be able to escape, either death or time in jail."

I read both notes and understood the message then in hand.
I saw they brought to me a firm, unshakable command,
For I had none to love and was not snared in love affairs.
They threw me and my guest into a deep and dark despair.

For I had Sir Shrove-Thursday at my table as a guest;
He got up very happily, which caused me no regret,

*The first is a Roman seaport town in Santander, the northeast region of Spain;
the second is a town in Old Castile. When the battle gets underway, Lady Lent's
fishy troops arrive from all over the country, naming the regions they presumably
have made famous as dishes.

And said, "Against this luckless Lent, I'm standard-bearer
   named,
And I shall joust with her; each year she feels my heavy
   weight."

He gave me many thanks for the abundant feast I spread,
And left; and I wrote out my notes and to Sir Friday said;
"Go to the Lord of Flesh tomorrow, tell him all of this,
And he must come on Tuesday next, prepared to fight till
   dead."

And when the letters were received, the haughty Lord of
   Flesh
Put on a show of being brave, but he was filled with fright.
He didn't want to send replies and quickly started out,
Leading a host of troops, for he was such a mighty knight.

So when the day came, after the appointed lapse of time,
The Lord of Flesh beforehand had arrived and in full force,
Accompanied by many men arrayed in battle gear.
Alexander would have been delighted by such regal corps.

A lot of fine foot soldiers in the front lines he displayed—
The chickens and the partridges, the capons and the hares,
And with them ducks and widgeons, too, and big fat geese;
   and there,
Around the smoldering fires, they drilled and passed in dress
   parade.

All of these bore the lances of the front-line foot soldiers—
The spits and skewers fashioned well from iron, wood and
   steel—
And all were guarded by their shields, the platters and the
   salvers.
These always come right at the start of any well-planned
   meal.

And after those with shields, there came the archers with
    their bows:
Wild ducks and dried corned beef and sides of mutton now
    appeared,
And roasted haunches of fresh pork and entire legs of ham.
And then behind all these, there came the mounted cavaliers:

Slices of roasted beef and cuts of suckling pigs and kids
Appeared there, leaping all about and uttering loud cries.
And next a whole armed guard—the many fritters made of
    cheese,
Which spur a man to using good red wine in large supplies.

And then there came a troop replete with old nobility—
A swarm of very fine pheasants, peacocks, proud in gay
    allure,
Arrived, accoutered brightly, with their banners held up high,
All wearing curious armor and impressive garniture.

Their arms were most elaborate, well wrought and very fine;
As helmets they wore stewpots of pure copper, or tureens,
And as their shields had kettles, frying pans and kitchen pots.
No such majestic, wealthy camp is owned by drab sardines!

There came then many buck deers and the powerful wild
    boar,
Who told him, "Now, my lord, don't go without me in this
    fight,
For many times already I have fought against the Moor.
As I am trained to fight, I'm always useful to a knight."

He never finished up his speech, he wasn't yet half through,
When straightway came along the very swift and fleet cerf-
    stag,
And said, "I bow to you, my lord, your servant tried and
    true;
So that I'll be of service, may I not be serf to you?"

To join the muster promptly came the very nimble hare.
"My lord," he said, "a fever on your lady-foe I'll cast,
I'll give her itch and boils, so she'll forget about her fight,
Except to want my skin when one of them should break at
    last."

The mountain goat with nimble deer and white-necked
    pigeons came,
Proclaiming his most braggart boasts in threatening loud
    tones.
"My lord," he said, "if you but wind this lady in my arms,
She'll have no power to harm you, not with all of her fish
    bones."

The thoroughbred old bullock came up slowly pace by pace.
"My lord," he said, "please turn me out to pasture. In my
    case
I am no longer good for work in fields or on highways,
But with my meat and hide, I'll do my service to your grace."

Sir Bacon too was there with many other good cured meats,
Big slabs of salted pork, rib joints—a kitchen stuffed and
    strewn
With all prepared and ready for the grand, malicious clash.
Lady Lent was a past master; she did not come too soon.

Because Lord Flesh is known to be a mighty emperor
And wields a prince's power across the world, both far and
    near,
The fowls and animals, out of their mighty love of him,
Came forth in deep humility, but they were full of fear.

The Lord of Flesh in splendor now had settled in his seat
Before a laden table in a lavish hall to eat,
With minstrels playing for him, like a highly honored man.
And he was well provided with a lot of kinds of meat.

And there in front of him his standard-bearer was in place
On bended knee, with wine keg, in his hand prepared to
    pour;
He crooked his elbow often, playing trumpet on the cask;
And Wine, the constable of all, was talking more and more.

When night had fallen and the feast had finished long before,
And everybody'd stuffed his campaign belly very tight,
So as to face the battle with the placid Lady Lent,
They all lay down to sleep, all wishing each a nice "good-
    night."

Through all that night the roosters felt exceedingly afraid
And stayed awake because of fear, slept not a wink nor
    stirred.
This wasn't such a wonder, as their mates were now all dead.
And so they were excited by the noises which they heard.

At midnight, right into the middle of these halls there came
Our Lady Lent and shouted, "Lord, God, do defend us now!"
The cocks raised up their voices and they flapped their wings
    about.
This bad news then was broken to the Lord of Flesh
    somehow.

But as that worthy gentleman had eaten much too much
And, with a great amount of meat, had drunk up too much
    wine,
He felt quite swollen and inert, indeed was half-asleep.
Through all his camp the call rang out to form a battle line.

But everyone was drowsy and marched sluggish into battle.
His soldiers were deployed in ranks; none sued for peace that
    day.
The sea battalion brought its weapons forward with a rattle,
Their spears were set to wound them all; they loudly cried,
    "Hurray!"

The first one of the lot who gave the Lord of Flesh a wound—
A pot of strong leek soup—hurt him severely with each
    bowl.
It made him spit up clots of phlegm, which was a hopeful
    sign;
The Lady Lent thought now she had the camp in full control.

To her assistance then the salty sardine quickly sped
And wounded very grievously the hen, fat and well fed.
It got stuck in her beak and quickly smothered her to death,
And later knocked the Lord of Flesh's helmet off his head.

Then came a troop of fox-sharks sent into the foremost lines,
With armed green fish and cuttlefish to stand guard on the
    flanks.
The fight was hard and rough, in many ways was turning
    bad,
And many valiant heads fell off on each side of the ranks.

From the region of Valencia there then came forth the eels
In many tiny schools pickled in brine and cured for weeks.
They struck the Lord Flesh hard, right in the middle of his
    ribs.
The fat trouts from Alberche smacked him soundly in the
    cheeks.

The giant tuna fish arrived, just like a big brave lion,
Met with Sir Bacon, challenged him with oaths on every part;
And were it not for Sir Corned Beef, who turned the shaft
    aside,
He would have hit Shrove-Thursday in the center of his heart.

From the region of Bayonne a host of little sharks came up,
Which killed the partridges and then castrated all the cocks.
Up from the river of Henares came the small crayfish
And to the Guadalquivir spread out their campaign tents in
    flocks.

The little cod and barbel fish were fighting with wild ducks.
The codfish called the hog: "Where are you, not to show
    somewhere?
If you appear before me, I'll mete out what you deserve;
Go hide out in a Moorish mosque, don't come to holy
    prayer."

The dogfish now arrived upon that scene of sure defeat.
He had sharp hooks in his tough skin, like sharp teeth of
    a rat,
And gave a painful time to fighters on their ribs and legs,
On which he seized and fastened just as if he were a cat.

Then in support, out of the ocean, swamps and ponds arose
Companies of outlandish fish of varied size and shape,
Who carried with them forceful arms and arrows and
    crossbows.
This rout was grimmer than we bore at Alarcos from our
    foes.

From Santandér there came the bright red lobsters, well
    aligned,
Who brought along with them their quivers full of many
    darts
And forced Lord Flesh to pay the full cost that they had
    assigned;
The battlefield, though broad, appeared quite narrow and
    confined.

A year of jubilee had been proclaimed for all the blest,
And everyone was very anxious then to save his soul.
All creatures that were living in the sea joined this contest;
The herrings and the breams came from Bermeo with the
    rest.

With many soldiers in his train the great otter attacked,
Both wounding and destroying troops of meat without a
    pause.

The valiant shads were slaughtering the pigeons and the
  doves;
The dolphin knocked the teeth out of the agèd ox's jaws.

The herrings, many daces and the noble sea lamprey
Came from Seville and Alcántara to take the spoils away;
And one by one they used their weapons on the Lord of
  Flesh.
To loosen up his leather belt would help him none today.

A stout and sturdy fellow came, the sturgeon, bravest known;
He carried in his hand the hefty handle of a plow.
He hit both hog and suckling pig across the forehead bone,
And ordered them to be put down in salt from Villenchón.

The octopus did not allow the peacocks any rest
Nor did he let the pheasants fly away from him in swoops,
And little kids and big buck deers he tried to choke to death.
Because he had so many arms, he could attack whole groups.

The oysters were embattled there against the hares' whole
  force;
Against the rabbits rugged crabs were jousting unsubdued.
From one side and the other they delivered many blows.
The little vales were running full of fish scales and red blood.

The strong Count of Laredo now was fighting valiantly—
The conger eel both fresh and dried—and with bad luck he
  pressed
The Lord of Flesh, pursued and drove him to the point of
  death.
This lord was sad and wanted only comfort and some rest.

And yet he gathered up some courage, raised his banner high
And, fired with fury, boldly marched against Lord Salmon
  there—
From Castro Urdiales seaport, he'd arrived just then.
This noble fish awaited him—no, did not flee his dare.

They battled for a long time and endured some grievous pain;
If they'd left Lord Flesh alone, he could have won quite out of
    hand.
But then to fight against him came the fat gigantic whale,
Who wrestled with him, knocked him down at once into the
    sand.

Most of his battle troops were down, already fallen now—
So many of them killed and many of them put to flight.
But though he was dismounted, he kept on with his attacks,
And fought as long as he could do it in his weakened plight.

As he had now so few of all his military force,
The wild boar and the stag fled to the hills to save their guts,
And other wild beasts all withdrew a distance from him, too,
Till those who stayed behind with him weren't worth two dry
    chestnuts.

So were it not for Dame Dried Meat with thick and fat Sir
    Bacon,
Who now with age were yellow and about to die right there
And in their fatness could not fight without their good Sir
    Wine,
He would have been alone, surrounded, and in deep despair.

The sea battalion readied for a rushing great assault,
Inflicting wounds with spurs, and all fell on him in a group;
They didn't want to kill their foe, they sympathized with
    him;
They tied him up securely in stout ropes with all his troops.

They took them bound up safely so that they might not
    escape
And gave them to the Lady thus, before they could get free.
Our Lady Lent gave orders that they guard well the Lord
    Flesh
And that they hang Sir Bacon and Lady Dried Meat instantly.

She ordered them to be hanged up, high as watchtowers rise,
That no one might go there to take them down at this late
　　date;
And then her forces hanged them high upon a beech-tree
　　beam.
The hangman said, "Let them who did such things, accept
　　this fate."

She then gave orders to Lord Flesh that he obey her Fast
And that Fast should be his jailor, so that none could visit
　　him,
Unless he should fall ill or want a father to confess;
　They gave him just one meal a day to eat, and that was slim.

—Translated by Saralyn R. Daly

Jean de la Fontaine

(French, 1621–1695)

The Little Fish and the Fisherman

It would seem to have been God's plan
For fry to mature if spared human guile;
But what a foolish fisherman
To free what he thinks he may catch afterwhile.
He might catch it, of course, but cannot be sure that he can.

A carp so small he was nearly an illusion
Was caught by an angler where a forest stream ran clear.
The man viewed his capture with exhilaration
And said, "Aha, first of a mess for my delectation:
　　There it goes," since a wicker creel lay near.

The poor thing in a tongue too fine for our ear
Asked, "Of what use am I? Must I make a fire roar—
      Half a mouthful when eaten!
      Let me grow, I implore:
      I'm certain to be retaken;
A gourmet will pay dear for a catch that is rare,
      Whereas compare the exertion
      Of catching a hundred such as I
For one meal. Meal? Mockery is the word to apply."
The angler said, "Mockery? Friend with the pulpit air,
Compose, if you will, a homily on despair.
You'll be laid in the frying pan. Preach till you tire,
      You'll sear tonight on a roaring fire."

A fish in the creel, so they say, is worth two you've not
    caught;
      The one, food in hand, and the second, for
      thought.

—Translated by Marianne Moore

Ogden Nash

(American, 1902–1971)

The Smelt

Oh, why does man pursue the smelt?
It has no valuable pelt,
It boasts of no escutcheon royal,
It yields no ivory or oil,
Its life is dull, its death is tame,

A fish as humble as its name.
Yet—take this salmon somewhere else.
And bring me half a dozen smelts.

The Eel

I don't mind eels
Except as meals.

William Cowper

(English, 1731–1800)

To the Immortal Memory of the Halibut

ON WHICH I DINED THIS DAY,
MONDAY, APRIL 26, 1784

Where hast thou floated, in what seas pursued
Thy pastime? when wast thou an egg new spawn'd,
Lost in th'immensity of ocean's waste?
Roar as they might, the overbearing winds
That rock'd the deep, thy cradle, thou wast safe—
And in thy minikin and embryo state,
Attach'd to the firm leaf of some salt weed,
Didst outlive tempests, such as wrung and rack'd
The joints of many a stout and gallant bark,
And whelm'd them in the unexplored abyss.
Indebted to no magnet and no chart,
Nor under guidance of the polar fire,
Thou wast a voyager on many coasts,

Grazing at large in meadows submarine,
Where flat Batavia, just emerging, peeps
Above the brine—where Caledonia's rocks
Beat back the surge—and where Hibernia shoots
Her wondrous causeway far into the main.
—Wherever thou hast fed, thou little thought'st,
And I not more, that I should feed on thee.
Peace, therefore, and good health, and much good fish
To him who sent thee! and success, as oft
As it descends into the billowy gulf,
To the same drag that caught thee!—Fare thee well!
Thy lot thy brethren of the slimy fin
Would envy, could they know that thou wast doom'd
To feed a bard, and to be praised in verse.

Thomas Love Peacock

(English, 1785–1866)

Fish Feast

All day we sat, until the sun went down—
'Twas summer, and the Dog-star scorch'd the Town—
At fam'd Blackwall, O Thames! upon thy shore,
Where Lovegrove's tables groan beneath their store,
We feasted full, on every famous dish,
Dress'd many ways, of sea and river fish—
Perch, mullet, eels, and salmon, all were there,
And whitebait, daintiest of our fishy fare—
Then meat of various kinds, and venison last,
Quails, fruits and ices, crown'd the rich repast.
Thy fields, Champagne, supplied us with our wine,

Madeira's island, and the rocks of Rhine.
The sun was set, and twilight veil'd the land:
Then all stood up—all who had strength to stand—
And pouring down, of Maraschino, fit
Libations to the gods of wine and wit,
In steam-wing'd chariots and on iron roads
Sought the great City, and our own abodes.

Sir Walter Scott
(Scottish, 1771–1832)

From *Redgauntlet*

LETTER IV
The Same to the Same
Shepherd's Bush

I mentioned in my last, that having abandoned my fishing-rod as an unprofitable implement, I crossed over the open downs which divided me from the margin of the Solway. When I reached the banks of the great estuary, which are here very bare and exposed, the waters had receded from the large and level space of sand, through which a stream, now feeble and fordable, found its way to the ocean. The whole was illuminated by the beams of the low and setting sun, who showed his ruddy front, like a warrior prepared for defence, over a huge battlemented and turreted wall of crimson and black clouds, which appeared like an immense Gothic fortress, into which the lord of day was descending. His setting rays glimmered bright upon the wet surface of the sands, and the numberless pools of water by which it was covered, where the inequality of the ground had occasioned their being left by the tide.

The scene was animated by the exertions of a number of horsemen, who were actually employed in hunting salmon.

Ay, Alan, lift up your hands and eyes as you will, I can give their mode of fishing no name so appropriate; for they chased the fish at full gallop, and struck them with their barbed spears, as you see hunters spearing boars in the old tapestry. The salmon, to be sure, take the thing more quietly than the boars; but they are so swift in their own element, that to pursue and strike them is the task of a good horseman, with a quick eye, a determined hand, and full command both of his horse and weapon. The shouts of the fellows as they galloped up and down in the animating exercise—their loud bursts of laughter when any of their number caught a fall—and still louder acclamations when any of the party made a capital stroke with his lance—gave so much animation to the whole scene, that I caught the enthusiasm of the sport, and ventured forward a considerable space on the sands. The feats of one horseman, in particular, called forth so repeatedly the clamorous applause of his companions, that the very banks rang again with their shouts. He was a tall man, well mounted on a strong black horse, which he caused to turn and wind like a bird in the air, carried a longer spear than the others, and wore a sort of fur cap or bonnet, with a short feather in it, which gave him on the whole rather a superior appearance to the other fishermen. He seemed to hold some sort of authority among them, and occasionally directed their motions both by voice and hand; at which times I thought his gestures were striking, and his voice uncommonly sonorous and commanding.

The riders began to make for the shore, and the interest of the scene was almost over, while I lingered on the sands, with my looks turned to the shores of England, still gilded by the sun's last rays, and, as it seemed, scarce distant a mile from me.

*   *   *

When [this] duenna had made all preliminary arrangements, she took from the well-filled pouch of my conductor, which he had hung up by the door, one or two salmon, or *grilses*, as the smaller sort are termed, and selecting that which seemed best, and in highest season, began to cut it into slices, and to prepare a *grillade;* the savoury smell of which

affected me so powerfully, that I began sincerely to hope that
no delay would intervene between the platter and the lip.

As this thought came across me, the man who had conducted the horse to the stable entered the apartment, and discovered to me a countenance yet more uninviting than that of
the old crone who was performing with such dexterity the
office of cook to the party. He was perhaps sixty years old;
yet his brow was not much furrowed, and his jet black hair
was only grizzled, not whitened, by the advance of age. All
his motions spoke strength unabated; and, though rather un-
dersized, he had very broad shoulders, was square-made,
thin-flanked, and apparently combined in his frame muscular
strength and activity; the last somewhat impaired perhaps by
years, but the first remaining in full vigour. A hard and harsh
countenance—eyes far sunk under projecting eyebrows,
which were grizzled like his hair—a wide mouth furnished
from ear to ear with a range of unimpaired teeth, of uncommon whiteness, and a size and breadth which might have become the jaws of an ogre, completed this delightful portrait.
He was clad like a fisherman, in jacket and trowsers of the
blue cloth commonly used by seamen, and had a Dutch case-
knife, like that of a Hamburgh skipper, stuck into a broad
buff belt, which seemed as if it might occasionally sustain
weapons of a description still less equivocally calculated for
violence.

This man gave me an inquisitive, and, as I thought, a
sinister look, upon entering the apartment; but without any
farther notice of me, took up the office of arranging the table,
which the old lady had abandoned for that of cooking the fish,
and, with more address than I expected from a person of his
coarse appearance, placed two chairs at the head of the table,
and two stools below; accommodating each seat to a cover,
beside which he placed an allowance of barley-bread, and a
small jug, which he replenished with ale from a large black
jack. Three of these jugs were of ordinary earthenware, but
the fourth, which he placed by the right-hand cover at the
upper end of the table, was a flagon of silver, and displayed
armorial bearings. Beside this flagon he placed a saltcellar of

silver, handsomely wrought, containing salt of exquisite whiteness, with pepper and other spices. A sliced lemon was also presented on a small silver salver.

*   *   *

My host, with a muttered remark on the cold of our ride, and the keen air of the Solway Sands, to which he did not seem to wish an answer, loaded my plate from Mabel's *grillade*, which, with a large wooden bowl of potatoes, formed our whole meal. A sprinkling from the lemon gave a much higher zest than the usual condiment of vinegar; and I promise you that whatever I might hitherto have felt, either of curiosity or suspicion, did not prevent me from making a most excellent supper.

Thomas Hood

(1799–1845)

The Supper Superstition

A PATHETIC BALLAD

"O flesh, flesh! how art thou fishified!"

—MERCUTIO

I

'Twas twelve o'clock by Chelsea chimes,
    When, all in hungry trim,
Good Mister Jupp sat down to sup,
    With wife, and Kate, and Jim.

II

Said he, "Upon this dainty cod
    How bravely I shall sup,"—
When, whiter than the tablecloth,
    A *ghost* came rising up!

III

"O father dear! O mother dear!
    Dear Kate, and brother Jim!
You know when some one went to sea,—
    Don't cry—but I am him!

IV

"You hope some day with fond embrace
    To greet your absent Jack,
But oh, I am come here to say
    I'm never coming back!

V

"From Alexandria we set sail,
    With corn, and oil, and figs,
But steering 'too much Sow,' we struck
    Upon the Sow and Pigs!

VI

"The ship we pump'd till we could see
    Old England from the tops,
When down she went with all our hands,
    Right in the Channel's Chops.

VII

"Just give a look in Norey's chart,
  The very place it tells;
I think it says twelve fathom deep,
  Clay bottom, mix'd with shells.

VIII

"Well, there we are till 'hands aloft,
  We have at last a call;
The pug I had for brother Jim,
  Kate's parrot too, and all.

IX

"But oh, my spirit cannot rest
  In Davy Jones's sod,
Till I've appear'd to you and said,—
  Don't sup on that 'ere cod!

X

"You live on land, and little think
  What passes in the sea;
Last Sunday week, at two P.M.,
  That cod was picking me!

XI

"Those oysters too, that look so plump,
  And seem so nicely done,
They put my corpse in many shells,
  Instead of only one.

XII

"Oh, do not eat those oysters then,
    And do not touch the shrimps;
When I was in my briny grave,
    They suck'd my blood like imps!

XIII

"Don't eat what brutes would never eat—
    The brutes I used to pat,
They'll know the smell they used to smell,
    Just try the dog and cat!"

XIV

The spirit fled—they wept his fate,
    And cried, "Alack, alack!"
At last up started brother Jim,—
    "Let's try if Jack was Jack!"

XV

They call'd the dog, they call'd the cat,
    And little kitten too,
And down they put the cod and sauce,
    To see what brutes would do.

XVI

Old Tray lick'd all the oysters up,
    Puss never stood at crimps,
But munch'd the cod,—and little Kit
    Quite feasted on the shrimps!

XVII

The thing was odd, and minus cod
And sauce, they stood like posts;
Oh, prudent folks, for fear of hoax,
Put no belief in ghosts!

Samuel Lover

(Irish, 1797–1868)

The White Trout

A LEGEND OF CONG

Oh! I would ask no happier bed
Than the chill wave my love lies under:
Sweeter to rest together, dead,
Far sweeter than to live asunder.

—LALLA ROOKH

The next morning I proceeded alone to the cave, to witness the natural curiosity of its subterranean river, my interest in the visit being somewhat increased by the foregoing tale. Leaving my horse at the little village of Cong, I bent my way on foot through the fields, if you may venture to give that name to the surface of this immediate district of the County Mayo, which, presenting large flat masses of lime-stone, intersected by patches of verdure, gives one the idea much more of a burial ground covered with monumental slabs, than a formation of nature. Yet, (I must make this remark *en passant*,) such is the richness of the pasture in these little verdant interstices, that cattle are fattened upon it in a much shorter time than on a meadow of the most cultured aspect; and though to the native of Leinster, this *land* (if we may be pardoned a premeditated *bull,*) would appear all *stones,* the Mayo farmer knows it from experience to be a profitable tenure. Sometimes deep clefts occur between these laminæ of lime-stone rock, which, closely overgrown with verdure, have not unfrequently occasioned serious accidents to man and beast; and one of these chasms, of larger dimensions than usual, forms the entrance to the celebrated cave in question. Very rude steps of unequal height, partly natural and partly artificial, lead the explorer of its quiet beauty, by an abrupt descent, to the bottom of the cave, which contains an enlightened area of some thirty or forty feet, whence a naturally-vaulted passage opens, of the deepest gloom. The depth of the cave may be about equal to its width at the bottom: the mouth is not more than twelve or fifteen feet across; and pendant from its margin clusters of ivy and other parasite plants hang and cling in all the fantastic variety of natural festooning and tracery. It is a truly beautiful and poetical little spot, and particularly interesting to the stranger, from being unlike any thing else one has ever seen, and having none of the noisy and vulgar pretence of regular *show-places,* which calls upon you every moment to exclaim "Prodigious!"

An elderly and decent looking woman had just filled her pitcher with the deliciously cold and clear water of the subterranean river that flowed along its bed of small, smooth, and many-coloured pebbles, as I arrived at the bottom, and perceiving at once that I was a stranger, she paused, partly perhaps with the pardonable pride of displaying her local knowledge, but more from the native peasant-politeness of her country, to become the temporary *cicerone* of the cave. She spoke some words of Irish, and hurried forth on her errand a very handsome and active boy, of whom, she informed me, she was great-grandmother.

"Great-grandmother!" I repeated, in unfeigned astonishment.

"Yes, your honour," she answered, with evident pleasure sparkling in her eyes, which time had not yet deprived of their brightness, nor the soul-subduing influence of this self-ish world bereft of their kind hearted expression.

"You are the youngest woman I have ever seen," said I, "to be a great-grandmother."

"Troth, I don't doubt you, Sir," she answered.

"And you seem still in good health, and likely to live many a year yet," said I.

"With the help of God, Sir," said she, reverently.

"But," I added, "I perceive a great number of persons about here of extreme age. Now, how long generally do the people in this country live?"

"Troth, Sir," said she, with the figurative drollery of her country, "we live here as long as we like."

"Well, that is no inconsiderable privilege," said I; "but you, nevertheless, must have married very young?"

"I was not much over sixteen, your honour, when I had my first child at my breast."

"That was beginning early," said I.

"Thrue for you, Sir; and faith, Noreen—(that's my daughter, Sir)—Noreen herself lost no time either; I suppose she thought she had as good a right as the mother before her—she was married at seventeen, and a likely couple her-self and her husband was. So you see, Sir, it was not long before I was a granny. Well, to make the saying good, 'as the owld cock crows, the young bird cherrups,' and faiks, the whole breed, seed, and generation, tuk after the owld woman (that's myself, Sir); and so, in coorse of time, I was not only a granny, but a *grate* granny; and, by the same token, here comes my darling Paudeen Bawn [Little Paddy], with what I sent him for."

Here the fine little fellow I have spoken of, with his long fair hair curling about his shoulders, descended into the cave, bearing some faggots of bog-wood, a wisp of straw, and a lighted sod of turf.

"Now, your honour, it's what you'll see the pigeon-hole to advantage."

"What pigeon-hole?" said I.

"Here where we are," she replied.

"Why is it so called?" I inquired.

"Because, Sir, the wild pigeons often builds in the bushes and the ivy that's round the mouth of the cave, and in here too," said she, pointing into the gloomy depth of the interior.

"Blow that turf, Paudeen;" and Paudeen, with distended cheeks and compressed lips, forthwith poured a few vigorous blasts on the sod of turf, which soon flickered and blazed, while the kind old woman lighted her faggots of bog-wood at the flame.

"Now, Sir, follow me," said my conductress.

"I am sorry you have had so much trouble on my account," said I.

"Oh, no throuble in life, your honour, but the greatest of pleasure;" and so saying, she proceeded into the cave, and I followed, carefully choosing my steps by the help of her torch-light, along the slippery path of rock that overhung the river. When she had reached a point of some little elevation, she held up her lighted pine branches, and waving them to and fro, asked me could I see the top of the cave.

The effect of her figure was very fine, illumined as it was, in the midst of utter darkness, by the red glare of the blazing faggots; and as she wound them round her head, and shook their flickering sparks about, it required no extraordinary stretch of imagination to suppose her, with her ample cloak of dark drapery, and a few straggling tresses of grey hair escaping from the folds of a rather Eastern head-dress, some Sybil about to commence an awful rite, and evoke her ministering spirits from the dark void, or call some water-demon from the river, which rushed unseen along, telling of its wild course by the turbulent dash of its waters, which the reverberation of the cave rendered still more hollow.

She shouted aloud, and the cavern-echoes answered to her summons.

"Look!" said she; and she lighted the wisp of straw, and flung it on the stream: it floated rapidly away, blazing in wild undulations over the perturbed surface of the river, and at length suddenly disappeared altogether. The effect was most picturesque and startling: it was even awful. I might almost say, sublime!

Her light being nearly expired, we retraced our steps, and emerging from the gloom, stood beside the river in the enlightened area I have described.

"Now, Sir," said my old woman, "we must thry and see the White Throut; and you never seen a throut o' that colour yet, I warrant."

I assented to the truth of this.

"They say it's a fairy throut, your honour, and tells mighty quare stories about it."

"What are they?" I inquired.

"Troth, it's myself doesn't know the half o' them—only partly: but sthrive and see it before you go, Sir; for there's them that says it isn't lucky to come to the cave, and lave it without seein' the white throut; an' if you're a bachelor, Sir, and didn't get a peep at it, throth you'd never be married; and sure that 'id be a murther!"

"Oh," said I, "I hope the fairies would not be so spiteful—"

"Whisht—whisht!" said she, looking fearfully around; then, knitting her brows, she gave me an admonitory look, and put her finger on her lip, in token of silence, and then coming sufficiently near me to make herself audible in a whisper, she said, "Never spake ill, your honour, of the good people—beyant all, in sitch a place as this—for it's in the likes they always keep; and one doesn't know who may be listenin'. God keep uz! But look, Sir! look!" And she pointed to the stream—"There she is."

"Who? what?" said I.

"The throut, Sir."

I immediately perceived the fish in question, perfectly a trout in shape, but in colour, a creamy white, heading up the stream, and seeming to keep constantly within the region of the enlightened part of it.

"There it is, in that very spot evermore," continued my guide, "and never anywhere else."

"The poor fish, I suppose, likes to swim in the light," said I.

"Oh, no, Sir," said she, shaking her head significantly, "the people here has a mighty owld story about that throut."

"Let me hear it, and you will oblige me."

"Och! it's only laughin' at me you'd be, and call me an owld fool, as the misthiss beyant in the big house often did afore, when she first kem among us—but she knows the differ now."

"Indeed I shall not laugh at your story," said I, "but on the contrary, shall thank you very much for your tale."

"Then sit down a minit, Sir," said she, throwing her apron upon a rock and pointing to the seat, "and I'll tell you to the best of my knowledge;" and seating herself on an adjacent patch of verdure, she began her legend.

"There was wanst upon a time, long ago, a beautiful young lady that lived in a castle up by the lake beyant, and they say she was promised to a king's son, and they wor to be married: when, all of a suddent, he was murther'd, the crathur, (Lord help uz) and threwn into the lake abow, and so, of coorse, he couldn't keep his promise to the fair lady,—and more's the pity.

"Well, the story goes that she wint out iv her mind, bekase av loosin' the king's son—for she was tindher-hearted, God help her, like the rest iv us!—and pined away after him, until, at last, no one about seen her, good or bad, and the story wint, that the fairies tuk her away.

"Well, Sir, in coorse o' time, the white throut, God bless it, was seen in the sthrame beyant; and sure the people didn't know what to think av the crathur, seein' as how a *white* throut was never heerd av afore nor sence, and years upon years the throut was there, just where you seen it this blessed minit, longer nor I can tell, aye throth, and beyant the memory o' th' owldest in the village.

"At last the people began to think it must be a fairy; for what else could it be?—and no hurt nor harm was iver put an the white throut, antil some wicked sinners of sojers [soldiers] kem to these parts, and laughed at all the people, and gibed and jeered them for thinkin' o' the likes; and one o' them in partic'lar, (bad luck to him!—God forgi' me for sayin' it,) swore he'd catch the throut, and ate it for his dinner—the blackguard!

"Well, what would you think o' the villiany of the sojer—sure enough he cotch the throut, and away wid him home, and puts an the fryin'-pan, and into it he pitches the purty little thing. The throut squealed all as one as a Chrishthan crathur, and, my dear, you'd think the sojer id split his sides laughin'—for he was a hardened villian. And when he thought one side was done, he turns it over to fry the other; and what would you think, but the divil a taste of a burn was an it, at all at all; and sure the sojer thought it was a *quare* throut that couldn't be briled; 'but,' says he, 'I'll give it another turn by and by'—little thinkin' what was in store for him, the haythen.

"Well, when he thought that side was done, he turns it agin—and lo and behould you, the divil a taste more done that side was nor the other—'Bad luck to me,' says the sojer, 'but that bates the world,' says he, 'but I'll thry you agin, my darlint,' says he, 'as cunnin' as you think yourself'—and so, with that, he turns it over and over; but the divil a sign av the fire was an the purty throut. 'Well,' says the desperate villian— (for sure, Sir, only he was a desperate villian *entirely*, he might know he was doin' a wrong thing, seein' that all his endayvours was no good). 'Well,' says he, 'my jolly little throut, maybe you're fried enough, though you don't seem over-well dress'd; but you may be better than you look, like a singed cat, and a tit-bit, afther all,' says he; and with that he ups with his knife and fork to taste a piece o' the throut, but, my jew'l, the minit he put his knife into the fish, there was a murtherin' screech, that you'd think the life id lave you if you heerd it, and away jumps the throut out av the fryin'-pan into the middle o' the flure; and an the spot where it fell, up riz a lovely lady—the beautifullest young crathur that eyes ever seen, dressed in white, with a band o' goold in her hair, and a sthrame o' blood runnin' down her arm.

" 'Look where you cut me, you villian,' says she, and she

held out her arm to him—and my dear, he thought the sight id lave his eyes.

" 'Couldn't you lave me, cool and comfortable in the river where you snared me, and not disturb me in my duty?' says she.

"Well, he thrimbled like a dog in a wet sack, and at last he stammered out somethin', and begged for his life, and ax'd her ladyship's pardin, and said he didn't know she was an duty, or he was too good a sojer not to know betther nor to meddle wid her.

" 'I *was* an duty, then,' says the lady; 'I was watchin' for my thrue love, that is comin' by wather to me,' says she; 'an' if he comes while I am away, an' that I miss iv him, I'll turn you into a pinkeen, [minnow] and I'll hunt you up and down for evermore, "while grass grows or wather runs." '

"Well, the sojer thought the life id lave him, at the thoughts iv his bein' turned into a pinkeen, and begged for marcy; and with that, says the lady—

" 'Renounce your evil coorses,' says she, 'you villian, or you'll repint it too late; be a good man for the futhur, and go to your duty reg'lar. And now,' says she, 'take me back, and put me into the river agin, where you found me.'

" 'Oh, my lady,' says the sojer, 'how could I have the heart to drownd a beautiful lady like you?'

"But before he could say another word, the lady was vanish'd, and there he saw the little throut an the ground. Well, he put it an a clane plate, and away he run for the bare life, for fear her lover would come while she was away; and he run, and he run, ever, till he came to the cave agin, and threw the throut into the river. The minit he did, the wather was as red as blood for a little while, by rayson av the cut, I suppose, until the sthrame washed the stain away; and to this day, there's a little red mark an the throut's side, where it was cut.

"Well Sir, from that day out, the sojer was an althered man, and reformed his ways, and wint to his duty reg'lar, and fasted three times a week, though it was never fish he tuk an fastin' days: for afther the fright he got, fish id never rest an his stomach, God bless us, savin' your presence. But anyhow, he was an althered man, as I said before; and in coorse o' time he left the army, and turned hermit at last; and they say he *used to pray evermore for the sowl of the White Trout.*"

Jorge Amado

(Brazilian, 1912–)

From *Dona Flor and Her Two Husbands*

DONA FLOR'S ENTREATY IN HER CLASSES AND IN HER REVERIES

Why don't they leave me alone with my mourning and my loneliness? Why do they have to talk about such things? Can't they respect my widowhood? Let's go to the stove. A fancy and elegant dish is *vatapá* of fish (or chicken), the most famous in the Bahian cuisine. None of that nonsense about my still being young; I am a widow who is dead to all those things. *Vatapá* sufficient for ten (with some left over, as there should always be).

Take two fresh groupers—other fish can be used, but are not as good. Salt and coriander, garlic and onions, several tomatoes and the juice of a lemon. Four tablespoons of olive oil, either Portuguese or Spanish; I have heard said that the Greek is even better. I don't know. I have never used it, as I have not seen it on sale.

If I were to find a suitor, what would I do? Someone who would revive my desire, buried in the coffin of the dead. What do you girls know about the intimate life of widows? The desire of a widow is the desire for debauchment and sin.

A seemly widow does not talk about such things, does not think about such things, does not bring the conversation around to such things. Just let me alone with my stove.

Sauté the fish in these seasonings and let it come to a boil with a mite of water, just a wee bit, almost none. Then all you have to do is strain the sauce, set it aside, and we proceed.

What if my bed is but a sad place to lay my body, with no other use, what does it matter? Everything in this world has its compensations. There is nothing better than a quiet life, without dreams, without desires, without being consumed by the flames of a burning womb. There is no better life than that of a serious, modest widow, a placid existence, free of ambition and desire. But what if my couch were not a bed in which to sleep, but a desert to be crossed, all fiery sands, and with no exit? What do you know of the secret life of widows, of their lonely bed, of their dead burden? You came here to learn to cook and not to find out the price of renunciation, the price in anxiety and loneliness to be an upright, modest widow. Let's get on with the lesson.

Take the grater and two well-fleshed coconuts, and grate. Grate hard. Go on—a little exercise never did anybody any harm (they say it dispels evil thoughts; I don't believe it). Gather up the grated white meat and warm it before you squeeze it; in that way the thick milk will come away more easily, the pure milk of the coconut. Put it to one side.

After squeezing out this first thick milk, do not throw away the coconut meat, don't be wasteful, for waste not, want not. Scald the meat in a quart of boiling water. Then squeeze it to get out the thin milk. After that you can throw the meat away, for by this time it is nothing but refuse.

A widow is nothing but refuse, limitation, and hypocrisy. In what country is it that they bury the widow in her husband's grave? Where is it that they set fire to her together with the body of her husband? It were better so than to be consumed in a slow, forbidden fire, consumed by longing and desire, outwardly hypocritical, a modesty of widow's weeds, veils hiding the rueful geography of fear and sin. A widow is nothing but refuse and suffering.

Cut the crust off stale bread, and then put the bread in the thin milk until it is moistened. In the meat grinder (well washed) grind up the bread moistened in coconut milk, and almonds, dried shrimp, cashew nuts, ginger, without forgetting the red pepper, bearing in mind the taste of the client. There are those who like their *vatapá* full of pepper, others who like just a pinch, the merest taste.

Ground and mixed, add these seasonings to the sauce of the grouper, mixing the one with the other, the ginger with the coconut, the salt with the pepper, the garlic with the cashew, and put it on the fire long enough to thicken the sauce.

Does not the *vatapá*, strong-flavored with ginger, pepper, almonds, affect people's dreams, lending them warmth and sensual seasoning? What do I know about such needs? I never needed ginger and almonds. It was the hand, the tongue, the word, his profile, his charm, it was he who stripped me of the sheet and my modesty for the wild astronomy of his kisses, to light me up with stars, in his nightly honey. Who bares me now of the veils of modesty in my dreams as a widow in my lonely bed? Whence comes this desire burning my breast and womb, if neither his hand nor his lip nor moonlit profile nor carefree laughter any longer exist? Why this desire, which is born of me alone? Why so many questions? Why this interest in knowing what goes on in the heart of a widow? Why don't they leave me with the black mourning veils on my face, veils prescribed by custom, to cover my divided face, divided between modesty and desire? I am a widow; it is not even proper for me to be talking about such things. A widow at the stove cooking *vatapá*, measuring the ginger, the almonds, the red pepper, and nothing more.

Add at once the coconut milk, the thick and pure, and at the very end the dendê oil, two full cups, flower of the dendê palm, the color of old gold, the color of *vatapá*. Let it cook for a long time over a low fire, stirring continually with a

wooden spoon, always in the same direction; do not stop stirring or the *vatapá* will curdle. Stir it, keep on stirring, without stopping, until it comes to just the right point.

Over a slow fire my dreams consume me. It is not my
fault: I am nothing but a widow divided in two, one half an
upright, modest widow, the other a dissolute widow, almost
hysterical, all swoons and sullenness. This robe of modesty is
smothering me; at night I run about the streets in search of a
husband. Of a husband to whom to serve the golden *vatapá*
of my copper-colored body of ginger and honey.

The *vatapá* is now ready. Doesn't it look beautiful! All it
needs is just a little dendê oil poured over it at the last minute. Serve it with ground hominy, and sweethearts and husbands will lick their chops.

And speaking of sweethearts, let me tell you so you will
all know: there is a young widow endowed with a certain
quiet charm and beauty, tea-colored, like gold and copper, a
cook who can hold her own with the best, so hard-working,
modest, and quiet that she had no equal in the whole city or
in the Recôncavo,* a first-class widow with an iron bed, the
modesty of a virgin, and a fire burning her womb. If you
should know of anyone whom this would interest, send him
here on the run, at any hour of the day or night, in the rain,
in the sunlight, send him at once, with the judge or the
priest, with a wedding license, send him quickly, as quickly as
you can.

I am launching this appeal to the four winds, to the mercy
of undersea currents, to the phases of the moon and the tide,
in the wake of any ship or coastwise vessel, for I am a port
whose harbor is hidden, a secluded gulf, a refuge for the ship-
wrecked. If you hear of any unmarried man whose object is
matrimony and who is looking for a widow, tell him that he
will find Dona Flor here beside the stove, standing over a
vatapá of fish, consumed by fire and accursed.

—*Translated by Harriet de Onís*

*The coastal farming district of East Bahia, Brazil.

James Wright

(American, 1927–1980)

Northern Pike

All right. Try this,
Then. Every body
I know and care for
And every body
Else is going
To die in a loneliness
I can't imagine and a pain
I don't know. We had
To go on living. We
Untangled the net, we slit
The body of this fish
Open from the hinge of the tail
To a place beneath the chin
I wish I could sing of.
I would just as soon we let
The living go on living.
An old poet whom we believe in
Said the same thing, and so
We paused among the dark cattails and prayed
For the muskrats,
For the ripples below their tails,
For the little movements that we knew the crawdads were
     making under water,
For the right-hand wrist of my cousin who is a policeman.
We prayed for the game warden's blindness.
We prayed for the road home.

We ate the fish.
There must be something very beautiful in my body,
I am so happy.

David Williams

(American, 1953–)

White Fish

Baskets of silver eyes
in the market,
onions, tomatoes, peppers
of every kind.
Old cathedral dust
kicked up by a donkey.
Indian children
moving up a hill.
Here, you wrap
raw fish in a tortilla
and call it lunch.
Here, on Sunday
shadows on
the plaza pass slowly
as you shake your wrist.
Here, we choose our rings
of silver and put them on.
Wound forever to each other.
Carrying the flesh of the lake
on our hands.

Ted Hughes

(English, 1930–)

Mackerel Song

While others sing the mackerel's armour
His stub scissor head, and his big blurred eye
And the flimsy savagery of his onset
I sing his simple hunger.

While others sing the mackerel's swagger
His miniature ocelot oil-green stripings
And his torpedo solidity of thump
I sing his gormless plenty.

While others sing the mackerel's fury
The belly-tug lightning-trickle of his evasions
And the wrist-thick muscle of his last word
I sing his loyal come-back.

While others sing the mackerel's acquaintance
The soap of phosphorous he lathers on your fingers
The midget gut and the tropical racer's torso
I sing his scorched sweetness.

While others sing the mackerel's demise
His ultimatum to be cooked instantly
And the shock of his decay announcement
I sing how he makes
           the rich summer seas
                    a million times richer
With the gift of his millions.

Rivers Carew

(Irish, 1935–)

Catching Trout

Each autumn, brown trout in the middle pond
Stocked by my grandfather, moved into the stream
And steered through shallow water over stones
Until they reached the spawning-beds upstream.

For an adventure we went fishing there.
Equipped with buckets. Water slithering past
Our ankles, we dipped and dipped again, and soon
We'd landed several on the bank. Aghast

To be precipitated into air
They beat in mortal anguish on the grass
And we, confronting terror, found that it
Was mimicked in our flesh as in a glass.

Dumb agony defeated us in the end.
We gave them back their atmosphere and scheme
Half glad to see them break the glossy water,
Harness it and zigzag up the stream.

Balked, with buckets empty, we trudged home.
But now it's different. Landing trout, I pounce,
Grip them and crack them sharply on the head.
They quiver and they die almost at once.

Nikos Kazantzakis

(1883–1957)

From *The Odyssey, A Modern Sequel*

BOOK II

"One day as I lay grunting in my fleshly sty,
I saw a light smoke rising on the shore, a fire,
and round it squatted men who with slit rushes pierced
a row of fish and roasted them on glowing coals.
A woman with a baby at her bosom stooped,
unbared her breasts till her son grasped her nipples tight,
and she refreshed him like a fountain of pure milk.
As the fish reddened and their fragrance smote the nostrils,
the fishermen pressed round the fire and sat cross-legged,
and when the mother came with outstretched hands, they filled
her palms with double portions of black bread and fish.
They ate with greed, munched silently, and watched the sea,
then wiped their long mustaches, tipped their flasks of wine,
drank deep, passed it from man to man, last to the mother.
O poor immortal comforts: fish, some bread and wine, . . ."

—Translated by Kimon Farir

Matthew, Chapter 16: 32–38

Then Jesus called his disciples unto him, and said, I have compassion on the multitude, because they continue with me now three days, and have nothing to eat: and I will not send them away fasting, lest they faint in the way.

And his disciples say unto him, Whence should we have so much bread in the wilderness, as to fill so great a multitude?

And Jesus saith unto them, How many loaves have ye? And they said, Seven, and a few little fishes.

And he commanded the multitude to sit down on the ground.

And he took the seven loaves and the fishes, and gave thanks, and brake them, and gave to his disciples, and the disciples to the multitude.

And they did all eat, and were filled: and they took up of the broken meat that was left seven baskets full.

And they that did eat were four thousand men, beside women and children.

The Staff of Life

Exodus, Chapter 16: 10–32

And it came to pass, as Aaron spake unto the whole congregation of the children of Israel, that they looked toward the wilderness, and, behold, the glory of the Lord appeared in the cloud.

And the Lord spake unto Moses, saying,

I have heard the murmurings of the children of Israel: speak unto them, saying, At even ye shall eat flesh, and in the morning ye shall be filled with bread; and ye shall know that I am the Lord your God.

And it came to pass, that at even the quails came up, and covered the camp: and in the morning the dew lay round about the host.

And when the dew that lay was gone up, behold, upon the face of the wilderness there lay a small round thing, as small as the hoar frost on the ground.

And when the children of Israel saw it, they said one to another, It is manna: for they wist not what it was. And Moses said unto them. This is the bread which the Lord hath given you to eat.

This is the thing which the Lord hath commanded, Gather of it every man according to his eating, an omer* for every man, according to the number of your persons; take ye every man for them which are in his tents.

And the children of Israel did so, and gathered, some more, some less.

And when they did mete it with an omer, he that gathered much had nothing over, and he that gathered little had no lack; they gathered every man according to his eating.

And Moses said, Let no man leave of it till the morning.

*A measure equal to about six pints.

Notwithstanding they hearkened not unto Moses; but some of them left of it until the morning, and it bred worms, and stank: and Moses was wroth with them.

And they gathered it every morning, every man according to his eating: and when the sun waxed hot, it melted.

And it came to pass, that on the sixth day they gathered twice as much bread, two omers for one man: and all the rulers of the congregation came and told Moses.

And he said unto them, This is that which the Lord hath said, Tomorrow is the rest of the holy sabbath unto the Lord: bake that which ye will bake today, and seethe that ye will seethe; and that which remaineth over lay up for you to be kept until the morning.

And they laid it up till the morning, as Moses bade: and it did not stink, neither was there any worm therein.

And Moses said, Eat that today; for today is a sabbath unto the Lord: today ye shall not find it in the field.

Six days ye shall gather it; but on the seventh day, which is the sabbath, in it there shall be none.

And it came to pass, that there went out some of the people on the seventh day for to gather, and they found none.

And the Lord said unto Moses, How long refuse ye to keep my commandments and my laws?

See, for that the Lord hath given you the sabbath, therefore he giveth you on the sixth day the bread of two days; abide ye every man in his place, let no man go out of his place on the seventh day.

So the people rested on the seventh day.

And the house of Israel called the name thereof manna: and it was like coriander seed, white; and the taste of it was like wafers made with honey.

And Moses said, This is the thing which the Lord commandeth, Fill an omer of it to be kept for your generations; that they may see the bread wherewith I have fed you in the wilderness, when I brought you forth from the land of Egypt.

Alphonse Daudet

(1840–1897)

Couscous

It was in Algeria; we were visiting an aga of the plain of
Chélif; in the great magnificent tent pitched for us before the
aga's house we watched the night descend, clad in hues of
half-mourning, dark violet at first, which deepened into the
purple of a magnificent sunset; through the freshness of the
evening a Kabyle* candlestick of palmwood was lighted in
the centre of the half-open tent, and the motionless flame
from its branches attracted night insects, who hovered about
it with a rustling of timid wings. Squatted upon mats we ate
in silence; whole sheep, all dripping in butter, were brought
in at the end of poles, honeyed pastry and perfumed confections followed, and, last of all, a great wooden platter,
upon which were chickens in the golden semolina of couscous.

Meanwhile night had fallen. Over the neighboring hills
the moon was rising, a tiny Oriental crescent, near which a
solitary star nestled. Out of doors a big bonfire was flaming
in front of the tent, surrounded by dancers and musicians. I
recall a gigantic negro, quite naked but for the ancient tunic
of the light regiment; he jumped about, causing long shadows
to dart all over the tent. This cannibal dance, those small
Arabian drums, rattling breathlessly when the beat was
hastened, the sharp barking of jackals responding from every
side of the plain,—all these things made the observer feel
that he was in a savage country. However, in the interior of
the tent, that refuge of these nomadic tribes, which resembles

*Berber Arab.

a motionless sail upon a waveless sea, the aga in his white woollen burnouses, seemed to me an apparition of primitive times, and as he gravely swallowed his couscous, I was wondering whether this national Arabian dish were not indeed that miraculous manna of the Hebrews of which so much is written in the Bible.

Traditional Navaho

The Corn Grows Up

The corn grows up.
The waters of the dark clouds drop, drop.
The rain descends.
The waters from the corn leaves drop, drop.
The rain descends.
The waters from the plants drop, drop.
The corn grows up.
The waters of the dark mists drop, drop.

Traditional Seminole

The Origin of White Corn

The Seminole always refer to themselves as "A jia tki," which means *white corn* and in the beginning they were white people.

An old woman was living with her grandchild. She made good *sofki** for the boy and it tasted good to him. He would go out and hunt, kill game and bring it to this grandmother. They all ate together, drank *sofki* and ate deer meat.

The boy did not know how his grandmother got the corn to make the *sofki*. He wanted to know where she got the corn, and he told his grandmother that he was going hunting again. Instead of going, he sneaked back to watch her make the *sofki*. He saw her go into a shack and sit down. She had very sore ankles that were so very dry that she could scrape off the flakes of skin. The boy watched her scrape off the flakes and bring them into the house. She got the pot and some water and put the flakes in the water. The boy found out that the *sofki* came from his grandmother's sore ankles.

After that he would not drink the *sofki*. His grandmother said, "Why don't you drink *sofki*?" He did not explain because he knew where it came from. The grandmother suspected that the boy had watched her, so she asked him, "Did you watch me doing something?" The boy did not reply, but said he would not drink *sofki* any more.

His grandmother told him that he must burn their house and everything. The reason was that the boy had found out her secret and she did not want to live any more. She told the boy to tell the people to burn the house over her, while she was in it.

A few days after the house was burned they came to see the ruins and found the old house restored and full of corn. From there the corn spread over all the earth.

That is the end of the story.

---

*A staple made from ground corn.

Joel Barlow

(American, 1754–1812)

The Hasty Pudding

CANTO I

Ye Alps audacious, through the heavens that rise,
To cramp the day and hide me from the skies;
Ye Gallic flags, that o'er their heights unfurled,
Bear death to kings and freedom to the world,
I sing not you. A softer theme I choose,
A virgin theme, unconscious of the muse,
But fruitful, rich, well suited to inspire
The purest frenzy of poetic fire.
　　Despise it not, ye bards to terror steeled,
Who hurl your thunders round the epic field;
Nor ye who strain your midnight throats to sing
Joys that the vineyard and the stillhouse bring;
Or on some distant fair your notes employ,
And speak of raptures that you ne'er enjoy.
I sing the sweets I know, the charms I feel,
My morning incense, and my evening meal,—
The sweets of Hasty Pudding. Come, dear bowl,
Glide o'er my palate, and inspire my soul.
The milk beside thee, smoking from the kine,
Its substance mingled, married in with thine,
Shall cool and temper thy superior heat,
And save the pains of blowing while I eat.
　　Oh! could the smooth, the emblematic song
Flow like the genial juices o'er my tongue,
Could those mild morsels in my numbers chime,
And, as they roll in substance, roll in rime,
No more thy awkward, unpoetic name
Should shun the muse or prejudice thy fame;

But, rising grateful to the accustomed ear,
All bards should catch it, and all realms revere!
　　Assist me first with pious toil to trace
Through wrecks of time, thy lineage and thy race;
Declare what lovely squaw, in days of yore,
(Ere great Columbus sought thy native shore)
First gave thee to the world; her works of fame
Have lived indeed, but lived without a name.
Some tawny Ceres, goddess of her days,
First learned with stones to crack the well-dried maize,
Through the rough sieve to shake the golden shower,
In boiling water stir the yellow flour:
The yellow flour, bestrewed and stirred with haste,
Swells in the flood and thickens to a paste,
Then puffs and wallops, rises to the brim,
Drinks the dry knobs that on the surface swim;
The knobs at last the busy ladle breaks,
And the whole mass its true consistence takes.
　　Could but her sacred name, unknown so long,
Rise, like her labors, to the son of song,
To her, to them I'd consecrate my lays,
And blow her pudding with the breath of praise.
If 'twas Oella whom I sang before,
I'd here ascribe her one great virtue more.
Nor through the rich Peruvian realms alone
The fame of Sol's sweet daughter should be known,
But o'er the world's wide climes should live secure,
Far as his rays extend, as long as they endure.
　　Dear Hasty Pudding, what unpromised joy
Expands my heart, to meet thee in Savoy!*
Doomed o'er the world through devious paths to roam.
Each clime my country, and each house my home,
My soul is soothed, my cares have found an end;
I greet my long-lost, unforgotten friend.
　　For thee through Paris, that corrupted town,
How long in vain I wandered up and down,

* Barlow wrote the poem when he was living in this southeastern region of France.

Where shameless Bacchus, with his drenching hoard
Cold from his cave, usurps the morning board.
London is lost in smoke and steeped in tea;
No Yankee there can lisp the name of thee;
The uncouth word, a libel on the town,
Would call a proclamation from the crown.
For climes oblique, that fear the sun's full rays,
Chilled in their fogs, exclude the generous maize;
A grain whose rich, luxuriant growth requires
Short, gentle showers, and bright, ethereal fires.

    But here, though distant from our native shore,
With mutual glee, we meet and laugh once more.
The same! I know thee by that yellow face,
That strong complexion of true Indian race,
Which time can never change, nor soil impair,
Nor Alpine snows, nor Turkey's morbid air;
For endless years, through every mild domain,
Where grows the maize, there thou art sure to reign.

    But man, more fickle, the bold licence claims,
In different realms to give thee different names.
Thee the soft nations round the warm Levant
Polanta call; the French, of course, *Polante*.
E'en in thy native regions, how I blush
To hear the Pennsylvanians call thee *Mush*!
On Hudson's banks, while men of Belgic spawn
Insult and eat thee by the name *Suppawn*.
All spurious appellations, void of truth;
I've better known thee from my earliest youth:
Thy name is *Hasty Pudding*! thus my sire
Was wont to greet thee fuming from his fire;
And while he argued in thy just defense
With logic clear he thus explained the sense:
"In haste the boiling caldron, o'er the blaze,
Receives and cooks the ready powdered maize;
In haste 'tis served, and then in equal haste,
With cooling milk, we make the sweet repast.
No carving to be done, no knife to grate
The tender ear and wound the stony plate;

But the smooth spoon, just fitted to the lip,
And taught with art the yielding mass to dip,
By frequent journeys to the bowl well stored,
Performs the hasty honors of the board."
Such is thy name, significant and clear,
A name, a sound to every Yankee dear,
But most to me, whose heart and palate chaste
Preserve my pure, hereditary taste.
   There are who strive to stamp with disrepute
The luscious food, because it feeds the brute;
In tropes of high-strained wit, while gaudy prigs
Compare thy nursling, man, to pampered pigs;
With sovereign scorn I treat the vulgar jest,
Nor fear to share thy bounties with the beast.
What though the generous cow gives me to quaff
The milk nutritious: am I then a calf?
Or can the genius of the noisy swine,
Though nursed on pudding, claim a kin to mine?
Sure the sweet song I fashion to thy praise,
Runs more melodious than the notes they raise.
   My song, resounding in its grateful glee,
No merit claims: I praise myself in thee.
My father loved thee through his length of days!
For thee his fields were shaded o'er with maize;
From thee what health, what vigor he possessed,
Ten sturdy freemen from his loins attest;
Thy constellation ruled my natal morn,
And all my bones were made of Indian corn.
Delicious grain, whatever form it take,
To roast or boil, to smother or to bake,
In every dish 'tis welcome still to me,
But most, my Hasty Pudding, most in thee.
   Let the green succotash with thee contend;
Let beans and corn their sweetest juices blend;
Let butter drench them in its yellow tide,
And a long slice of bacon grace their side;
Not all the plate, how famed soe'er it be,
Can please my palate like a bowl of thee.

Some talk of hoe-cake, fair Virginia's pride!
Rich johnny-cake this mouth has often tried;
Both please me well, their virtues much the same,
Alike their fabric, as allied their fame,
Except in dear New England, where the last
Receives a dash of pumpkin in the paste,
To give it sweetness and improve the taste.
But place them all before me, smoking hot,
The big, round dumpling, rolling from the pot;
The pudding of the bag, whose quivering breast,
With suet lined, leads on the Yankee feast;
The charlotte brown, within whose crusty sides
A belly soft the pulpy apple hides;
The yellow bread whose face like amber glows,
And all of Indian that the bakepan knows,—
You tempt me not; my favorite greets my eyes,
To that loved bowl my spoon by instinct flies.

CANTO II

To mix the food by vicious rules of art,
To kill the stomach and to sink the heart,
To make mankind to social virtue sour,
Cram o'er each dish, and be what they devour;
For this the kitchen muse first framed her book,
Commanding sweats to stream from every cook;
Children no more their antic gambols tried,
And friends to physic wondered why they died.
   Not so the Yankee: his abundant feast,
With simples furnished and with plainness dressed,
A numerous offspring gathers round the board,
And cheers alike the servant and the lord;
Whose well-bought hunger prompts the joyous taste,
And health attends them from the short repast.
   While the full pail rewards the milkmaid's toil,
The mother sees the morning caldron boil;
To stir the pudding next demands her care;

To spread the table and the bowls prepare;
To feed the household as their portions cool
And send them all to labor or to school.
    Yet may the simplest dish some rules impart,
For nature scorns not all the aids of art.
E'en Hasty Pudding, purest of all food,
May still be bad, indifferent, or good,
As sage experience the short process guides,
Or want of skill, or want of care presides.
Whoe'er would form it on the surest plan,
To rear the child and long sustain the man;
To shield the morals while it mends the size,
And all the powers of every food supplies,—
Attend the lessons that the muse shall bring,
Suspend your spoons, and listen while I sing.
    But since, O man! thy life and health demand
Not food alone, but labor from thy hand,
First, in the field, beneath the sun's strong rays,
Ask of thy mother earth the needful maize;
She loves the race that courts her yielding soil,
And gives her bounties to the sons of toil.
    When now the ox, obedient to thy call,
Repays the loan that filled the winter stall,
Pursue his traces o'er the furrowed plain,
And plant in measured hills the golden grain.
But when the tender germ begins to shoot,
And the green spire declares the sprouting root,
Then guard your nursling from each greedy foe,
The insidious worm, the all-devouring crow.
A little ashes sprinkled round the spire,
Soon steeped in rain, will bid the worm retire;
The feathered robber with his hungry maw
Swift flies the field before your man of straw,
A frightful image, such as schoolboys bring
When met to burn the Pope or hang the King.
    Thrice in the season, through each verdant row,
Wield the strong plowshare and the faithful hoe;
The faithful hoe, a double task that takes,

To till the summer corn and roast the winter cakes.
   Slow springs the blade, while checked by chilling rains,
Ere yet the sun the seat of Cancer gains;
But when his fiercest fires emblaze the land,
Then start the juices, then the roots expand;
Then, like a column of Corinthian mold,
The stalk struts upward and the leaves unfold;
The bushy branches all the ridges fill,
Entwine their arms, and kiss from hill to hill.
Here cease to vex them; all your cares are done:
Leave the last labors to the parent sun;
Beneath his genial smiles, the well-dressed field,
When autumn calls, a plenteous crop shall yield.
   Now the strong foliage bears the standards high,
And shoots the tall top-gallants to the sky;
The suckling ears their silky fringes bend,
And pregnant grown, their swelling coats distend;
The loaded stalk, while still the burden grows,
O'erhangs the space that runs between the rows;
High as a hop-field waves the silent grove,
A safe retreat for little thefts of love,
When the fledged roasting-ears invite the maid
To meet her swain beneath the new-formed shade;
His generous hand unloads the cumberous hill,
And the green spoils her ready basket fill;
Small compensation for the twofold bliss,
The promised wedding, and the present kiss.
   Slight depredations these; but now the moon
Calls from his hollow tree the sly raccoon;
And while by night he bears his prize away,
The bolder squirrel labors through the day.
Both thieves alike, but provident of time,
A virtue rare, that almost hides their crime.
Then let them steal the little stores they can,
And fill their granaries from the toils of man;
We've one advantage where they take no part—
With all their wiles, they ne'er have found the art
To boil the Hasty Pudding; here we shine

Superior far to tenants of the pine;
This envied boon to man shall still belong,
Unshared by them in substance or in song.
   At last the closing season browns the plain,
And ripe October gathers in the grain;
Deep-loaded carts the spacious corn-house fill;
The sack distended marches to the mill;
The laboring mill beneath the burden groans,
And showers the future pudding from the stones;
Till the glad housewife greets the powdered gold,
And the new crop exterminates the old.
Ah, who can sing what every wight must feel,
The joy that enters with the bag of meal.
A general jubilee pervades the house,
Wakes every child and gladdens every mouse.

CANTO III

   The days grow short; but though the falling sun
To the glad swain proclaims his day's work done,
Night's pleasing shades his various tasks prolong,
And yield new subjects to my various song.
For now, the corn-house filled, the harvest home,
The invited neighbors to the husking come;
A frolic scene, where work, and mirth, and play,
Unite their charms to chase the hours away.
   Where the huge heap lies centered in the hall,
The lamp suspended from the cheerful wall,
Brown, corn-fed nymphs, and strong, hard-handed beaux,
Alternate ranged, extend in circling rows,
Assume their seats, the solid mass attack;
The dry husks rustle, and the corncobs crack;
The song, the laugh, alternate notes resound,
And the sweet cider trips in silence round.
   The laws of husking every wight can tell;
And sure no laws he ever keeps so well:
For each red ear a general kiss he gains,

With each smut ear* she smuts the luckless swains;
But when to some sweet maid a prize is cast,
Red as her lips and taper as her waist,
She walks the round and culls one favored beau,
Who leaps the luscious tribute to bestow.
Various the sport, as are the wits and brains
Of well-pleased lasses and contending swains;
Till the vast mound of corn is swept away,
And he that gets the last ear wins the day.
   Meanwhile, the housewife urges all her care,
The well-earned feast to hasten and prepare.
The sifted meal already waits her hand,
The milk is strained, the bowls in order stand,
The fire flames high; and as a pool—that takes
The headlong stream that o'er the milldam breaks—
Foams, roars, and rages with incessant toils,
So the vexed caldron rages, roars, and boils.
   First with clean salt she seasons well the food,
Then strews the flour, and thickens all the flood.
Long o'er the simmering fire she lets it stand;
To stir it well demands a stronger hand;
The husband takes his turn: and round and round
The ladle flies; at last the toil is crowned;
When to the board the thronging huskers pour,
And take their seats as at the corn before.
   I leave them to their feast. There still belong
More useful matters to my faithful song.
For rules there are, though ne'er unfolded yet,
Nice rules and wise, how pudding should be eat.
   Some with molasses line the luscious treat,
And mix, like bards, the useful with the sweet.
A wholesome dish, and well deserving praise,
A great resource in those bleak wintry days,
When the chilled earth lies buried deep in snow,
And raging Boreas dries the shivering cow.
   Blest cow! thy praise shall still my notes employ,

---

* A diseased ear contaminated by a black fungus.

Great source of health, the only source of joy;
Mother of Egypt's god,*—but sure, for me,
Were I to leave my God, I'd worship thee.
How oft thy teats these pious hands have prest!
How oft thy bounties proved my only feast!
How oft I've fed thee with my favorite grain!
And roared, like thee, to see thy children slain!
   Ye swains who know her various worth to prize,
Ah! house her well from winter's angry skies.
Potatoes, pumpkins, should her sadness cheer,
Corn from your crib, and mashes from your beer;
When spring returns, she'll well acquit the loan,
And nurse at once your infants and her own.
Milk then with pudding I should always choose;
To this in future I confine my muse,
Till she in haste some further hints unfold,
Well for the young, nor useless to the old.
First in your bowl the milk abundant take,
Then drop with care along the silver lake
Your flakes of pudding; these at first will hide
Their little bulk beneath the swelling tide;
But when their growing mass no more can sink,
When the soft island looms above the brink,
Then check your hand; you've got the portion due;
So taught my sire, and what he taught is true.
   There is a choice in spoons. Though small appear
The nice distinction, yet to me 'tis clear.
The deep-bowled Gallic spoon, contrived to scoop
In ample draughts the thin, diluted soup,
Performs not well in those substantial things,
Whose mass adhesive to the metal clings;
Where the strong labial muscles must embrace
The gentle curve, and sweep the hollow space.
With ease to enter and discharge the freight,
A bowl less concave, but still more dilate,
Becomes the pudding best. The shape, the size,

*Hathor, sometimes associated with the god Horus.

A secret rests, unknown to vulgar eyes.
Experienced feeders can alone impart
A rule so much above the lore of art.
These tuneful lips that thousand spoons have tried,
With just precision could the point decide,
Though not in song; the muse but poorly shines
In cones, and cubes, and geometric lines;
Yet the true form, as near as she can tell,
Is that small section of a goose-egg shell,
Which in two equal portions shall divide
The distance from the center to the side.
    Fear not to slaver; 'tis no deadly sin.
Like the fine Frenchman, from your joyous chin
Suspend the ready napkin; or, like me,
Poise with one hand your bowl upon your knee;
Just in the zenith your wise head project,
Your full spoon, rising in a line direct,
Bold as a bucket, heeds no drops that fall;
The wide-mouthed bowl will surely catch them all!

Thomas Carlyle

(English, 1795–1881)

The Sower's Song

Now hands to seedsheet, boys,
We step and we cast; old Time's on wing;
And would ye partake of Harvest's joys,
The corn must be sown in Spring.

Fall gently and still, good corn,
Lie warm in thy earthy bed;

And stand so yellow some morn,
For beast and man must be fed.

Old Earth is a pleasure to see
In sunshiny cloak of red and green;
The furrow lies fresh; this Year will be
As Years that are past have been.

    Fall gently, etc.

Old Mother, receive this corn,
The son of six Thousand golden sires:
All these on thy kindly breast were born;
One more thy poor child requires.

    Fall gently, etc.

Now steady and sure again,
And measure of stroke and step we keep;
Thus up and thus down we cast our grain:
Sow well, and you gladly reap.

    Fall gently and still, good corn,
    Lie warm in thy earthy bed;
    And stand so yellow some morn,
    For beast and man must be fed.

Charles Dickens

(1812–1870)

From *Oliver Twist*

"Make a bow to the gentleman, Oliver," said Mrs. Mann.

Oliver made a bow, which was divided between the beadle on the chair and the cocked hat on the table.

"Will you go along with me, Oliver?" said Mr. Bumble in a majestic voice.

Oliver was about to say that he would go along with anybody with great readiness, when, glancing upward, he caught sight of Mrs. Mann, who had got behind the beadle's chair, and was shaking her fist at him with a furious countenance. He took the hint at once, for the fist had been too often impressed upon his body not to be deeply impressed upon his recollection.

"Will *she* go with me?" inquired poor Oliver.

"No, she can't," replied Mr. Bumble. "But she'll come and see you sometimes."

This was no very great consolation to the child; but, young as he was, he had sense enough to make a feint of feeling great regret at going away. It was no very difficult matter for the boy to call tears into his eyes. Hunger and recent ill-usage are great assistants if you want to cry; and Oliver cried very naturally indeed. Mrs. Mann gave him a thousand embraces, and, what Oliver wanted a great deal more, a piece of bread and butter, lest he should seem too hungry when he got to the workhouse. With the slice of bread in his hand, and the little brown-cloth parish cap on his head, Oliver was then led away by Mr. Bumble from the wretched home where one kind word or look had never lighted the gloom of his infant years. And yet he burst into an agony of childish grief as the cottage-gate closed after him. Wretched as were the little companions in misery he was leaving behind, they were the only friends he had ever known; and a sense of his loneliness in the great wide world sank into the child's heart for the first time.

Mr. Bumble walked on with long strides, and little Oliver, firmly grasping his gold-laced cuff, trotted beside him, inquiring at the end of every quarter of a mile whether they were "nearly there." To these interrogations Mr. Bumble returned very brief and snappish replies; for the temporary blandness which gin-and-water awakens in some bosoms had by this time evaporated, and he was once again a beadle.

Oliver had not been within the walls of the workhouse a quarter of an hour, and had scarcely completed the demolition of a second slice of bread, when Mr. Bumble, who had handed him over to the care of an old woman, returned, and, telling him it was a board night, informed him that the board had said he was to appear before it forthwith.

Not having a very clearly defined notion of what a live board was, Oliver was rather astounded by this intelligence, and was not quite certain whether he ought to laugh or cry. He had no time to think about the matter, however; for Mr. Bumble gave him a tap on the head with his cane to wake him up, and another on the back to make him lively, and bidding him follow, conducted him into a large whitewashed room where eight or ten fat gentlemen were sitting round a table, at the top of which, seated in an arm-chair rather higher than the rest, was a particularly fat gentleman with a very round, red face.

"Bow to the board," said Bumble. Oliver brushed away two or three tears that were lingering in his eyes, and seeing no board but the table, fortunately bowed to that.

"What's your name, boy?" said the gentleman in the high chair.

Oliver was frightened at the sight of so many gentlemen, which made him tremble; and the beadle gave him another tap behind, which made him cry; and these two causes made him answer in a very low and hesitating voice; whereupon a gentleman in a white waistcoat said he was a fool. Which was a capital way of raising his spirits, and putting him quite at his ease.

"Boy," said the gentleman in the high chair, "listen to me. You know you're an orphan, I suppose?"

"What's that, sir?" inquired poor Oliver.

"The boy *is* a fool—I thought he was," said the gentleman in the white waistcoat, in a very decided tone. If one member of a class be blessed with an intuitive perception of others of the same race, the gentleman in the white waistcoat was unquestionably well qualified to pronounce an opinion on the matter.

"Hush!" said the gentleman who had spoken first. "You know you've got no father or mother, and that you were brought up by the parish, don't you?"

"Yes, sir," replied Oliver, weeping bitterly.

"What are you crying for?" inquired the gentleman in the white waistcoat. And to be sure it was very extraordinary. What *could* the boy be crying for?

"I hope you say your prayers every night," said another gentleman in a gruff voice, "and pray for the people who feed you, and take care of you, like a Christian."

"Yes, sir," stammered the boy. The gentleman who spoke last was unconsciously right. It would have been *very* like a Christian, and a marvellously good Christian, too, if Oliver had prayed for the people who fed and took care of *him*. But he hadn't, because nobody had taught him.

"Well! You have come here to be educated, and taught a useful trade," said the red-faced gentleman in the high chair.

"So you'll begin to pick oakum* tomorrow morning at six o'clock," added the surly one in the white waistcoat.

For the combination of both these blessings in the one simple process of picking oakum, Oliver bowed low by the direction of the beadle, and was then hurried away to a large ward, where, on a rough, hard bed, he sobbed himself to sleep. What a noble illustration of the tender laws of this

*Loose fiber from old ropes, used as a caulking material.

favoured country! They let the paupers go to sleep!

Poor Oliver! He little thought, as he lay sleeping in happy unconsciousness of all around him, that the board had that very day arrived at a decision which would exercise the most material influence over all his future fortunes. But they had. And this was it:

The members of this board were very sage, deep, philosophical men, and when they came to turn their attention to the workhouse, they found out at once, what ordinary folks would never have discovered—the poor people liked it! It was a regular place of public entertainment for the poorer classes; a tavern where there was nothing to pay; a public breakfast, dinner, tea, and supper all the year round; a brick and mortar elysium, where it was all play and no work. "Oho!" said the board, looking very knowing, "we are the fellows to set this to rights; we'll stop it all, in no time." So, they established the rule, that all poor people should have the alternative (for they would compel nobody, not they), of being starved by a gradual process in the house, or by a quick one out of it. With this view, they contracted with the water-works to lay on an unlimited supply of water; and with a corn-factor to supply periodically small quantities of oatmeal; and issued three meals of thin gruel a day, with an onion twice a week, and half a roll on Sundays. They made a great many other wise and humane regulations having reference to the ladies, which it is not necessary to repeat; kindly undertook to divorce poor married people, in consequence of the great expense of a suit in Doctors' Commons; and, instead of compelling a man to support his family, as they had theretofore done, took his family away from him, and made him a bachelor! There is no saying how many applicants for relief, under these last two heads, might have started up in all classes of society, if it had not been coupled with the workhouse; but the board were long-headed men, and had provided for this difficulty. The relief was inseparable from the workhouse and the gruel; and that frightened people.

For the first six months after Oliver Twist was removed, the system was in full operation. It was rather expensive at first, in consequence of the increase in the undertaker's bill, and the necessity of taking in the clothes of all the paupers, which fluttered loosely on their wasted, shrunken forms, after a week or two's gruel. But the number of workhouse inmates got thin as well as the paupers; and the board were in ecstasies.

The room in which the boys were fed was a large stone hall, with a copper at one end, out of which the master, dressed in an apron for the purpose, and assisted by one or two women, ladled the gruel at meal-times; of which composition each boy had one porringer, and no more—except on festive occasions, and then he had two ounces and a quarter of bread besides. The bowls never wanted washing. The boys polished them with their spoons till they shone again; and when they had performed this operation (which never took very long, the spoons being nearly as large as the bowls), they would sit staring at the copper with such eager eyes as if they could have devoured the very bricks of which it was composed; employing themselves, meanwhile, in sucking their fingers most assiduously, with the view of catching up any stray splashes of gruel that might have been cast thereon. Boys have generally excellent appetites. Oliver Twist and his companions suffered the tortures of slow starvation for three months: at last they got so voracious and wild with hunger, that one boy, who was tall for his age, and hadn't been used to that sort of thing (for his father had kept a small cookshop), hinted darkly to his companions, that unless he had another basin of gruel *per diem*, he was afraid he might some night happen to eat the boy who slept next him, who happened to be a weakly youth of tender age. He had a wild, hungry eye; and they implicitly believed him. A council was held; lots were cast who should walk up to the master after supper that evening, and ask for more; and it fell to Oliver Twist.

The evening arrived; the boys took their places. The master, in his cook's uniform, stationed himself at the copper; his pauper assistants ranged themselves behind him; the gruel was served out; and a long grace was said over the short commons. The gruel disappeared; the boys whispered to each other, and winked at Oliver, while his next neighbours nudged him. Child as he was, he was desperate with hunger, and reckless with misery. He rose from the table, and advancing to the master, basin and spoon in hand, said: somewhat alarmed at his own temerity:

"Please, sir, I want some more."

The master was a fat, healthy man; but he turned very pale. He gazed in stupefied astonishment on the small rebel for some seconds, and then clung for support to the copper. The assistants were paralysed with wonder; the boys with fear.

"What!" said the master at length, in a faint voice.

"Please, sir," replied Oliver, "I want some more."

The master aimed a blow at Oliver's head with the ladle, pinioned him in his arms, and shrieked aloud for the beadle.

The board were sitting in solemn conclave, when Mr. Bumble rushed into the room in great excitement, and addressing the gentleman in the high chair, said,

"Mr. Limbkins, I beg your pardon, sir! Oliver Twist has asked for more!" There was a general start. Horror was depicted on every countenance.

"For *more*!" said Mr. Limbkins. "Compose yourself, Bumble, and answer me distinctly. Do I understand that he asked for more, after he had eaten the supper allotted by the dietary?"

"He did, sir," replied Bumble.

"That boy will be hung," said the gentleman in the white waistcoat; "I know that boy will be hung."

Premchand
[Srivastava Dhanpatrai]

(Indian, 1881–1936)

A Handful of Wheat

In a certain village there was a low-caste peasant named
Shanker. He was a simple and poor fellow who was absorbed
in his own toil and did not try to interfere in the affairs of
other folk. He had no tricks up his sleeve at all; he knew no
cunning or deceit. He was not worried about being cheated
and he himself cheated none. He had a meal, if he could. If he
could not, then he would eat a little gram* and be content
with it. If he did not even get gram to eat, he just drank some
water and went off to sleep. But when a guest came to his
door, he had to give up these ways of renunciation. Specially
when some *sadhu* or *mahatma* arrived, he had inevitably to
resort to worldliness in his dealings. He could sleep on a hungry stomach himself, but he could not possibly ask a *sadhu* to
do the same, *sadhus* being devotees of God!

One evening a *mahatma* came and settled down at his place
for a night's rest. He was an impressive figure with his yellow
robe, long hair, a brass receptacle in his hands, sandalled feet
and spectacles. His whole rig-out was reminiscent of those
mahatmas who practise renunciation in the mansions of the
rich, tour holy places in luxurious carriages and consume rich
meals for the attainment of singular powers of the body and
the mind! Shanker had only barley flour at his house. How
could he offer this to a *mahatma*? Barley might have been
supposed to possess great merit in ancient times, but in the
modern age barley is indigestible for people who possess great

*Pottage made from leguminous seeds, such as lentils or chick-peas.

and mysterious powers. Shanker was very worried as to what he could offer to the *mahatma* by way of food. He could find no wheat flour in any home in the village. There were mere men living in the village. There was not one single god among them. How could he then find food in the village which only gods eat? Fortunately, he found a little wheat at the house of the village priest. He borrowed a seer* and a quarter of wheat from him and asked his wife to grind it. The *mahatma* dined well and later on slept well. In the morning he offered his blessings to Shanker and went his way.

It was customary to make two offerings of grain to the priest during the year. Shanker thought to himself that there was no point in his returning a small amount like a seer and a quarter of wheat. He would make an addition to the usual offering of five seers. They would both know and understand. When the priest came for his offering at harvest time, Shanker offered him the usual amount and half as much over and above this. He imagined he had cleared his debt, but made no mention of it to the priest. And the priest, too, never reminded Shanker about it. How could poor Shanker imagine that his present life would not suffice to clear his debt?

Seven years passed by. The priest gradually changed into a moneylender. Shanker deteriorated from a peasant into a labourer. His younger brother, Mangal, had separated from him. They were peasants when they lived together; having parted they both became labourers. Shanker tried his level best to calm down the flames of bitterness, but circumstances ultimately forced his hands. When the home-fires burnt separately, Shanker cried bitterly. The two brothers would now live in hostility! If one of them cried, the other would laugh; if one of them was mourning, the other would be feasting. The ties of blood, the ties of love were being snapped that day. He had planted this tree of family good-name after terrific toil; he had nursed it with his sweat and blood. His heart was sore to find that same tree being uprooted. For a whole

---

*A variable measure in India, usually equal to about two pounds.

week he could neither eat nor drink. He laboured the whole day long in the terrible summer heat and at night he lay in bed eating his heart out in loneliness and sorrow. His body was consumed by this grief and hard labour and he was reduced to a mere skeleton. He fell ill and could not move from his bed for months. How were they to live now? There were only half their fields left to them now, measuring five *bighas** and just one bullock. What farming was it possible to do with such resources? In the end things came to such a pass that cultivation was merely a pretence for maintaining the family tradition. As far as livelihood was concerned, it had to be earned by labour.

Seven years had passed. One evening when Shanker was returning home after work, the priest stopped him on the way and said, "Shanker, come tomorrow and settle your account. You have to pay me five and a half maunds† of wheat, but you don't seem to take any notice of this matter. Do you wish to disown your debt?"

Shanker was amazed and said, "When did I borrow wheat from you that it should now grow into five and a half maunds? You are making a mistake. I owe nobody either an ounce of corn or as much as a pice!"‡

Priest: "It is due to this attitude of yours that you are starving!"

Saying this the priest mentioned the seer and quarter of wheat which he had lent to Shanker seven years ago. Shanker was flabbergasted at this. O God! He had made him annual offerings of corn so often and what had the priest ever done for him in return? Whenever he had come to calculate an auspicious moment or to look into a horoscope, he had always received an offering in return for it. Such selfishness! He had been roosting over this seer and a quarter of wheat and now raised a monster which would gobble him up! If he had mentioned it even once, he would have measured out the grain for

---

*About one and a half acres.
†A coin worth a quarter of an anna; a very small amount.
‡Another variable weight, now standardized at one hundred pounds.

him. Had he kept silent precisely for this reason? He said, "It is true that I never made a specific mention of it, but I often added an extra seer or two to my annual gifts to you. And now, you are asking me to give five and a half maunds to you! Where am I to get it from?"

Priest: "Accounts are one thing: gifts another. Whatever you gave me, must have been by way of gifts. No account is preserved of a gift, though instead of five seers you may offer twenty! There are five and a half maunds against your name in my accounts book. You may ask anyone to calculate this. If you return it, I shall strike out your name: otherwise the account will continue to multiply."

Shanker: "Pandey! Why do you trouble a poor man? I have not enough to eat; where am I to get so much wheat?"

Priest: "You may get it from where you please! I am not going to give up even a grain from my account. If you don't pay me here, you will have to pay it in the next world!"

Shanker shivered with fear. If he had been an educated person, he might have said, "Very well, we shall pay it in the next world. The account there could not be worse than it is here! At least we have no evidence that it is so. Then why should we worry about that?" But Shanker was not so logical or practical. A debt—and that too owing to a Brahmin! If he did not clear it, he was bound to go straight to Hell! He trembled to think so. He said, "*Maharaj!* I shall pay whatever I owe you, here. Why should I wait to pay it in the next world? I am suffering torment here; why should I spoil my next world too? But there is no justice in this. You have made a mountain out of a molehill. You should not have done this; you are a *Brahmin!* You should have asked for it and realised it earlier. Then it would not have been such a burden for me. I shall repay you, but you will have to answer before God for this!"

"I am not afraid of that; you might be so. There I shall have cousins and friends all round me. The sages and saints there are all *Brahmins!* They shall take care of my interests, if anything goes wrong. Well, when are you going to clear your debt?"

Shanker: "I have nothing with me. I shall have to beg or borrow it from someone. Then only can I pay you."

Priest: "I shall not accept this. Seven years have already gone by. I shall not grant you even a day's respite now. If you cannot repay the wheat, you must execute a deed accepting the debt."

Shanker: "I have to pay you, whether it is wheat or a deed makes no difference to me. Let us write it down. What rate will you charge?"

Priest: "The market rate is five seers. I may charge you at the rate of five and a quarter."

Shanker: "When I am paying you, then let it be at the market rate. Why should I feel guilty for a quarter of a seer?"

The debt was calculated and came to sixty rupees. A deed for sixty rupees was executed with three per cent interest. If he did not clear the debt within a year, the rate of interest would increase to three and a half per cent. Eight annas for the stamp and a rupee for the execution of the deed had to be paid by Shanker.

The whole village cursed the priest, but not to his face. Everyone has to have dealings with the moneylender. Who is there so brave as to defy him?

II

Shanker toiled hard for a year. He had taken a vow to pay the money within the time-limit. Even previously no food was cooked in the morning; they had only taken some gram. Now they gave up that also. They kept some bread for their son from the night's cooking. Shanker used to smoke a pice worth of tobacco; this had been his one luxury which he had never been able to renounce. Now this addiction too was sacrificed in the terrible ordeal facing him. He threw away his *chilum,** smashed the hubble-bubble, and broke up the pot containing his tobacco. His clothes had already attained in

* Tobacco bowl of the hookah (hubble-bubble).

earlier times extreme limits of sacrifice; now they assumed the thinnest lines possible in nature's scheme. He faced the severe rigours of winter with the help of fires. The fruits of this grim determination exceeded all hopes. He had collected sixty rupees at the end of the year. He thought, he would give this money to Panditji and say, "*Maharaj*! I shall offer you the rest of the money quite soon!" He had only to pay an extra fifteen rupees. Panditji would surely be forbearing! He took the money and placed it at Panditji's feet. Panditji was surprised and asked, "Did you borrow them from someone?"

Shanker: "No, sir. I found good wages this year, thanks to your blessings."

Priest: "But these are only sixty rupees!"

Shanker: "Yes, *Maharaj*! Kindly accept them now. I shall pay the rest in another two or three months. Please release me now from my bondage."

Priest: "You can only be released after paying back every pice. Please go and bring another fifteen rupees."

Shanker: "Take pity on me now, Sir. I do not even know what I am to eat in the evening. I am in the village and bound to repay the rest."

Priest: "No. I am not fond of much talk or of such transactions. If I do not receive the whole sum, then you will have to pay interest at the rate of three and a half per cent. You can take your money with you or leave it here, just as you please!"

Shanker: "All right. Please keep what I have brought. I shall try to get the rest from somewhere."

Shanker went round the whole village, but no one gave him the money; not because they did not trust him or because they did not have the money, but because nobody dared to come between Panditji and his victim.

III

It is the eternal law that action is followed by reaction. When Shanker failed to achieve his salvation after a year's grim toil, his discipline yielded to despair. He realised that if he had been unable to collect more than sixty rupees after such hardship, how could he now collect together twice this sum of money? If he were to be weighed down under the load of debt, then what did it matter whether it was a maund or a maund and a quarter? He lost heart and started to hate toil. Hope is the mother of zest: in hope there is life, strength and glory. Hope is the motive force of all life. Shanker lost hope and grew indifferent. The necessities which he had been denying to himself for a whole year, appeared no longer as beggars at his threshold, but rather as monsters gripping his throat who would not let go their hold without receiving the offering which was their due! There is a limit beyond which cloth cannot be patched. When Shanker received his wages now, he no longer hoarded them, but bought either cloth or something to eat. Whereas formerly he had been smoking only tobacco, he now developed a taste for other intoxicating drugs too. He no longer worried about repaying his debt, as though he owed no one a single pice. Formerly, he had gone to work, even if he had a fever. Now he looked for excuses not to have to go to work.

Three years went by in this fashion. The priest did not give him a single reminder all this time. Like a cunning hunter he wished to strike a mortal blow. It was against his policy to startle his victim prematurely.

One day Panditji called Shanker and showed the accounts to him. After deducting the sixty rupees which had been deposited with him, Shanker had still one hundred and twenty rupees to pay.

Shanker: "I can pay so much money only in my next life! I cannot pay it in this one."

Priest: "I shall take it in this life, at least the interest, if not the capital!"

Shanker: "I have a bullock; take that. I have a hut; you can take that too. What else have I for you to take?"

Priest: "I don't need your bullocks, etc. You have much that you can still pay to me."

Shanker: "What else do I possess?"

Priest: "If there is nothing else, there is you yourself! You go to work somewhere or other; I too need a labourer to work on my fields. You work on my fields as payment of interest; you may pay the capital, when convenient to you. The truth is, you cannot go to work anywhere now, unless you have cleared my debt! You possess no property; how can I risk losing such a big sum without any security? Who is going to stand security that you will be paying me interest every month? And when you are unable to pay me even interest from your earnings elsewhere, then how can you pay the capital?"

Shanker: "I am to work for you in lieu of interest; then what shall I live on?"

Priest: "There are your wife and sons. Will they sit at home like cripples? As for me, I shall give you half a seer of barley every day for breakfast. I shall give you a blanket in the year to cover yourself; I may give you a jacket too. What else do you want? It is true that others pay six annas a day. But that is no concern of mine. I have to give you work to realise my interest."

Shanker was sunk in deep anxiety for a time; then he said: "*Maharaj!* This is slavery for life!"

Priest: "Call it what you please, service or slavery! I shall not release you without obtaining payment of my debt. If you escape, I shall catch hold of your son. If there is none left to repay me, that would be another matter!"

No appeal could be made against such a decision anywhere. Who would stand security for a labourer? Nowhere could he run away. Who would offer him refuge? He started working for the priest for the sake of a handful of wheat! If any idea could comfort the poor wretch now, it was that the deeds of a previous existence were bearing fruit now! His wife had now to undertake labour which she had never previously done. His children were nearly starved. But Shanker could do nothing about it except look on helplessly. Those few grains of wheat burdened his back through life like the curse of a god.

IV

Shanker departed from this purposeless world after a servitude of twenty years. He was yet burdened with a debt of one hundred and twenty rupees. Panditji did not like the idea of troubling the poor fellow in the next world; he was not so cruel and unjust. He clutched the throat of his young son. He works at the priest's place to this day. God only knows when he will achieve his salvation, if ever at all!

Reader! This is no imaginary story! This is the living truth. The world still has such priests and such Shankers!

—Translated by P. C. Gupta

oats. A grain, which in England is generally given to horses, but in Scotland supports the people.

—SAMUEL JOHNSON, *The Dictionary*

Jonathan Swift
(1667–1745)

From *Gulliver's Travels*
A VOYAGE TO THE LAND OF THE HOUYHNHNMS

About noon, I saw coming towards the house a kind of vehicle, drawn, like a sledge, by four Yahoos. There was in it an old steed, who seemed to be of quality; he alighted with his hind feet forward, having, by accident, got a hurt in his fore-

foot. He came to dine with our horse, who received him with
great civility. They dined in the best room and had oats
boiled in milk for the second course, which the old horse eat
warm, but the rest cold. Their mangers were placed circular
in the middle of the room, and divided into several partitions,
round which they sat on their haunches upon bosses of straw.
In the middle was a large rack, with angles answering to
every partition of the manger; so that each horse and mare
ate their own hay, and their own mash of oats and milk, with
much decency and regularity. The behaviour of the young
colt and foal appeared very modest; and that of the master
and mistress extremely cheerful and complaisant to their
guest. The grey ordered me to stand by him; and much dis-
course passed between him and his friend concerning me, as I
found by the stranger's often looking on me, and the frequent
repetition of the word Yahoo.

I happened to wear my gloves, which the master grey observing, seemed perplexed, discovering signs of wonder what
I had done to my fore-feet; he put his hoof three or four
times to them, as if he would signify, that I should reduce
them to their former shape, which I presently did, pulling off
both my gloves, and putting them into my pocket. This occasioned further talk, and I saw the company was pleased with
my behaviour, whereof I soon found the good effects. I was
ordered to speak the few words I understood; and while they
were at dinner, the master taught me the names for oats,
milk, fire, water, and some others; which I could readily pronounce after him, having from my youth a great facility in
learning languages.

When dinner was done, the master horse took me aside,
and by signs and words, made me understand the concern
that he was in, that I had nothing to eat. Oats, in their
tongue, are called *hluunh*. This word I pronounced two or
three times; for although I had refused them at first, yet,
upon second thoughts, I considered that I could contrive to
make of them a kind of bread, which might be sufficient, with
milk, to keep me alive, till I could make my escape to some

other country, and to creatures of my own species. The horse immediately ordered a white mare servant, of his family, to bring me a good quantity of oats on a sort of wooden tray. These I heated before the fire, as well as I could, and rubbed them till the husks came off, which I made a shift to winnow from the grain; I ground and beat them between two stones, then took water, and made them into a paste or cake, which I toasted at the fire, and ate warm with milk. It was at first a very insipid diet, though common enough in many parts of Europe, but grew tolerable by time; and, having been often reduced to hard fare in my life, this was not the first experiment I had made, how easily nature is satisfied. And I cannot but observe, that I never had one hour's sickness while I stayed in this island.

O. Henry

(American, 1862–1910)

The Pimienta Pancakes

While we were rounding up a bunch of the Triangle-O cattle in the Frio bottoms, a projecting branch of a dead mesquite caught my wooden stirrup and gave my ankle a wrench that laid me up in camp for a week.

On the third day of my compulsory idleness I crawled out near the grub wagon, and reclined helpless under the conversational fire of Judson Odom, the camp cook. Jud was a monologist by nature, whom Destiny, with customary blundering, had set in a profession wherein he was bereaved, for the greater portion of his time, of an audience.

Therefore, I was manna in the desert of Jud's obmutescence.

Betimes I was stirred by invalid longings for something to eat that did not come under the caption of "grub." I had visions of the maternal pantry "deep as first love, and wild with all regret," and then I asked:

"Jud, can you make pancakes?"

Jud laid down his sixshooter, with which he was preparing to pound an antelope steak, and stood over me in what I felt to be a menacing attitude. He further indorsed my impression that his pose was resentful by fixing upon me with his light blue eyes a look of cold suspicion.

"Say, you," he said, with candid, though not excessive, choler, "did you mean that straight, or was you trying to throw the gaff into me? Some of the boys been telling you about me and that pancake racket?"

"No, Jud," I said, sincerely, "I meant it. It seems to me I'd swap my pony and saddle for a stack of buttered brown pancakes with some first crop, open kettle, New Orleans sweetening. Was there a story about pancakes?"

Jud was mollified at once when he saw that I had not been dealing in allusions. He brought some mysterious bags and tin boxes from the grub wagon and set them in the shade of the hackberry where I lay reclined. I watched him as he began to arrange them leisurely and untie their many strings.

"No, not a story," said Jud, as he worked, "but just the logical disclosures in the case of me and that pink-eyed snoozer from Mired Mule Cañada and Miss Willella Learight. I don't mind telling you.

"I was punching then for old Bill Toomey, on the San Miguel. One day I gets all ensnared up in aspirations for to eat some canned grub that hasn't ever mooed or baaed or grunted or been in peck measures. So, I gets on my bronc and pushes the wind for Uncle Emsley Telfair's store at the Pimienta Crossing on the Neuces.

"About three in the afternoon I throwed my bridle over a mesquite limb and walked the last twenty yards into Uncle

Emsley's store. I got up on the counter and told Uncle Emsley that the signs pointed to the devastation of the fruit crop of the world. In a minute I had a bag of crackers and a long-handled spoon, with an open can each of apricots and pineapples and cherries and green-gages beside of me with Uncle Emsley busy chopping away with the hatchet at the yellow clings. I was feeling like Adam before the apple stampede, and was digging my spurs into the side of the counter and working with my twenty-four-inch spoon when I happened to look out of the window into the yard of Uncle Emsley's house, which was next to the store.

"There was a girl standing there—an imported girl with fixings on—philandering with a croquet maul and amusing herself by watching my style of encouraging the fruit canning industry.

"I slid off the counter and delivered up my shovel to Uncle Emsley.

" 'That's my niece,' says he; 'Miss Willella Learight, down from Palestine on a visit. Do you want that I should make you acquainted?'

" 'The Holy Land,' I says to myself, my thought milling some as I tried to run 'em into the corral. 'Why not? There was sure angels in Pales—Why yes, Uncle Emsley,' I says out loud, 'I'd be awful edified to meet Miss Learight.'

"So Uncle Emsley took me out in the yard and gave us each other's entitlements.

"I never was shy about women. I never could understand why some men who can break a mustang before breakfast and shave in the dark, get all left-handed and full of perspiration and excuses when they see a bolt of calico draped around what belongs in it. Inside of eight minutes me and Miss Willella was aggravating the croquet balls around as amiable as second cousins. She gave me a dig about the quantity of canned fruit I had eaten, and I got back at her, flat-footed, about how a certain lady named Eve started the fruit trouble in the first free-grass pasture—'Over in Palestine, wasn't it?' says I, as easy and pat as roping a one-year-old.

"That was how I acquired cordiality for the proximities of Miss Willella Learight; and the disposition grew larger as time passed. She was stopping at Pimienta Crossing for her health, which was very good, and for the climate, which was forty per cent hotter than Palestine. I rode over to see her once every week for a while; and then I figured it out that if I doubled the number of trips I would see her twice as often.

"One week I slipped in a third trip; and that's where the pancakes and the pink-eyed snoozer busted into the game.

"That evening, while I set on the counter with a peach and two damsons in my mouth, I asked Uncle Emsley how Miss Willella was.

" 'Why,' says Uncle Emsley, 'she's gone riding with Jackson Bird, the sheep man from over at Mired Mule Cañada.'

"I swallowed the peach seed and the two damson seeds. I guess somebody held the counter by the bridle while I got off; and then I walked out straight ahead till I butted against the mesquite where my roan was tied.

" 'She's gone riding,' I whispered in my bronc's ear, 'with Birdstone Jack, the hired mule from Sheep Man's Cañada. Did you get that, old Leather-and-Gallops?''

"That bronc of mine wept, in his way. He'd been raised a cow pony and he didn't care for snoozers.

"I went back and said to Uncle Emsley: 'Did you say a sheep man?'

" 'I said a sheep man,' says Uncle again. 'You must have heard tell of Jackson Bird. He's got eight sections of grazing and four thousand head of the finest Merinos south of the Arctic Circle.'

"I went out and sat on the ground in the shade of the store and leaned against a prickly pear. I sifted sand into my boots with unthinking hands while I soliloquized a quantity about this bird with the Jackson plumage to his name.

"I never had believed in harming sheep men. I see one, one day, reading a Latin grammar on hossback, and I never touched him! They never irritated me like they do most cowmen. You wouldn't go to work now, and impair and disfigure snoozers, would you, that eat on tables and wear little shoes and speak to you on subjects? I had always let 'em pass, just as you would a jack-rabbit; with a polite word and a guess about the weather, but no stopping to swap canteens. I never thought it was worth while to be hostile with a snoozer. And because I'd been lenient, and let 'em live, here was one going around riding with Miss Willella Learight!

"An hour by sun they come loping back, and stopped at Uncle Emsley's gate. The sheep person helped her off; and they stood throwing each other sentences all sprightful and sagacious for a while. And then this feathered Jackson flies up in his saddle and raises his little stewpot of a hat, and trots off in the direction of his mutton ranch. By this time I had turned the sand out of my boots and unpinned myself from the prickly pear; and by the time he gets half a mile out of Pimienta, I singlefoots up beside him on my bronc.

"I said that snoozer was pink-eyed, but he wasn't. His seeing arrangement was gray enough, but his eye-lashes was pink and his hair was sandy, and that gave you the idea. Sheep man—he wasn't more than a lamb man, anyhow—a little thing with his neck involved in a yellow silk hand-kerchief, and shoes tied up in bowknots.

"'Afternoon!' says I to him. 'You now ride with an equestrian who is commonly called Dead-Moral-Certainty Judson, on account of the way I shoot. When I want a stranger to know me I always introduce myself before the draw, for I never did like to shake hands with ghosts.'

"'Ah,' says he, just like that—'Ah, I'm glad to know you, Mr. Judson. I'm Jackson Bird, from over at Mired Mule Ranch.'

"Just then one of my eyes saw a roadrunner skipping down the hill with a young tarantula in his bill, and the other eye noticed a rabbit-hawk sitting on a dead limb in a water-elm. I popped over one after the other with my forty-five, just to show him. 'Two out of three,' says I, 'Birds just naturally seem to draw my fire wherever I go.'

"'Nice shooting,' says the sheep man, without a flutter.

'But don't you sometimes ever miss the third shot? Elegant fine rain that was last week for the young grass, Mr. Judson?' says he.

" 'Willie,' says I, riding over close to his palfrey, 'your infatuated parents may have denounced you by the name of Jackson, but you sure moulted into a twittering Willie—let us slough off this here analysis of rain and the elements, and get down to talk that is outside the vocabulary of parrots. That is a bad habit you have got of riding with young ladies over at Pimienta. I've known birds,' says I, 'to be served on toast for less than that. Miss Willella,' says I, 'don't ever want any nest made out of sheep's wool by a tomtit of the Jacksonian branch of ornithology. Now, are you going to quit, or do you wish for to gallop up against this Dead-Moral-Certainty attachment to my name, which is good for two hyphens and at least one set of funeral obsequies?'

"Jackson Bird flushed up some, and then he laughed.

" 'Why, Mr. Judson,' says he, 'you've got the wrong idea. I've called on Miss Learight a few times; but not for the purpose you imagine. My object is purely a gastronomical one.'

"I reached for my gun.

" 'Any coyote,' says I, 'that would boast of dishonorable—'

" 'Wait a minute,' says this Bird, 'till I explain. What would I do with a wife? If you ever saw that ranch of mine! I do my own cooking and mending. Eating—that's all the pleasure I get out of sheep raising. Mr. Judson, did you ever taste the pancakes that Miss Learight makes?'

" 'Me? No,' I told him. 'I never was advised that she was up to any culinary maneuvers.'

" 'They're golden sunshine,' says he, 'honey-browned by the ambrosial fires of Epicurus. I'd give two years of my life to get the recipe for making them pancakes. That's what I went to see Miss Learight for,' says Jackson Bird, 'but I haven't been able to get it from her. It's an old recipe that's been in the family for seventy-five years. They hand it down from one generation to another, but they don't give it away to outsiders. If I could get that recipe, so I could make them

pancakes for myself on my ranch, I'd be a happy man,' says
Bird.

" 'Are you sure,' I says to him, 'that it ain't the hand that
mixes the pancakes that you're after?'

" 'Sure,' says Jackson. 'Miss Learight is a mighty nice girl,
but I can assure you my intentions go no further than the
gastro—' but he seen my hand going down to my holster and
he changed his similitude—'than the desire to procure a copy
of the pancake recipe,' he finishes.

" 'You ain't such a bad little man,' says I, trying to be fair.
'I was thinking some of making orphans of your sheep, but
I'll let you fly away this time. But you stick to pancakes,'
says I, 'as close as the middle one of a stack; and don't go and
mistake sentiments for syrup, or there'll be singing at your
ranch, and you won't hear it.'

" 'To convince you that I am sincere,' says the sheep man,
'I'll ask you to help me. Miss Learight and you being closer
friends, maybe she would do for you what she wouldn't for
me. If you will get me a copy of that pancake recipe, I give
you my word that I'll never call upon her again.'

" 'That's fair,' I says, and I shook hands with Jackson Bird.
'I'll get it for you if I can, and glad to oblige.' And he turned
off down the big pear flat on the Piedra, in the direction of
Mired Mule; and I steered northwest for old Bill Toomey's
ranch.

"It was five days afterward when I got another chance to
ride over to Pimienta. Miss Willella and me passed a gratifying evening at Uncle Emsley's. She sang some, and exasper-
ated the piano quite a lot with quotations from the operas. I
gave imitations of a rattlesnake, and told her about Snaky
McFee's new way of skinning cows, and described the trip I
made to Saint Louis once. We was getting along in one another's estimations fine. Thinks I, if Jackson can now be per-
suaded to migrate, I win. I recollect his promise about the
pancake receipt, and I thinks I will persuade it from Miss
Willella and give it to him; and then if I catches Birdie off of
Mired Mule again, I'll make him hop the twig.

"So, along about ten o'clock, I put on a wheedling smile and says to Miss Willella: 'Now, if there's anything I do like better than the sight of a red steer on green grass it's the taste of a nice hot pancake smothered in sugarhouse molasses.'

"Miss Willella gives a little jump on the piano stool, and looked at me curious.

" 'Yes,' says she, 'they're real nice. What did you say was the name of that street in Saint Louis, Mr. Odom, where you lost your hat?'

" 'Pancake Avenue,' says I, with a wink, to show her that I was on about the family receipt, and couldn't be side-corralled off of the subject. 'Come, now, Miss Willella,' I says; 'let's hear how you make 'em Pancakes is just whirling in my head like wagon wheels. Start her off, now—pound of flour, eight dozen eggs, and so on. How does the catalogue of constituents run?'

" 'Excuse me for a moment, please,' says Miss Willella, and she gives me a quick kind of sideways look, and slides off the stool. She ambled out into the other room, and directly Uncle Emsley comes in in his shirt sleeves, with a pitcher of water. He turns around to get a glass on the table, and I see a forty-five in his hip pocket. 'Great post-holes!' thinks I, 'but here's a family thinks a heap of cooking receipts, protecting it with firearms. I've known outfits that wouldn't do that much by a family feud.'

" 'Drink this here down,' says Uncle Emsley, handing me the glass of water. 'You've rid too far to-day, Jud, and got yourself over-excited. Try to think about something else now.'

" 'Do you know how to make them pancakes, Uncle Emsley?' I asked.

" 'Well, I'm not as apprised in the anatomy of them as some,' says Uncle Emsley, 'but I reckon you take a sifter of plaster of paris and a little dough and saleratus* and corn meal, and mix 'em with eggs and buttermilk as usual. Is old Bill going to ship beeves to Kansas City again this spring, Jud?'

*Baking soda.

"That was all the pancake specifications I could get that night. I didn't wonder that Jackson Bird found it uphill work. So I dropped the subject and talked with Uncle Emsley a while about hollow-horn and cyclones. And then Miss Willella came and said 'Good-night,' and I hit the breeze for the ranch.

"About a week afterward I met Jackson Bird riding out of Pimienta as I rode in, and we stopped in the road for a few frivolous remarks.

"'Got the bill of particulars for them flap-jacks yet?' I asked him.

"'Well, no,' says Jackson. 'I don't seem to have any success in getting hold of it. Did you try?'

"'I did,' says I, 'and 'twas like trying to dig a prairie dog out of his hole with a peanut hull. That pancake receipt must be a jooka-lorum, the way they hold on to it.'

"'I'm 'most ready to give it up,' says Jackson, so discouraged in his pronunciations that I felt sorry for him; 'but I did want to know how to make them pancakes to eat on my lonely ranch,' says he. 'I lie awake at nights thinking how good they are.'

"'You keep on trying for it,' I tells him, 'and I'll do the same. One of us is bound to get a rope over its horns before long. Well, so-long, Jacksy.'

"You see, by this time we was on the peacefullest of terms. When I saw that he wasn't after Miss Willella I had more endurable contemplations of that sandy-haired snoozer. In order to help out the ambitions of his appetite I kept on trying to get that receipt from Miss Willella. But every time I would say 'pancakes' she would get sort of remote and fidgety about the eye, and try to change the subject. If I held her to it she would slide out and round up Uncle Emsley with his pitcher of water and hip-pocket howitzer.

"One day I galloped over to the store with a fine bunch of blue verbenas that I cut out of a herd of wild flowers over on Poisoned Dog Prairie. Uncle Emsley looked at 'em with one eye shut and says:

"'Haven't ye heard the news?'

" 'Cattle up?' I asks.

" 'Willella and Jackson Bird was married in Palestine yesterday,' says he. 'Just got a letter this morning.'

"I dropped them flowers in a cracker-barrel, and let the news trickle in my ears and down toward my upper left-hand shirt pocket until it got to my feet.

" 'Would you mind saying that over again once more, Uncle Emsley?' says I. 'Maybe my hearing has got wrong, and you only said that prime heifers was 4.80 on the hoof, or something like that.'

" 'Married yesterday,' says Uncle Emsley, 'and gone to Waco and Niagara Falls on a wedding tour. Why, didn't you see none of the signs all along? Jackson Bird has been courting Willella ever since that day he took her out riding.'

" 'Then,' says I, in a kind of a yell, 'what was all this zizzaparoola he gives me about pancakes? Tell me *that*.'

"When I said 'pancakes' Uncle Emsley sort of dodged and stepped back.

" 'Somebody's been dealing me pancakes from the bottom of the deck,' I says, 'and I'll find out. I believe you know. Talk up,' says I, 'or we'll mix a panful of batter right here.'

"I slid over the counter after Uncle Emsley. He grabbed at his gun, but it was in a drawer, and he missed it two inches. I got him by the front of his shirt and shoved him in a corner.

" 'Talk pancakes,' says I, 'or be made into one. Does Miss Willella make 'em?'

" 'She never made one in her life and I never saw one,' says Uncle Emsley, soothing. 'Calm down now, Jud—calm down. You've got excited, and that wound in your head is contaminating your sense of intelligence. Try not to think about pancakes.'

" 'Uncle Emsley,' says I, 'I'm not wounded in the head except so far as my natural cogitative instincts run to runts. Jackson Bird told me he was calling on Miss Willella for the purpose of finding out her system of producing pancakes, and he asked me to help him get the bill of lading of the ingredients. I done so, with the results as you see. Have I been sodded down with Johnson grass by a pink-eyed snoozer, or what?'

"'Slack up your grip on my dress shirt,' says Uncle Emsley, 'and I'll tell you. Yes, it looks like Jackson Bird has gone and humbugged you some. The day after he went riding with Willella he came back and told me and her to watch out for you whenever you got to talking about pancakes. He said you was in camp once where they was cooking flapjacks, and one of the fellows cut you over the head with a frying pan. Jackson said that whenever you got over-hot or excited that wound hurt you and made you kind of crazy, and you went raving about pancakes. He told us to just get you worked off of the subject and soothed down, and you wouldn't be dangerous. So, me and Willella done the best by you we knew how. Well, well,' says Uncle Emsley, 'that Jackson Bird is sure a seldom kind of a snoozer.'"

During the progress of Jud's story he had been slowly but deftly combining certain portions of the contents of his sacks and cans. Toward the close of it he set before me the finished product—a pair of red-hot, rich-hued pancakes on a tin plate. From some secret hoarding place he also brought a lump of excellent butter and a bottle of golden syrup.

"How long ago did these things happen?" I asked him.

"Three years," said Jud. "They're living on the Mired Mule Ranch now. But I haven't seen either of 'em since. They say Jackson Bird was fixing his ranch up fine with rocking chairs and window curtains all the time he was putting me up the pancake tree. Oh, I got over it after a while. But the boys kept the racket up."

"Did you make these cakes by the famous recipe?" I asked.

"Didn't I tell you there wasn't no receipt?" said Jud. "The boys hollered pancakes till they got pancake hungry, and I cut this receipt out of a newspaper. How does the truck taste?"

"They're delicious," I answered. "Why don't you have some, too, Jud?"

I was sure I heard a sigh.

"Me?" said Jud. "I don't never eat 'em."

Eugene Field

(1850–1895)

The Remorseful Cakes

A little boy named Thomas ate
    Hot buckwheat cakes for tea—
A very rash proceeding, as
    We presently shall see.

He went to bed at eight o'clock,
    As all good children do,
But scarce had closed his little eyes,
    When he most restless grew.

He flopped on this side, then on that,
    Then keeled upon his head,
And covered all at once each spot
    Of his wee trundle-bed.

He wrapped one leg around his waist
    And t' other round his ear,
While mamma wondered what on earth
    Could ail her little dear.

But sound he slept, and as he slept
    He dreamt an awful dream
Of being spanked with hickory slabs
    Without the power to scream.

He dreamt a great big lion came
    And ripped and raved and roared—

While on his breast two furious bulls
　　In mortal combat gored.

He dreamt he heard the flop of wings
　　Within the chimney-flue—
And down there crawled, to gnaw his ears,
　　An awful bugaboo!

When Thomas rose next morn, his face
　　Was pallid as a sheet;
"I nevermore," he firmly said,
　　"Will cakes for supper eat!"

Robert Herrick

(English, 1591–1674)

Charms

Bring the holy crust of bread,
Lay it underneath the head;
'Tis a certain charm to keep
Hags away while children sleep.

Another

If ye fear to be affrighted,
When ye are by chance benighted,
In your pocket, for a trust,
Carry nothing but a crust:
For that holy piece of bread
Charms the danger and the dread.

B. C. Leale

(English, 1930–)

Loaves

How slowly they are brought out
wrapped in a hot
spicy steam

a careless finger
could disfigure their
piping sides

crusts nutty-flavoured
hot-buttered
honeyed

those distant days
sliding down ricks
of glossy cornstalks

climbing ladders
to yeasty heights
of cloudless nowheres

loaves baked to the rich
dark colour of
contentment.

Thomas Hardy

(English, 1840–1928)

The Pat of Butter

Once, at the Agricultural Show,
We tasted—all so yellow—
Those butter-pats, cool and mellow!
Each taste I still remember, though
It was so long ago.

This spoke of the grass of Netherhay,
And this of Kingcomb Hill,
And this of Coker Rill:
Which was the prime I could not say
Of all those tried that day,

Till she, the fair and wicked-eyed,
Held out a pat to me:
Then felt I all Yeo-Lea
Was by her sample sheer outvied;
And, "This is the best," I cried.

Sholem Asch

(American, 1880–1957)

God's Bread

There once lived in a certain town two bakers, one rich and one poor. The rich one was of course a distinguished house-holder, one of the notables of the town, a man of learning, the follower of a great Rabbi. The poor one was simple, obscure, and unlettered. The rich one baked for his own kind, that is, for the other rich people—great, white twisted loaves, tasty rolls shining with oil, and the special bread of the Sab-bath and the holy days. The poor one baked for his kind, too, for penniless laborers, for peddlers who carried their packs into the villages, and for peasants. So it fell out that the rich baker never had occasion to use his trade for the performance of good deeds. He forgot that there were such as needed bread and could not buy it or could buy it only by the sweat of their brows. The wealthy householders whom he supplied with his produce always paid him on time; no one ever owed him anything, and never was he asked for a favor. But the poor baker was the daily witness of the want and poverty of his customers. A woman from a neighboring street, or a peasant from the village, would come into his bakery and look long and earnestly at the loaves of bread, would think long and earnestly before digging down for the last few coppers. Some-times his customers were short of a groschen or two to make the purchase, and the baker, knowing what their life was like, would give them the bread nevertheless.

When a rich family arranged a marriage, or celebrated a circumcision, it was of course *their* baker who supplied the

cakes, rolls, loaves, pastries, cookies, and other baked delicacies, for he knew how to prepare the bread of the rich. He
used only the finest white flour, with the best fresh eggs; and
he besprinkled the loaves with the sweetest poppyseed. His
loaves shone like the sun. The poor baker had no occasion to
bake a costly loaf of delicate white flour. His bread was thick,
coarse, and black, compounded of cornmeal and rye, and
heavy, like the lot and food of the poor everywhere; and what
he had learned in his apprenticeship of the finer kind of baking he gradually forgot, from lack of practice.

A famous Rabbi, a wonder worker and a descendant of a
dynasty of wonder workers, whose name was uttered with
awe wherever Jews congregated and whose followers were
legion, came to settle in this town. He made his home, as was
to be expected, in the house of the richest Jew, one of the
customers of the rich baker; and when Sabbath was approaching the proud and happy householder told the rich baker to
prepare him twelve pairs of Sabbath loaves, such as the town
had never seen before.

The whole town spoke of the twelve loaves over which the
great Rabbi would utter the benediction on the forthcoming
Sabbath and which would be served at the Sabbath meal. The
rich baker sought out the finest meal and put into the labor
all the skill at his command; and before the loaves were delivered he displayed them in the window of his bakery, and Jews
came from every corner of the town to admire his handiwork.

The poor baker heard of all this, and his heart bled in him,
because he too wanted to be represented at the table of the
great Rabbi. But he had never baked for the rich, and his
bread was the bread of the poor. Nevertheless, he made up
his mind that he would bring half a dozen loaves to the table
of the Rabbi, in order that the benediction might be said over
them and that they might be eaten at the feast while the
Rabbi edified the assembly with words of learning and piety.
He chose, from his poor store, the best flour he had, and he
put into the baking whatever he remembered out of the days
of his apprenticeship. What was lacking in the quality of the

ingredients and in the skill of his labor, he sought to make up in devotion. He kneaded the dough lovingly, put the loaves in the oven, and watched tremblingly that they should be neither raw nor overdone; he smeared the tops of the loaves with the white of egg and sprinkled poppyseed on them, and when everything was ready he carried his offering to the house in which the Rabbi would celebrate the Sabbath.

There was laughter in the kitchen of the rich man when the poor baker came with his half dozen loaves. "What? He too brings bread for the Rabbi?" they asked. And they turned him away, saying that his loaves were unfit for the feast, and that an unlettered man such as he did not merit the attention of the Rabbi.

The man went home broken-hearted, carrying with him his rejected gift, and, being indeed unlettered, he bethought himself that if the Rabbi would not take his bread for the Sabbath feast, perhaps God would. For he believed that God too needed loaves on His table for the Sabbath feast. Late that night, then, he stole into the street of the synagogue and, having looked round carefully to make certain he was not observed, he broke into the synagogue, went up to the Ark, and opened the doors, saying:

"God, O God, I have baked six loaves for You, for Your Sabbath table. Take them and use them, and do not shame me."

And with that he closed the Ark and went home.

There lived in this same town an old tailor, a man of great piety and no possessions. All his life he had earned his daily bread with the ten fingers of his hands. But he had not eaten his daily bread; he and his wife had made it a practice to all but fast from week end to week end and to save his earnings for the celebration of the Sabbath. From Sunday to Friday they went short of food; but on Friday morning the tailor's wife went out into the marketplace and bought the best piece of meat in the butcher's shop, the handsomest loaf on the baker's stall. She also bought many candles, so that on the eve of the Sabbath her poor home shone like the home of a prince. There were many who, not knowing how the hunger of a week went into the preparation of the Sabbath, were amazed and angry at the wife of the tailor and behind her back spoke sneeringly of her extravagance, especially when she outbid a rich buyer for the best-looking morsel on the butcher's block. But the tailor had made up his mind that, being too poor to observe all the commandments of God, he would concentrate on the observance of one of them, and he picked out the commandment to keep the Sabbath day holy and to make it a day of rest and rejoicing. He said, "On this day, which is God's day, I will forget all poverty, all pain and all humiliation; I will rejoice, even as the Law enjoins, in the beauty and peace of the Sabbath, and no memory of the week's want shall disturb my repose."

As the tailor grew older he found it harder and harder to observe the one commandment which he had singled out for his special devotion, for his hands began to tremble and he worked slowly; his eyes were dimmed, and he could no longer undertake the tasks which brought better pay. Therefore he could not prepare for the Sabbath as he had always been wont to do, except by selling, one after the other, the few things that stood in his home. But he sold them, one after the other. For, besides his determination to make the Sabbath his province, he had also taken a vow not to make his Sabbath an object of charity. He would ask help of no man of flesh and blood but would depend on God, and on God alone, for the means to carry out his resolve.

The time came when the last of his household things were gone and his earnings of the week, which he and his wife had saved, did not suffice even for the purchase of the Sabbath bread. Late on Thursday night, when he had been wont to give his wife the week's money to make her purchases for the Sabbath, he left the house and stole into the street of the synagogue. Having looked round carefully to make certain he was not observed, he broke into the synagogue and went up to the Ark, and laying hold of the doors of the Ark he said:

"God, O God, You know that as long as I could work and earn something, I saved whatever I made for the proper celebration of Your Sabbath. Now I am old, and my eyes are darkened, and my fingers tremble, and I can earn no more. And I have put my trust in You and have not turned to man of flesh and blood for succor. So I implore You, send me at least the loaves for the celebration of the Sabbath. For the rest of the week we will live, my wife and I, on crusts and water; but help us to observe Your commandment to keep the Sabbath day holy."

With that he opened the doors of the Ark, and there, at the foot of the Scrolls, lay half a dozen loaves of Sabbath bread, fresh, crisp, and warm, as if they had just been sent down from the heavenly bakery. They were shiny with divine oil and fragrant with divine poppyseeds.

The tailor knew at once that the loaves had been delivered from above in answer to his prayer. He gathered them up, stole out of the synagogue, and ran home with the gift to his wife.

Ever since then the custom continued in town. Every Thursday night the poor baker brought God's bread into the synagogue and deposited it in the Ark, and shortly thereafter the tailor would come and would pick up the Sabbath bread which God had sent down for him and his wife.

Before the tailor died he entrusted his secret to another Jew, as poor and as pious as he; and the baker continued to deliver, and God continued to take from him. As long as the baker lived and delivered his bread, there was peace and plenty in the town. No pestilence came near it; childbirths were easy; no fires broke out; and little children grew up strong and went gladly to school to learn the word of God.

They said everywhere that this was due to the loaves which the rich baker prepared for the Rabbi and over which the Rabbi made the Sabbath benediction before he sat down with his disciples to edify them with words of learning and piety.

—Translated by Maurice Samuel

Leo Tolstoy

(Russian, 1828–1910)

Three Rolls and a Pretzel

Feeling hungry one day, a peasant bought himself a large roll and ate it. But he was still hungry, so he bought another roll and ate it. Still hungry, he bought a third roll and ate it. When the three rolls failed to satisfy his hunger, he bought some pretzels. After eating one pretzel he no longer felt hungry.

Suddenly he clapped his hand to his head and cried:

"What a fool I am! Why did I waste all those rolls? I ought to have eaten a pretzel in the first place!"

—Translated by Ann Dunnigan

David Ignatow

(American, 1914–)

The Bagel

I stopped to pick up the bagel
rolling away in the wind,
annoyed with myself

for having dropped it
as it were a portent.
Faster and faster it rolled,
with me running after it
bent low, gritting my teeth,
and I found myself doubled over
and rolling down the street
head over heels, one complete somersault
after another like a bagel
and strangely happy with myself.

César Vallejo

(Peruvian, 1892–1938)

Our Daily Bread

I drink my breakfast . . . Damp earth
of the cemetery freezes the precious blood.
City of winter . . . the biting crusade
of a wheelbarrow appears, hauling
a feeling of starvation in chains.

I wish I could beat on all the doors,
and ask for somebody; and then
look at the poor, and, while they wept softly,
give bits of fresh bread to them.
And plunder the rich of their vineyards
with my two blessed hands
which, with one blow of light,
could blast nails from the Cross!

Eyelash of morning, Thou wilt not rise!
Give us our daily bread,
Lord . . . !

Every bone in me belongs to others;
and maybe I robbed them.

I came to take something for myself that maybe
was meant for some other man;
and so I start thinking that, if I had not been born,
another poor man could have drunk this coffee.
I feel like a dirty sneak-thief . . . Wherever I go!

And in this frigid hour, when the earth
transcends human dust and is so sorrowful,
I wish I could beat on all the doors
and beg pardon from someone,
and make bits of fresh bread with it
here, in the oven of my heart . . . !

—Translated by James Wright

Robert Coles

(American, 1929–)

Spanish Bread

We are the old ones;
Dough, rising growing bursting
Almost a ferment I start
But it is God's doing
I only sing to it.
Seventy years of dough

Seventy years of hands working at it
The words are inside
Outside, too: the butter.
I do not boast
The dough pulls my hands
My voice too. Sing!
Sí, I say *sí,* and begin
I feel the music in the bread
I eat the old songs
Words from the old country
Spanish words, Spanish bread.

Bertolt Brecht

(1898–1956)

The Bread of the People

Justice is the bread of the people.
Sometimes it is plentiful, sometimes it is scarce.
Sometimes it tastes good, sometimes it tastes bad.
When the bread is scarce, there is hunger.
When the bread is bad, there is discontent.

Throw away the bad justice
Baked without love, kneaded without knowledge!
Justice without flavour, with a grey crust
The stale justice which comes too late!

If the bread is good and plentiful
The rest of the meal can be excused.
One cannot have plenty of everything all at once.
Nourished by the bread of justice
The work can be achieved
From which plenty comes.

As daily bread is necessary
So is daily justice.
It is even necessary several times a day.

From morning till night, at work, enjoying oneself.
At work which is an enjoyment.
In hard times and in happy times
The people requires the plentiful, wholesome
Daily bread of justice.

Since the bread of justice, then, is so important
Who, friends, shall bake it?

Who bakes the other bread?

Like the other bread
The bread of justice must be baked
By the people.

Plentiful, wholesome, daily.

—*Translated by Christopher Middleton*

Frank Norris

(American, 1870–1902)

From *The Octopus*

". . . We are well met, indeed, the farmer and the man-
ufacturer, both in the same grist between the two millstones
of the lethargy of the Public and the aggression of the Trust,
the two great evils of modern America. Pres, my boy, there is
your epic poem ready to hand."

But Cedarquist was full of another idea. Rarely did so favourable an opportunity present itself for explaining his theories, his ambitions. Addressing himself to Magnus, he continued:

"Fortunately for myself, the Atlas Company was not my only investment. I have other interests. The building of ships—steel sailing ships—has been an ambition of mine—for this purpose, Mr. Derrick, to carry American wheat. For years, I have studied this question of American wheat, and at last I have arrived at a theory. Let me explain. At present, all our California wheat goes to Liverpool, and from that port is distributed over the world. But a change is coming. I am sure of it. You young men," he turned to Presley, Lyman, and Harran, "will live to see it. Our century is about done. The great word of this nineteenth century has been Production. The great word of the twentieth century will be—listen to me, you youngsters—Markets. As a market for our Production—or let me take a concrete example—as a market for our *Wheat*, Europe is played out. Population in Europe is not increasing fast enough to keep up with the rapidity of our production. In some cases, as in France, the population is stationary. *We*, however, have gone on producing wheat at a tremendous rate. The result is over-production. We supply more than Europe can eat, and down go the prices. The remedy is *not* in the curtailing of our wheat areas, but in this, we *must have new markets, greater markets*. For years we have been sending our wheat from East to West, from California to Europe. But the time will come when we must send it from West to East. We must march with the course of empire, not against it. I mean, we must look to China. Rice in China is losing its nutritive quality. The Asiatics, though, must be fed; if not on rice, then on wheat. Why, Mr. Derrick, if only one half the population of China ate a half ounce of flour per man per day all the wheat areas in California could not feed them. Ah, if I could only hammer that into the brains of every rancher of the San Joaquin, yes, and of every owner of every bonanza farm in Dakota and Minnesota. Send your wheat to China; handle it yourselves; do away with the mid-

dleman; break up the Chicago wheat pits and elevator rings
and mixing houses. When in feeding China you have de-
creased the European shipments, the effect is instantaneous.
Prices go up in Europe without having the least effect upon
the prices in China. We hold the key, we have the wheat,
infinitely more than we ourselves can eat. Asia and Europe
must look to America to be fed. What fatuous neglect of opportunity to continue to deluge Europe with our surplus food
when the East trembles upon the verge of starvation!"

*   *   *

Directly in front of where he sat on the platform was the
chute from the cleaner, and from this into the mouth of a
half-full sack spouted an unending gush of grain, winnowed,
cleaned, threshed, ready for the mill.

The pour from the chute of the cleaner had for S. Behrman an immense satisfaction. Without an instant's pause, a
thick rivulet of wheat rolled and dashed tumultuous into the
sack. In half a minute—sometimes in twenty seconds—the
sack was full, was passed over to the second sewer, the mouth
reeved up, and the sack dumped out upon the ground, to be
picked up by the wagons and hauled to the railroad.

S. Behrman, hypnotized, sat watching that river of grain. All
that shrieking, bellowing machinery, all that gigantic organism, all
the months of labour, the ploughing, the planting, the prayers for
rain, the years of preparation, the heartaches, the anxiety, the
foresight, all the whole business of the ranch, the work of horses,
of steam, of men and boys, looked to this spot—the grain chute
from the harvester into the sacks. Its volume was the index of
failure or success, of riches or poverty. And at this point, the
labour of the rancher ended. Here, at the lip of the chute, he parted
company with his grain, and from here the wheat streamed forth
to feed the world. The yawning mouths of the sacks might well
stand for the unnumbered mouths of the People, all agape for
food; and here, into these sacks, at first so lean, so flaccid, attenu-
ated like starved stomachs, rushed the living stream of food,
insistent, interminable, filling the empty, fattening the shrivelled,
making it sleek and heavy and solid.

Lu Yu

(Chinese, 1125–1210)

It has snowed repeatedly and we can count on a good crop of wheat and barley; in joy I made this song.

Bitter cold, but don't complain when Heaven sends down
    snow;
snow comes to bring us next year's grain!
Third month: emerald waves dancing in the east wind;
fourth month: clouds of yellow hiding paths in the southern
    field.
How easy to see it—rows of houses raising shouts of joy,
already certain that officials will ease their load of taxes.
Sickle at waist, every young man in the village turns out;
gleaning kernels, little boys each day by the hundred and
    thousand.
Dust of white jade spills from the mill wheel, whirling up to
    the rafters;
noodles, silver threads into the pot, to be melted in boiling
    water.
Winter wine beginning to work, cakes of steamed malt
    bursting;
in oil pressed from fresh sesame, Cold Food dumplings
    smelling sweet;
the wife steps down from her loom, neglecting her morning
    weaving;
little sister helps in the kitchen, forgetful of evening makeup.
Old men, stuffed with food, laugh and thump their bellies;

under the trees, beating time on the ground, they sing of this
season of peace.

—Translated by Burton Watson

Yeh Shao-Chün

(Chinese, 1894–?)

Three to Five Bushels More

Open boats, newly arrived from upcountry and heavily
laden with the year's new rice, were tied up this way and that
at the Wan Sheng Rice Shop landing. A thick white foam
clinging to the leaves and rubbish floated like waves in the
spaces between the boats. The Wan Sheng Rice Shop stood a
few steps up from the landing across a narrow street up which
no more than three men could walk abreast. The early sun
cast long, slanting columns of light through the slits in the
old awning over the shop and shone down in golden bars on
the torn felt hats of the men crowded outside at the counter.
The boats had barely come alongside and the ropes were
scarcely fastened before these men had leaped ashore and
rushed up to the shop to learn their fate.

"How much?"

"Five dollars for coarse rice and three for grain," replied
the man in the shop, showing no particular interest either in
the men or in their rice.

"Eh?" The men in the torn felt caps stared incredulously
across the counter. Beautiful, blooming hopes shriveled up
inside of them. They stood stupefied.

"Wasn't it thirteen dollars in the sixth month?"

"More, it was fifteen."

"How could it fall so far?"

"Don't you fools know what season it is? Rice is flowing out of the country like a tide. The price will go down still more in a few days' time."

The ready energy with which they had sculled their boats downstream, swiftly as though they were racing a dragon boat, ebbed from them. Blessed by Heaven this year with timely rains and protected against harmful insects and pests, they had reaped a rich harvest of three to five extra bushels a *mow*, and everyone had looked to the future for relief from their many heavy troubles. But now at the last stage of things, they were struck down more heavily than ever before.

"Let's row back without selling!" cried one angry villager.

"Tsi!" sneered the man behind the counter. "You think anybody will starve if you don't sell your rice? There's a lot of foreign rice and wheat everywhere. Before the first lot is gone the great foreign ships come with more."

Talk of foreign rice and foreign ships meant nothing to his listeners. But they knew that to refuse to sell their rice down by the river landing was madness. How could they hold on to the rice? Rent had to be paid. Money borrowed for fertilizer and food and help had to be repaid.

"Let's go to Fan Mu!" Somebody thought they might have better luck there.

"Hmph!" mocked the shopkeeper, feeling his scanty beard. "Talk about Fan Mu! You can go right on down to the city and find the same thing. We've all decided on the price among ourselves. Five for coarse and three for grain."

"We won't get anything by going to Fan Mu," broke in one of the peasants. "There are two tax stations to pass on the way, and who knows how much they'll charge us? And where is the money to pay them?"

"Can't you make it a little higher, sir?" they turned, pleading.

"Easy to say higher. It took money to open this shop.

Capital. If we pay you a better price what are we going to get out of it? Who's going to do any such fool thing?"

"We never thought the price would be so low. Last year we sold at seven and a half. This year you sold rice at thirteen. No, you just said fifteen! We were sure it would have to be better than seven and a half and now we find it's only five!"

"Look here, how about keeping the old price, seven and a half?"

"We're poorer than you are. Have pity and lower your profit a little. . . ."

"Don't sell if you don't like the price," said another man behind the counter, impatiently flicking his cigarette into the street. "We didn't invite you here. You came yourselves. What's the use of all this babbling? Others will take our money for their rice. There are two more boats pulling in now." He pointed to the landing.

Three or four men, faces ruddy with hope, jumped up onto the planks and rushed over to join them. The slanting sun was shining on the shoulders of their old padded jackets.

"How much?"

"Worse than last year. Only five dollars," replied somebody in the crowd.

"Eh?" Three or four more men saw their hopes burst like so many bubbles.

But the rice had to be sold, and, as fate would have it, it had to be sold right there to the Wan Sheng shop. The shop had the dollars and the men with the rice had none. The argument lengthened into disputes over the quality of the rice and the fullness of the bushels. Gradually the laden boats were emptied and rose in the water. The scum and the rubbish between the boats slid from view. The men carried their rice into the shop and were given bank notes in return.

"Give us silver dollars, will you? Yuan Shih-kai dollars too—" was this a new trick, these colored papers? They looked suspiciously at the shopkeeper.

"Village bumpkins!" said that gentleman contemp-

tuously, fingering his brush and his abacus. He looked up at
them over the rims of his glasses. "One dollar bank note
equals one dollar silver. Not a copper less," he said. "We've
only got notes here, no silver."

"Then give us Bank of China notes," said one peasant,
who could not find the familiar design of the Bank of China
on the notes he received.

"Stop being a nuisance! These are Central Bank notes.
You refuse to accept them. Do you want to taste the kindness
of the law?"

None of them knew why the law should have anything to
do with it. But nobody dared ask any more questions. They
looked dubiously at the figures on the notes and, with questioning glances at each other they pocketed them in their rag-
ged jackets or tucked them into little pouches hanging from
waist bands. They left, murmuring discontentedly. By this
time another group of open boats had come up to the landing
and the men were jostling and joking over the lines and
brushing past them into the shop. The same scene was repeated. The joyous thrill they had known looking at their rich
and heavy paddies ever since autumn was dissipated in anger
and confusion. But they also, and those who followed, reluctantly poured their rice into the granary of the shop and went
off in the end with their notes instead of clinking silver
dollars.

The street with its open shops pulsed with the life of harvest time. Back in their fields and on the way downstream the
villagers had, with great anticipation, checked off one by one
the things they were going to buy on this street. Soap had
given out, and they would buy more. They would also stock
up on boxes of matches. And oil. They had always lost
heavily buying oil from itinerant dealers at ten coppers a
spoonful. They figured that if several families could get together and buy a whole tin that would save a great deal. And
the women remembered longingly the gaudy cloth in the
shops which they heard cost only eight and a half cents a
foot. So they clamored to come to town with their men when

the rice was loaded on the boats, figuring so much for Ah Ta, so much for Ah Erh and so much for themselves. Some of them dreamed of the shining foreign hand mirrors or of a white towel or of a delicately knitted baby's cap made of real wool. Blessings from Heaven, they had harvested three to five bushels more to every *mow* of their land! Who would blame them for loosening the purse strings a little? If everything went well they would be able to pay rent, debts, and taxes. And maybe there would still be money left after that. Thinking thus, some even planned with a new thrill of expectation to buy a Thermos bottle, a wonderful contraption with which they could keep water hot without a fire. What an improvement on the warmer made of rice stalks and reeds which they used around their teapots! As different as Heaven must be from earth!

But now, like men leaving a gambling house where luck has been steadily against them, the villagers grumbled as they left the Wan Sheng Rice Shop. Lost again. How much they had lost they had no idea. They would not be able to keep for themselves even one or a half or a tenth of one of these bank notes! More—somewhere, somehow they would have to find more to pay what they owed, and other people would dictate how much that came to. But they stood irresolutely on the narrow street. What was lost was lost. They were here in town now. Would it matter so much if they added a little to their burden by making the most necessary of their contemplated purchases? Almost all of them decided that there was no use in just getting back into their boats and rowing away. Instead they walked down the street past the shops, their short shadows trailing behind them. The street now took on a lively aspect.

In groups of threes and fives they straggled along the narrow street, going over again and again the money they had received and cursing the heartless rice merchants. Holding their children's hands and with baskets on their arms the women peered into the shops with interest and curiosity. The children were hypnotized by the foreign dolls, tigers, dogs, and brightly colored bells and gongs and trumpets of tin. They dawdled and refused to leave when their mothers pulled them away.

"Get one for little brother!" wheedled the storekeeper. "Get a little foreign drum or a horn. What fun! Look!" and he struck the drum—tung-tung-tung—and he blew on the horn—pa-pa-pa. . . .

"Tong-tong-tong—this enameled basin of highest quality. Really cheap at forty cents. Take one home, neighbors!"

"Wei! Wei! Neighbors, here are all kinds of flowered cloth. Eight and a half cents a foot with a few inches thrown in to boot! Take some? Buy some to take back?"

The shopkeepers vied for their trade and often they stepped out into the street and grabbed a "neighbor" by his torn cotton sleeve and tried to drag him inside. Everybody knew this was one of the rare events of the year—when farmers appeared with money in their pockets! After much indecision and calculation, what to buy, what not to buy, the notes were handed over, one by one, to the eager salesmen. Matches and soap were bought in small quantities. The tin of oil proved a bit too steep. They would have to go on buying it spoonful by spoonful. If they had planned for two shirts, they bought cloth for one. If mother and child were both to get something, the child's was bought and the mother went without. The foreign mirror was handled and looked into, but finally put back with a last, yearning look. The knitted woolen cap was fitted on baby's head but father said no and it was handed back. Nobody dared even ask the price of the Thermos bottle. It would probably cost a whole dollar or dollar and a half. If they bought one, the older folks would frown and scold:

"All that money for such idle things in these times! You'll never know a better life, that's sure! When we were young, did we ever have anything like that?"

But some of the women found it harder to resist their children than to listen to their elders. And they bought small, cheap baby dolls. The dolls' arms and legs could be moved, and they could be made to sit or stand or to raise their hands. Not only did the other children pop their eyes with envy; some of the older people too looked on and even played with pleasure gleaming in their eyes.

The last money they dared spend went for some wine and some cooked meat. With their bundles they went back to their boats, still tied up at the Wan Sheng Rice Shop landing. Taking some salted vegetables and bean curd soup they had brought in bowls, the men sat down in the forward part of the boat to drink the wine and the women busied themselves in the stern with the cooking. Columns of smoke rose from their stoves, one after another, and the breeze blew it into their faces, making their eyes smart. The children tumbled into the empty holds of the boats or picked away in the trash that flowed past, looking for anything they could play with. Only the children were filled with happiness. Among the men, the unaccustomed wine had loosened tongues. Whether they were neighbors or not, here they were at the same place, drinking the same wine and sharing the same troubles. One of them would speak and flourish his bowl of wine in his hand. Somebody would answer, slapping down his chopsticks. When they agreed they shouted "Sure!" When they spoke of their troubles they swore. Bitterness was high in them. They needed outlets.

"Five dollars! The devil's on us!"

"Last year we lost out because of the bad harvest owing to the flood. This year we've had a good harvest and we've lost out again!"

"Lost more this year than last. We got seven and a half last year, don't forget."

"Had to sell the rice kept for ourselves again. Can't even eat our own rice!"

"The devil, what did you sell for? I'm going to hold mine for my wife and family. I'm just not going to pay my rent. I'd rather be put in jail!"

"That's the only way, stop paying rent! Rent means more debts. What do we get by borrowing and paying four or five

328 FOOD FOR THOUGHT

percent interest a month? Just to have more of a debt to pay off next year?"

"What's the use in working the land?"

"Give up the land and run away like refugees from a famine—that sounds good!"

"Run away from debts and payments. It's a good plan. Let's all go together!"

"Let somebody lead and we'll all take orders from him!"

"Let's go to work in Shanghai. I've heard it's not so bad there. They say in the factories you get fifteen dollars a month! That's worth three bushels of rice according to today's prices! Didn't Little Wang from our village go down to Shanghai?"

"What do you think you're yapping about? Many of the factories have closed down since the fighting with the Japanese. Don't you know Little Wang is a beggar down there now?"

Almost everyone had to have his say and then all fell silent. Little Wang was a beggar now. The sun and the wine deepened the red in their faces until they seemed bloated.

"Whom do we work for anyway, when we work on the land year after year?" somebody finally asked gloomily, sipping some wine.

His neighbor pointed to the shore and the worn gilded characters swayed on the sign over the Wan Sheng Rice Shop.

"Those are the people we work for. We suffer all kinds of hardship, we get ourselves into debt, and finally we produce our rice. Then they—with a silent movement of their lips—just enough to say 'five dollars'—they take it all away from us."

"Wouldn't it be good if we could fix the price ourselves? Eight dollars a bushel. That's all, eight dollars, all I'd ask, honestly, I would not ask for more."

"What are you doing, spinning dreams? Didn't you hear him say he used capital to open the shop and that they wouldn't work for us without a profit?"

"But we've spent money on our land too. Why should we

work for them without making any profit? And why should we work for the landlords the same way?"

"When I was up in the granary there," he pointed to the shop and lowered his voice, his bloodshot eyes casting sidelong glances toward shore, "I said to myself—well, let them have the upper hand, taking our rice now. When we have nothing to eat later on, we'll know where to find some."

"If we really had nothing to eat, it wouldn't be a crime, would it, to take some where we could find it?" Everybody agreed in strong voices.

"Didn't they attack the rice stores at Fung Chiao last spring?"

"The soldiers opened fire and killed two men."

"Any of us here now might be fired on some day, who knows?"

Nothing came of their aimless talk. When they were done with the wine and the food they took up their oars and pulled away homeward, leaving a gentle wake behind, the dirty, black-green water washing up against the planks of the Wan Sheng Rice Shop landing after they left. More came after them and left the same way in this town and in towns and cities throughout the district. There was nothing at all unusual.

In the cities "Cheap rice is ruining the peasant" became a favorite headline for newspaper editorials. Landlords anticipated tough measures would be needed to collect rents, so they met and issued joint statements to this effect: Good harvest meant surplus rice and falling prices. Farmers would soon experience the pinch and require outside help. Pompous financiers, who would not miss the opportunity to do business in any case, announced plans to "bring relief" to the peasants: (1) Banks and money changers should mobilize capital to buy up rice for stocking up at suitable depots. The following spring, when demand became high, supply of rice would be gradually released to the market so as to insure a stable price. (2) Promote the use of grain as security against payments, thus preventing rice merchants from buying up too much rice for hoarding. (3) Financial circles should raise subscriptions to buy rice for storage, calculating profit or loss after sales were completed. Factory owners made no comment. Lower rice prices brought benefits by cutting the cost of food allowances. Social scientists busily published articles on the subject, saying that neither fact nor theory could support the ridiculous argument on a grain surplus. But then, one could hardly say that "cheap rice prices ruin the peasant" either, since without that the peasant suffered just the same under the double yoke of imperialism and feudalism.

These were all speculations in the cities; those who lived in the countryside knew nothing. Some of the farmers sold the last of their own rice or their beloved oxen, or raised new loans at four or five percent a month. Some of them offered themselves to the district prison as prisoners, lamenting the twenty or thirty cents food cost they must hand over each day. Some of them gambled away what money they had left in hopes of winning enough to pay part of their debts. Some begged middlemen to approach the landlords for them and plead for rent reductions. Or else they gave up their land and became half-naked beggars along the roadsides. A few stole arms from the militia and ran away. And still others slipped into fourth class cars on the train bound for Shanghai.

Matsuo Bashō

(Japanese, 1644–1694)

The Beginning

Spring starts:
  new year; old rice,
    five quarts.

The Poor Man's Son

Poverty's child—
  he starts to grind the rice,
    and gazes at the moon.

—*Translated by Harold G. Henderson*

Vegetables

Fredrich Steinway

(American, ?–)

The Day I Became a Vegetarian

I woke from a dream that all my friends were scallions
I heard bravos from the lumps of beef I had left behind
From the ground round porterhouse and tartar
As they cleaved like peas and sent out shoots.

The sprouts I had eaten
Rejoiced within the striations of my iris
Arched in delight tickling tight curls of chromosomes

I read leaves in a wadded lettuce heart
   for news of the world
I dug up sweet tuberous poems
I discovered myself counting the chambers in a tomato
I made ink from spores I signed my checks with it

The day I became a vegetarian
I found letters from all the fish in the seas

B. C. Leale

(1930-)

A Vegetation to Be Read by the Parsnip

Aubergine aubergine
Lettuce pray for the marrow
For no one radishes the end
We have all cucumbered our unworthy chives
With foul swedes
It ill beetroots us to publicly sprout pea
From the endive our fennels
None escapes the cabbages of thyme
Even the wisest sage comes to a spinach
Celery celery I say unto you
This is the cauliflower
When salsifiers all
Artichoke and kale.

Ogden Nash

(1902-1971)

Celery

Celery, raw,
Develops the jaw,
But celery, stewed,
Is more quietly chewed.

Marge Piercy

(1936–)

Attack of the Squash People

And thus the people every year
in the valley of humid July
did sacrifice themselves
to the long green phallic god
and eat and eat and eat.

They're coming, they're on us,
the long striped gourds, the silky
babies, the hairy adolescents,
the lumpy vast adults
like the trunks of green elephants.
Recite fifty zucchini recipes!

Zucchini tempura; creamed soup;
sauté with olive oil and cumin,
tomatoes, onion; frittata;
casserole of lamb; baked
topped with cheese; marinated;
stuffed; stewed; driven
through the heart like a stake.

Get rid of old friends: they too
have gardens and full trunks.
Look for newcomers: befriend
them in the post office, unload
on them and run. Stop tourists
in the street. Take truckloads

to Boston. Give to your Red Cross.
Beg on the highway: please
take my zucchini, I have a crippled
mother at home with heartburn.

Sneak out before dawn to drop
them in other people's gardens,
in baby buggies at churchdoors.
Shot, smuggling zucchini into
mailboxes, a federal offense.

With a suave reptilian glitter
you bask among your raspy
fronds sudden and huge as
alligators. You give and give
too much, like summer days
limp with heat, thunderstorms
bursting their bags on our heads,
as we salt and freeze and pickle
for the too little to come.

Charles Kingsley

(English, 1819–1875)

The Poetry of a Root Crop

Underneath their eider-robe
Russet swede and golden globe,
Feathered carrot, burrowing deep,
Steadfast wait in charmèd sleep;
Treasure-houses wherein lie,

Locked by angels' alchemy,
Milk and hair, and blood, and bone,
Children of the barren stone;
Children of the flaming Air,
With his blue eye keen and bare,
Spirit-peopled smiling down
On frozen field and toiling town—
Toiling town that will not heed
God His voice for rage and greed;
Frozen fields that surpliced lie,
Gazing patient at the sky;
Like some marble carven nun,
With folded hands when work is done,
Who mute upon her tomb doth pray,
Till the resurrection day.

William Fahey

(American, 1923–)

Parsnips

Fragrant roots; old codgers' winter handles, dreaming of
young breasts and sweet erections.

Grandfather's steaming underwear hung from the back
porch on Saturday night. Yellow tusks dug from the
frozen earth. Legs supporting the torso bearing the witch's
tit.

A kitchen supper, snow feathering the dark glass and the
stove turning pink.

Mashed, with a little butter, they counter the ravages of
age damp, and the spleen.

John Haines

(American, 1938–)

The Cauliflower

I wanted to be a cauliflower,
all brain and ears,
thinking on the origin of gardens
and the divinity of him
who carefully binds my leaves.

With my blind roots touched
by the songs of the worms,
and my rough throat throbbing
with strange, vegetable sounds,
perhaps I'd feel the parting stroke
of a butterfly's wing . . .

Not like my cousins, the cabbages,
whose heads, tightly folded,
see and hear nothing of this world,
dreaming only on the yellow
and green magnificence
that is hardening within them.

Carl Sandburg
(American, 1878–1967)

Nocturn Cabbage

Cabbages catch at the moon.
It is late summer, no rain, the pack of the soil
    cracks open, it is a hard summer.

In the night the cabbages catch at the moon, the
    leaves drip silver, the rows of cabbages are
    series of little silver waterfalls in the moon.

Edward Thomas
(English, 1878–1917)

Swedes

They have taken the gable from the roof of clay
On the long swede pile. They have let in the sun
To the white and gold and purple of curled fronds
Unsunned. It is a sight more tender-gorgeous
At the wood-corner where Winter moans and drips
Than when, in the Valley of the Tombs of Kings,
A boy crawls down into a Pharaoh's tomb

And, first of Christian men, beholds the mummy,
God and monkey, chariot and throne and vase,
Blue pottery, alabaster, and gold.

But dreamless long-dead Amen-hotep lies.
This is a dream of Winter, sweet as Spring.

Anthelme Brillat-Savarin

(1755–1826)

From *The Physiology of Taste*

THE ASPARAGUS

M. Cortois de Quincey, Bishop of Belley, was told one day
that a head of a marvellous size had just appeared above one
of the asparagus beds of his kitchen garden.

Immediately everybody ran to the spot to ascertain the
truth of the story; for, even in episcopal palaces, people are
delighted with having something to do.

The news was found to be neither false nor exaggerated:
the head stuck out the earth, and appeared already above the
ground. It was round, shiny, variegated, and gave promise of
an asparagus the size of a column, and so thick that the hand
could hardly span it.

This horticultural phenomenon was the talk of every one.
It was clear that the bishop alone had the right of cutting it,
and an order was immediately given to a neighbouring cutler
to make a knife specially for this lofty purpose.

For several days the asparagus continued to grow, and to
look more charming and beautiful; its progress was slow, but
gradual, and soon people began to perceive that part of the
white stalk which is not fit to be eaten.

The time for cutting it having come, a good dinner was

first given, and then the operation was delayed until after the bishop and his guests had come back from their walk.

Then the bishop advanced, with the official knife in his hand, stooped gravely, and began to separate the proud vegetable from its stalk, while the whole of the attendants of the episcopal court showed some impatience to examine its fibres and contexture.

But, to their surprise, disappointment, and sorrow, the knife would not cut, and the prelate rose with nothing in his hands. The asparagus was a wooden one.

This joke, perhaps carried a little too far, was planned by the Canon Rousset, a native of Saint-Claude,* an admirable turner, and a very fair artist.

He had carved a wooden asparagus in perfect imitation of a real one, had stuck it by stealth into the bed, and lifted it a little every day to imitate the nocturnal growth.

The bishop did not know how he ought to take this mystification, for it was really one; but seeing a grin on the faces of all the bystanders, he smiled, and the smile was followed by a general explosion of really Homeric laughter. The *corpus delicti* was then removed, and without taking any further notice of the perpetration of the joke, for the whole of that evening at least the monster asparagus had the honours of the drawing-room.

*A town in Jura.

Jonathan Swift

(1667–1745)

Asparagus

Ripe 'sparagrass,
Fit for lad or lass,
To make their water pass:
Oh, 'tis pretty picking
With a tender chicken!

Onions

Come, follow me by the smell,
Here are delicate onions to sell;
I promise to use you well.
They make the blood warmer;
You'll feed like a farmer:
For this is every cook's opinion,
No savoury dish without an onion;
But, lest your kissing should be spoil'd,
Your onions must be thoroughly boil'd:
Or else you may spare
Your mistress a share,
The secret will never be known;
She cannot discover
The breath of her lover,
But think it as sweet as her own.

" If your mother is an onion and your father a garlic, how could your smell be sweet."

ARAB PROVERB

Stéphane Mallarmé

(French, 1842–1898)

Le Marchand d'Ail et d'Oignons

A clove of garlic can keep
off the boredom of a call.
With onions cut small
an elegy's easy to weep.

—Translated by C. F. MacIntyre

Pablo Neruda

(Chilean, 1904–1973)

Artichoke

The artichoke
of delicate heart
erect
in its battle-dress, builds

its minimal cupola;
keeps
stark
in its scallop of
scales.
Around it,
demoniac vegetables
bristle their thicknesses,
devise
tendrils and belfries,
the bulb's agitations;
while under the subsoil
the carrot
sleeps sound in its
rusty mustaches.
Runner and filaments
bleach in the vineyards,
whereon rise the vines.
The sedulous cabbage
arranges
its petticoats;
oregano
sweetens a world;
and the artichoke
dulcetly there in a gardenplot,
armed for a skirmish,
goes proud
in its pomegranate
burnishes.
Till, on a day,
each by the other,
the artichoke moves
to its dream
of a market place
in the big willow
hoppers:
a battle formation.
Most warlike

of defilades—
with men
in the market stalls,
white shirts
in the soup-greens,
artichoke
field marshals,
close-order conclaves,
commands, detonations,
and voices,
a crashing of crate staves.

And
Maria
come
down
with her hamper
to
make trial
of an artichoke:
she reflects, she examines,
she candles them up to the light like an egg,
never flinching;
she bargains,
she tumbles her prize
in a market bag
among shoes and a
cabbage head,
a bottle
of vinegar; is back
in her kitchen.
The artichoke drowns in an olla.

So you have it:
a vegetable, armed,
a profession
(call it an artichoke)
whose end

is millenial.
We taste of that
sweetness,
dismembering
scale after scale.
We eat of a halcyon paste:
it is green at the artichoke heart.

—Translated by Ben Belitt

François Rabelais

(1483-95?–1553)

XXXVIII

From *Gargantua and Pantagruel*

HOW GARGANTUA ATE SIX PILGRIMS IN A SALAD

We must now relate what happened to six pilgrims who were returning from St. Sebastien-d'Aigne, near Nantes. Afraid of the enemy, they sought shelter that night in the garden, crouched among the cabbage, lettuce and peas.

Gargantua, being somewhat thirsty, asked for some lettuce salad. When they told him the lettuce in that garden was the greatest and finest in the land (some heads were tall as plum trees or walnut trees) he determined to pick it himself. Plucking what he thought good, he also carried off in the hollow of his hand the six pilgrims, who were too terrified to cough, let alone to speak.

While Gargantua was washing the heads of lettuce in the fountain, the pilgrims plucked up their courage and held a whispered consultation.

"What can we do?"

"We're drowning in all this lettuce!"

"Dare we speak?"

"If we speak, he'll kill us for spies."

Amid their deliberations, Gargantua put them with the lettuce in a bowl of Grangousier's large as the tun at the Abbey of Cîteaux, in Burgundy, a fine huge cask reputed to hold three hundred hogsheads. Then he doused the leaves (and pilgrims) with salt, vinegar and oil, and, for refreshment before supper, began to eat. He had already swallowed five pilgrims and the sixth lay under a leaf, completely invisible save for his staff, when Grangousier pointed to the latter.

"Look, Gargantua, that's a snail's horn. Don't eat it!"

"Why not? Snails are good this month."

Picking up staff and pilgrim, he swallowed them neat, then drank a terrific draught of red Burgundy while awaiting his supper.

The pilgrims thus devoured crept out of his gullet as best they could, avoiding the millstones of his teeth. They believed they had been cast into the pit of the lowest dungeon in a prison. When Gargantua downed his wine, they all but drowned; the crimson torrent almost swept them down again into the abyss of his belly. However, leaping on their staffs as the Mont St. Michel pilgrims do, they found shelter in the chinks between his teeth. Unhappily one of them, sounding the lay of the land with his staff to ascertain its safety, struck hard into the cavity of a sore tooth and hit the mandibulary nerve. Gargantua screamed with pain, then, for relief, reached for his toothpick. Strolling out towards the great walnut tree in the garden, he proceeded to dislodge our six gentlemen pilgrims. He jerked one out by the legs, another by the shoulders, a third by his scrip, a fourth by his pouch, a fifth by his neckerchief and the last, the poor devil who had hurt him, he pulled out by the codpiece. This turned out to be a piece of great good fortune for the pilgrim, since Gargantua in the process broke a chancre that had been torturing him since they left Ancenis on the Loire.

The pilgrims, thus dislodged, scurried away, at top speed. Gargantua's toothache subsided, just as Eudemon announced dinner.

"Very well," said Gargantua. "I shall piss away my misfortune."

Which he proceeded to do so copiously that the pilgrims'
road was washed away and they were forced to wade through
this vast, foamy salt lake.

Virgil

(Roman, 70–19 B.C.)

From *The Salad*

   Close to his cottage lay a garden-ground,
With reeds and osiers sparely girt around;
Small was the spot, but liberal to produce,
Nor wanted aught that serves a peasant's use;
And sometimes even the rich would borrow thence,
Although its tillage was his sole expense.
For oft, as from his toils abroad he ceased,
Homebound by weather or some stated feast,
His debt of culture here he duly paid,
And only left the plough to wield the spade.
He knew to give each plant the soil it needs,
To drill the ground, and cover close the seeds;
And could with ease compel the wanton rill
To turn, and wind, obedient to his will.
There flourished starwort, and the branching beet,
The sorrel acid, and the mallow sweet,
The skirret, and the leek's aspiring kind,
The noxious poppy—quencher of the mind!
Salubrious sequel of a sumptuous board,
The lettuce, and the long huge-bellied gourd;

But these (for none his appetite controlled
With stricter sway) the thrifty rustic sold;
With broom-twigs neatly bound, each kind apart
He bore them ever to the public mart;
Whence, laden still, but with a lighter load,
Of cash well earned, he took his homeward road,
Expending seldom, ere he quitted Rome,
His gains, in flesh meat for a feast at home.
There, at no cost, on onions, rank and red,
Or the curled endive's bitter leaf, he fed;
On scallions sliced, or with a sensual gust
On rockets*—foul provocatives of lust;
Nor even shunned, with smarting gums, to press
Nasturtium, pungent face-distorting mess!
　　Some such regale now also in his thought,
With hasty steps his garden-ground he sought;
There delving with his hands, he first displaced
Four plants of garlic, large, and rooted fast;
The tender tops of parsley next he culls,
Then the old rue-bush shudders as he pulls,
And coriander last to these succeeds,
That hangs on slightest threads her trembling seeds.
　　Placed near his sprightly fire, he now demands
The mortar at his sable servant's hands;
When stripping all his garlic first, he tore
The exterior coats, and cast them on the floor,
When cast away with like contempt the skin,
Flimsier concealment of the cloves within.
These searched, and perfect found, he one by one
Rinsed and disposed within the hollow stone;
Salt added, and a lump of salted cheese,
With his injected herbs he covered these,
And tucking with his left his tunic tight,
And seizing fast the pestle with his right,
The garlic bruising first he soon expressed,
And mixed the various juices of the rest.
He grinds, and by degrees his herbs below

*Arugula.

Lost in each other their own powers forgo,
And with the cheese in compound, to the sight
Nor wholly green appear, nor wholly white.
His nostrils oft the forceful fume resent;
He cursed full oft his dinner for its scent,
Or with wry faces, wiping as he spoke
The trickling tears, cried—"Vengeance on the smoke!"
The work proceeds: not roughly turns he now
The pestle, but in circles smooth and slow;
With cautious hand that grudges what it spills,
Some drops of olive oil he next instills;
Then vinegar with caution scarcely less;
And gathering to a ball the medley mess,
Last, with two fingers frugally applied,
Sweeps the small remnant from the mortar's side:
And thus complete in figure and in kind,
Obtains at length the Salad he designed.

—Translated by William Cowper

Alberto Moravia

(1907–)

From *Two Women*

. . . Our greatest resource at this time was chicory; not the
chicory that is eaten in Rome, which is always the same plant
and never changes, but rather any kind of herb that can be
eaten. I myself made more and more use of this so-called
chicory; and sometimes I spent the morning picking it on the
terraces with Rosetta and Michele. We would get up early,

354   FOOD FOR THOUGHT

each of us armed with a small knife and a basket, and go off
along the slope of the mountainside, sometimes below, sometimes above, gathering herbs. People have no idea of how
many herbs there are which can be eaten—almost all of
them, in fact. I already knew a little about them from having
gathered them when I was a child, but I had almost entirely
forgotten their names and species. Luisa, Paride's wife, went
with me the first time in order to teach me, and quite soon I
had become as good at it as the peasants and knew the various
kinds of "chicory" both by name and by shape. I remember
only a few of them now. We used to go, as I say, up and
down over the terraces, and we were not the only ones, for
everyone was picking chicory now and it was a strange sight
to see the mountain slope dotted all over with people moving
about with their heads down, one step at a time, like so many
souls in purgatory. It looked as if everyone was searching for
some lost object, instead of which it was hunger that caused
them to search, not for something they had lost, but for
something which they hoped to find. This chicory-gathering
took a long time, two or three hours or even more, for in
order to make a bare soup bowl of it you had to collect an
apronful. It was not so plentiful that it sufficed for all the
people who were looking for it, and, as time went on, you had
to go farther and farther away and spend longer and longer
hunting for it. All this hard work had little result; once
boiled, two or three apronfuls of chicory became two or three
green balls each of them the size of an orange. After boiling it
I used to put it in a frying pan with just a taste of lard, and
this, if it provided no nourishment, at least served to fill our
bellies and to cheat our hunger. But the labor of collecting the
chicory left us dead tired for the rest of the day. And at night,
when I lay down beside Rosetta on our hard bed, with its sack
of dried maize leaves, instead of seeing darkness when I
closed my eyes I saw nothing but chicory, plants and plants of
chicory dancing in front of me. In vain I would try to go to
sleep, but for a long time I would see the chicory crossing and
re-crossing and dissolving before my eyes, until at last, after

long wakefulness, I would fall right into the chicory and go to sleep.

—*Translated by Angus Davidson*

Zahrad (Zareh Yaldizčiyan)

(Armenian, 1924–)

The Woman Cleaning Lentils

A lentil, a lentil, a lentil, a stone. A lentil, a lentil, a lentil, a
    stone.
A green one, a black one, a green one, a black. A stone.
A lentil, a lentil, a stone, a lentil, a lentil, a word.
Suddenly a word. A lentil.
A lentil, a word, a word next to another word. A sentence.
A word, a word, a word, a nonsense speech. Then an old
    song.
Then an old dream.
A life, another life, a hard life. A lentil. A life.
An easy life. A hard life. Why easy? Why hard?
Lives next to each other. A life. A word. A lentil.
A green one, a black one, a green one, a black one, pain.
A green song, a green lentil, a black one, a stone.
A lentil, a stone, a stone, a lentil.

—*Translated by Ralph Setian*

Bernard Dadié

(African [Ivory Coast], 1916–)

The Yam Field

The field stretched as far as the eye could see. It belonged to Kacou Ananzè. The yam stalks gracefully entwined their supporting props and indolently trailed along the ground like fat women in the men's courtyard; they crept up the roots and trunks of the trees and the maize plants. . . .

Here and there were planted *taros, gombos,** pimentos, white egg-plants, and flower-beds full of sweet potatoes with dark-green leaves. Mingled with all these were yellow-flowered ground-nut plants. Truly, this field was beautiful, especially at sunset!

All these leaves and stalks, intoxicated with freshness and perfume, drunk with air and vitality, rippled under the caressing breeze.

The yams adopted these airs and graces! One could have said that they were gallants going to their lovers, with loincloths turned up like this, and silk kerchiefs, in which the zephyr was joyfully playing, turned up like that . . . kerchiefs in battle-order.

The yams were affected creatures, each day unfurling themselves and parading new shades of colour, each hour taking on different tints according to whether the sun was rising or setting, according to the zenith, whether the sun shone with all its force or whether the sky was cloudy. Only the haricot beans and *taros* had those colours which could whet the appetite.

*The first is a root staple, the second a fruit eaten as a legume and used for seasoning.

Kacou Ananzè never became bored with looking at the yams, the *gombos*, the *taros*, the peony-red of the pimentos, the haricot beans whose tendrils fastened themselves hither and thither on to the stalks, the twigs, the feet of the talkative maize plants and the banana-trees which were rapidly growing and whose large leaves acted as a parasol for the other plants. . . .

In the forest, curtains of mist persisted through the rifts in the clouds. Like a whip, the sun burnt the skin, penetrated the body, warmed the blood and struck the skull as if to open it and expose one's thoughts to broad daylight. In this it did not succeed, and contented itself with making everybody sweat. Between two clouds, it shone for a long time in the small valleys, happy to expand and stretch itself, to hunt out the shadows and to nibble, absorb, and dissolve them. And the shadows, impelled by the ardent burden of this heavenly body, took refuge under the banana leaves and the thick foliage of the large trees. Unimpeded, the sun hunted them out, chased them, peppered them with holes and placed hedges of light between them.

What a spectacle! Butterflies flutter about, land on one leaf, lightly touch another, climb, descend, dive, disappear and reappear. They are white, yellow, and spotted. Two, four, or several of them gallivant in this way. Vagabonds, they sing indolence, caprice, inconstancy, and laziness. They wander about while mocking the burning sun, who through shame, comes from behind a mountain of cloud to withdraw into himself, as people say, in order to more strongly project his concentrated rays afterwards. But, the gallant sun laughs! He ignores the stubbornness of moths.

Below, the monkeys are shrieking. It is their habit. They never keep quiet. They are always scratching themselves and jumping from branch to branch, dozing a little and then set about asking questions: "Kpa! Koun! Kpa! Koun!" Farther on, the raucous cries of the black monkey and the alarmed voice of the capuchin monkey reply; the latter is the most elegant animal in the forest.

The singing birds come and go. The maize plants allow

their beards to be combed by the wind which takes away their tufts. All the yams shake their leaves which are beginning to dry and indicate the approaching day of their gathering. The birds leave the field and fly over the trees. Some of them return and perch on the stalks, the branches, the twigs, and the trunks which have continued to waste away since the day the field was set on fire. The smoke rises calmly in the air, forms circles, crawls about, meanders about the earth, straightens itself, rolls itself up, unrolls itself and straightens up again. And as for the dragonflies! They do not tarry on any perch as they are always in a hurry to go goodness knows where. With their filigree wings which have quickly learnt their job, they come absent-mindedly and caress one's ears and cheek. They flutter for a moment in front of one and whisper something in one's ear, then, proving that one is deaf and that they are talking with a stranger, they fly away with a "zinn! zinn!" of their wings.

And over the yam field, which stretches as far as the eye can see, the sun is always shedding its light and reviving all the colours!

The yams were certainly welcome! No yams had ever been more so! But then all those who passed near the field could not contain themselves from murmuring jealously. It had cost Kacou Ananzè many months of hard assiduous labour to have such a beautiful field and this fact was ignored by the jealous passers-by. They saw the field but not the labour and privations. Now, does one ever see the labour and privations which one gives oneself, to which one submits when one is obscurely pursuing an aim?

But something was running around his head like a beast. It was lying there under his skull. . . .

"Now, look! Follow his route with your finger. He is here . . . he is there. . . . What? Don't you see him? Don't you feel him? He is running under my skin and under my skull! Ah, poor me! Poor Kacou Ananzè! I am always the victim of other people."

Chased away, the thing found refuge in the nape of Kacou's neck and again came back and settled under his forehead.

"But is it really under my forehead this 'something' which is always at my heels? No! No! I don't want it!"

"But yes, Kacou Ananzè . . . it is possible . . ."

"What? What do you take me for?"

"Yes . . . do it, Kacou Ananzè! For you, this will be a new chapter of glory . . . a new element which will take you into legend."

"Go away from me . . . And my wife and my children?"

"Come on! Come on, Kacou Ananzè. You know very well that your wife and children . . ."

"Then you will ask me: 'Are you going to eat all these yams by yourself?'"

"That's it! Such lovely yams! Look at them. Look at this field. —Your field! Do you think it is necessary to share this with others? What have they done? They have only helped you. Who has done the hard work? You have done it."

"You're right . . . I have cut down all these trees . . . It's a good idea after all. . . ."

"If you eat all these yams by yourself? Of course! Don't give any to a soul."

"Nothing is more succulent than a good plate of yams with mashed sweet-potato leaves, seasoned with coarse salt which crackles between the teeth and a little honey as an extra condiment!"

"You know, Kacou Ananzè, you are a gourmet!"

"Some good bitter palm-wine scratching the throat after eating a good yam cooked in ashes—nothing like it!"

"About these yams. . . , Kacou Ananzè, you will eat them all by yourself, just like that, without giving any to a soul?"

"Yes, I must eat them all by myself."

Such had been the continuous inner thoughts of Kacou Ananzè ever since the leaves of the yams had begun to turn yellow. . . .

Came evening and a sad Ananzè went back to the house, sad because he had not yet found the means to eat all those good things by himself. And all the time he was rummaging around his bag of tricks. And in his bag he found once more what he had been looking for, ever since that morning when something had murmured in his ear "If you eat all these yams by yourself?"

He had to die. It was the only solution. He had to die in order to eat by himself all those yams which were already being gathered and whose tubers were larger than the thighs of overfat women. Yes, he had to die. It was the only solution.

Consequently one day Kacou Ananzè and his family were in the field. They had been working since morning. The sun had slowly climbed to the tops of the trees and reflected metallically on the leaves of the banana-trees. They were still working despite the stifling heat. Everywhere one could see the skeletons of insects, the ringlets of centipedes and the shells of snails and other molluscs which had been taken unawares by the flames when the field had been set on fire. Here and there, the rain had formed small irrigating canals.

They were working, when all of a sudden, Kacou Ananzè fell into a swoon. His wife and children carried him to the village where he came to his senses and heard Côlou, his wife, saying to Eban, his eldest son:

"Your father is in the act of . . . You understand?"

"What are you thinking about, mother?"

"I think nothing good will come of this swoon at harvest-time. I have never seen your father fall into a swoon. It isn't even a family illness. Itches, scurvy, a swollen stomach perhaps, but a swoon . . . Hum! Let's keep our eyes open, my son."

"I shall do so, mother."

The harvest was finished. On one side of the field were placed the pimentos, the *taros*, the *gombos;* on the other, the yams, haricot beans, bananas, and sweet potatoes.

And there is Kacou Ananzè falling sick!

"Hum! Eban. . . ," said Côlou once again.

"I have my eye on him, mother."

"Your father is the slyest and most artful being in the whole world!"

"I am of the same breed and can see into father's trick."

One morning, Kacou Ananzè said to his family:

"Last night I had a fantastic dream. I am going to die."

"What did you say? You're going to die? What will become of your children, and me, your wife?"

"My poor wife! Alas! I am going to die. Somebody came to me and said as clearly as I am speaking to you: 'Kacou Ananzè, you are going to die. But when you die . . .'"

"Oh! Father's going to die!" cried the children.

"Let me tell you about the dream. The voice told me: 'But when you die, nobody must wash or dress you, but you must be buried in your field near the yams for which you have given so much labour.'"

"What!" I replied, "I must be neither washed nor dressed but be buried in a field? Never! I shall be buried in the cemetery with my own kin. But the voice continued to say: 'It is for the happiness of your kin, your wife, and above all, for your children.'"

"Therefore I tell you I am going to die and you must do what was said to me in my dream last night. Hold on! I forgot something. He recommended that a mortar, a pestle, a pot, some salt and some oil be placed on my tomb. What else was there? Ah! my memory is growing old!! I think that is all he said. I shall be happy to die, really happy. At last I shall be spared all bad language."

Two days later, Kacou Ananzè died. He was buried in the field near the yams.

In the village, the funeral ceremonies dragged on. Each night saw the offering of libations, dancing, interminable palavers, and even fighting, because everybody had drunk excessively. All the village tam-tams were split (through over-use) because everybody was happy to have buried Kacou Ananzè. Some people, instead of throwing a pinch of sand over the poor corpse, had several times even violently thrown handfuls of earth over it. There was no trace of sorrow on any face. On the contrary, eyes were laughing and seemed to say: "At last! About time too!"

The funeral ceremonies ended because all the tam-tams were split and there was nothing to summon people to offer libations.

Each night, Kacou left his tomb and stuffed himself with yams. As he listened to the roaring tam-tams he said to himself: "Poor people, since when does one learn of one's death through a dream? Since when have they had themselves buried in a yam field? I, Kacou Ananzè, to die like this without even having attempted to cheat Death?"

After the funeral ceremonies people again took to the plantations, hoe on shoulder and matchet in hand, taking large strides to avoid being soaked by the dew-drenched grass. Here, heads were bent under a canopy of foliage; there, people crawled almost under a tree which several years before had blown across the path by a storm.

Eban and Côlou, like the others, came to the field. The mound of yams had become smaller.

"Eban, I told you to keep your eyes open."

"I have done so, mother."

"Then what about these diminishing yams?"

"But father is dead!"

"Who else could possibly be responsible?"

"We will soon know. I have an idea."

Night came. The whole bush was asleep. The animals, satiated, made no cry. Even those which hunted their food at night were drowsy. One could hardly hear the occasional hiccup of a parrot, the hoot of an owl, and the rustling of a branch which unhooked itself from another after an amorous embrace. Even the insects, those indefatigable singers, had lowered the pitch of their chorus because they also were overtaken by sleep. Under the weight of darkness, the fruit, tired by their struggle, had fallen to the ground. The trees no longer had the strength to snort against the wind, which, awaking with a start, continued its journey. Not succeeding in stirring the billow of the ravelled and shadow-covered peaks, it subsided, also overtaken by sleep. Only the grass stirred, but not for long. Peace became so profound that not a soul wished to disturb it. The fire-flies tried to set light to this immense green forest, which they goaded with twinkling fire, fleeting rays, and shooting stars. Waking chimpanzees chattered "kpa koun!" Peace returned, only disturbed in the undergrowth by some watching serpent, a continually walking blind centipede, the falling of a branch or a creeper, by all the multiple sighs and the innumerable murmurs of creatures in the night.

Leaving his tomb, Kacou Ananzè went towards the mound of yams. But there was somebody by the side of it.

Kacou broke a branch but this "somebody" did not move.

He coughed a little and repeatedly and let fall an old root. There was still no movement.

"Eh! Eh! Where are you bound for tonight, friend?"

SILENCE . . .

"Yes, it's true, you've come to pay me a visit."

SILENCE . . .

"You have been entrusted with guarding the harvest. I am also doing that. The elephants, buffaloes, and monkeys love such things as yams, bananas, sweet-potatoes, and *taros*, therefore I am obliged each night to come and chase them away. Since my death, I do not sleep. I am awake every night. Can you succeed in sleeping?"

SILENCE . . .

"You won't reply? I shall get angry. I shall strike you! Yes, I shall! Thief! You know me! I am the spider."

SILENCE . . .

"Ah! You aren't running away? Being brave are you? You therefore don't know me. I am Kacou Ananzè! I'll tell you again. I don't like this type of joke. If I get annoyed, look after yourself. You won't reply? You are ill-mannered? You won't answer an old man like me? Ah, well! Take that! That will teach you to come and beard me in my field!"

And then came the sound of a slap.

SILENCE . . .

"What? You dare take hold of my hand? What cheek! Let me go."

SILENCE . . .

"What about my other hand? It's free. Watch out! . . ."

And then came another slap.

"Ah, but you're exaggerating. Your insolence is beyond measure. One can joke but not go as far as that. You're holding both my hands! What will you do with my feet?"

And quickly both his feet were seized by this "somebody" who never spoke a word.

"Ah! I understand. You have come to provoke me. But nobody ever provokes me. You have seized my hands and legs. What are you going to do with my stomach?"

And quickly his stomach was glued against this thing which Kacou had taken for a human being but which was only a scarecrow made of bird-lime.

Day drew near. One by one the tree tops took off their shadowy cloaks. Gaps could be seen through the dissolving gloom. The pagoda cocks and the thousands of bush inhabitants greeted each other in diverse tongues. The sun was climbing. A fine powder of dew remained on the leaves. The turacos noisily alighted on the ripening cabbage-trees and wrangled over the seeds.

Ananzè remained a prisoner. After having rummaged in his bag once more, he pretended to be dead as soon as he heard his children coming.

They cried: "We have captured the thief!"

"He looks so like father!"

"But our father is dead!"

"Our father is not a thief!"

Côlou came in her turn. She looked at him. Ananzè opened an eye. He even made a sign at his wife who, with hands on hips, slowly said to her children:

"This man isn't your father."

"What shall we do with him?"

"We shall burn him," replied Côlou.

They set fire to the twigs and dead leaves which were piled around Kacou's feet.

The smoke rises. It enters Kacou Ananzè's nose and ears. The poor man is suffocating. Suddenly, the flame attacks him. At first it is rose-coloured and then it reddens. It licks him, lightly touches him, claws at him and bites him.

What? Will he allow himself to be burnt like a cabbage-tree rat, enclosed in his hole? He is either Kacou Ananzè or he isn't!

Côlou fanned the flames with all her might as if the wind were not strong enough.

The bird-lime melts. Kacou Ananzè moves. He shakes a leg, an arm.

In flames, he pulls himself from the stake, hurls himself upon his wife and children and drags them to the stream which is flowing near by.

Some of his family glide away, others survive.

And ever since that day one can see spiders floating on the springs, streams, and rivers. . . .

—Translated by H. G. Jones

Chinese Folk Song

A Sweet Potato Rolls Off the Hill

A crystal river flows to the east of our commune,
From its bank rises a gentle slope.
On the slope the communers are digging sweet potatoes
In a happy hum of laughing chatter.

Suddenly I heard a noise in the river.
Water splashed up over ten feet high.
And I heard my own frightened voice shouting,
"Who is the careless one that fell down?"

Everybody heard me and roared and roared,
One girl answered:
"Nobody fell off, nobody at all,
It's only a sweet potato!"

—*Translated by Kai-Yu Hsu*

Richard Wilbur

(American, 1921–)

Potato

for André du Bouchet

An underground grower, blind and a common brown;
Got a misshapen look, it's nudged where it could;
Simple as soil yet crowded as earth with all.

Cut open raw, it looses a cool clean stench,
Mineral acid seeping from pores of prest meal;
It is like breaching a strangely refreshing tomb:

Therein the taste of first stones, the hands of dead slaves,
Waters men drank in the earliest frightful woods,
Flint chips, and peat, and the cinders of buried camps.

Scrubbed under faucet water the planet skin
Polishes yellow, but tears to the plain insides;
Parching, the white's blue-hearted like hungry hands.

All of the cold dark kitchens, and war-frozen grey
Evening at window; I remember so many
Peeling potatoes quietly into chipt pails.

"It was potatoes saved us, they kept us alive."
Then they had something to say akin to praise
For the mean earth-apples, too common to cherish or steal.

Times being hard, the Sikh and the Senegalese,
Hobo and Okie, the body of Jesus the Jew,
Vestigial virtues, are eaten; we shall survive.

What has not lost its savour shall hold us up,
And we are praising what saves us, what fills the need.
(Soon there'll be packets again, with Algerian fruits.)

Oh, it will not bear polish, the ancient potato,
Needn't be nourished by Caesars, will blow anywhere,
Hidden by nature, counted-on, stubborn and blind.

You may have noticed the bush that it pushes to air,
Comical-delicate, sometimes with second-rate flowers
Awkward and milky and beautiful only to hunger.

Tony Curtis

(1946 –)

Jack Watts

squints across a sprouting field,
chews at a leaf, then weighs your crop
to the nearest bag.

Soft cap down to the eyes
and what had been somebody's suit
held by baling cord;
he is pigmented with dirt
as if washing would have drained
away the years' knowledge.

The whole country waits:
in April the Pembrokeshire Earlies come
a stiff, dark green out of the ground.
Jack and his tribe pout
like Winter rats from their cottage.

Jack stops at the stile,
pushes the cap back to the perch of his head,
then walks along a row to what becomes
the centre of the field.
He delivers a potato from the earth,
soil spilling from the web of tubers,
shaking from the clumps.
He scrapes through dirt and skin;
the sweet flesh goes between his leather lips,
a nugget lodging in the jags of his teeth.

He closes his eyes on the taste—
it is the soil crumbling, the crush
of frost, the rain carried in on the sea,
the sweat of planting.

He holds the ridged sweetness to his nose,
between finger and thumb it glistens,
the rarest egg, the first
potato and the last.

Nora Ephron

(American, 1941–)

From *Heartburn*

POTATOES AND LOVE: SOME REFLECTIONS
The Beginning

I have friends who begin with pasta, and friends who begin with rice, but whenever I fall in love, I begin with potatoes. Sometimes meat and potatoes and sometimes fish and potatoes, but always potatoes. I have made a lot of mistakes falling in love, and regretted most of them, but never the potatoes that went with them.

Not just any potato will do when it comes to love. There are people who go on about the virtues of plain potatoes—plain boiled new potatoes with a little parsley or dill, or plain baked potatoes with crackling skins—but my own feeling is that a taste for plain potatoes coincides with cultural antecedents I do not possess, and that in any case, the time for plain potatoes—if there is ever a time for plain potatoes—is never at the beginning of something. It is also, I should add, never at the end of something. Perhaps you can get away with plain potatoes in the middle, although I have never been able to.

All right, then: I am talking about crisp potatoes. Crisp potatoes require an immense amount of labor. It's not just the peeling, which is one of the few kitchen chores no electric device has been invented to alleviate; it's also that the potatoes, once peeled, must be cut into whatever shape you intend them to be, put into water to be systematically prevented from turning a loathsome shade of bluish-brownish-black, and then meticulously dried to ensure that they crisp properly. All this takes time, and time, as any fool can tell you, is what true romance is about. In fact, one of the main reasons why you must make crisp potatoes in the beginning is that if you don't make them in the beginning, you never will. I'm sorry to be so cynical about this, but that's the truth.

There are two kinds of crisp potatoes that I prefer above all others. The first are called Swiss potatoes, and they're essentially a large potato pancake of perfect hash browns; the flipping of the pancake is so wildly dramatic that the potatoes themselves are almost beside the point. The second are called potatoes Anna; they are thin circles of potato cooked in a shallow pan in the oven and then turned onto a plate in a darling mound of crunchy brownness. Potatoes Anna is a classic French recipe, but there is something so homely and old-fashioned about them that they can usually be passed off as either an ancient family recipe or something you just made up.

For Swiss potatoes: Peel 3 large (or 4 small) russet potatoes (or all-purpose if you can't get russets) and put them in cold water to cover. Start 4 tablespoons butter and 1 table-spoon cooking oil melting in a nice heavy large frying pan. Working quickly, dry the potatoes and grate them on the grating disk of the Cuisinart. Put them into a colander and squeeze out as much water as you can. Then dry them again on paper towels. You will need more paper towels to do this than you ever thought possible. Dump the potatoes into the frying pan, patting them down with a spatula, and cook over medium heat for about 15 minutes, until the bottom of the pancake is brown. Then, while someone is watching, loosen the pancake and, with one incredibly deft motion, flip it over. Salt it generously. Cook 5 minutes more. Serves two.

For potatoes Anna: Peel 3 large (or 4 small) russet po-tatoes (or Idahos if you can't get russets) and put them in water. Working quickly, dry each potato and slice into 1/16-inch rounds. Dry them with paper towels, round by round. Put 1 tablespoon clarified butter into a cast-iron skillet and line the skillet with overlapping potatoes. Dribble clarified butter and salt and pepper over them. Repeat twice. Put into a 425° oven for 45 minutes, pressing the potatoes down now and then. Then turn up the oven to 500° and cook 10 more minutes. Flip onto a round platter. Serves two.

The Middle (I)

One day the inevitable happens. I go to the potato drawer to make potatoes and discover that the little brown buggers I bought in a large sack a few weeks earlier have gotten soft and mushy and are sprouting long and quite uninteresting vines. In addition, one of them seems to have developed an odd brown leak, and the odd brown leak appears to be the cause of a terrible odor that in only a few seconds has perme-ated the entire kitchen. I throw out the potatoes and look in the cupboard for a box of pasta. This is the moment when the beginning ends and the middle begins.

The Middle (II)

Sometimes, when a loved one announces that he has decided
to go on a low-carbohydrate, low-fat, low-salt diet (thus ruling out the possibility of potatoes, should you have been so
inclined), he is signaling that the middle is ending and the
end is beginning.

The End

In the end, I always want potatoes. Mashed potatoes. Nothing like mashed potatoes when you're feeling blue. Nothing
like getting into bed with a bowl of hot mashed potatoes already loaded with butter, and methodically adding a thin cold
slice of butter to every forkful. The problem with mashed
potatoes, though, is that they require almost as much hard
work as crisp potatoes, and when you're feeling blue the last
thing you feel like is hard work. Of course, you can always
get someone to make the mashed potatoes for you, but let's
face it: the reason you're blue is that there *isn't* anyone to
make them for you. As a result, most people do not have
nearly enough mashed potatoes in their lives, and when they
do, it's almost always at the wrong time.

   (You can, of course, train children to mash potatoes, but
you should know that Richard Nixon spent most of his childhood making mashed potatoes for his mother and was extremely methodical about getting the lumps out. A few lumps
make mashed potatoes more authentic, if you ask me, but
that's not the point. The point is that perhaps children should
not be trained to mash potatoes.)

   For mashed potatoes: Put 1 large (or 2 small) potatoes in a
large pot of salted water and bring to a boil. Lower the heat
and simmer for at least 20 minutes, until tender. Drain and
place the potatoes back in the pot and shake over low heat to
eliminate excess moisture. Peel. Put through a potato ricer
and immediately add 1 tablespoon heavy cream and as much
melted butter and salt and pepper as you feel like. Eat immediately. Serves one.

Emily Dickinson

(American, 1830–1886)

1298

The Mushrooms is the Elf of Plants—
At Evening, it is not—
At Morning, in a Truffled Hut
It stop upon a Spot

As if it tarried always
And yet its whole Career
Is shorter than a Snake's Delay
And fleeter than a Tare*—

'Tis Vegetation's Juggler—
The Germ of Alibi—
Doth like a Bubble antedate
And like a Bubble, hie—

I feel as if the Grass was pleased
To have it intermit—
This surreptitious scion
Of Summer's circumspect.

Had Nature any supple Face
Or could she one contemn—
Had Nature an Apostate—
That Mushroom—it is Him!

*A weed, member of the vetch family.

Martin Tucker

(American, 1928–)

The Inveterate Hesitater

He buys a truffle every five years
and keeps it for ten,
because he can find no proper reason
to celebrate eating them,
or so he feels.
Which is an exaggeration,
since he feels little at any one time,
not even the greed
of money melting in his mouth,
at 50 bucks a bite,
which is what truffling matters are made of.

He suffers in his way:
he stays with a vegetable he defers to eat,
he dreams of mushrooms to greet
him on a new day and consume him away
to a new birth—
or at least refine the nature of his earth.

Fruits

Andrew Marvell

(English, 1621–1678)

From *The Garden*

What wondrous life is this I lead!
Ripe apples drop about my head;
The luscious clusters of the vine
Upon my mouth do crush their wine;
The nectarene, and curious peach,
Into my hands themselves do reach;
Stumbling on melons, as I pass,
Ensnared with flowers, I fall on grass.

John Milton

(English, 1608–1674)

From *Paradise Lost*, Book IX

Great are thy Vertues, doubtless, best of Fruits,
Though kept from Man, and worthy to be admir'd,
Whose taste, too long forborn, at first assay
Gave elocution to the mute, and taught
The Tongue not made for Speech to speak thy praise:

Thy praise hee also who forbids thy use,
Conceales not from us, naming thee the Tree
Of Knowledge, knowledge both of good and evil;
Forbids us then to taste, but his forbidding
Commends thee more, while it inferrs the good
By thee communicated, and our want:
For good unknown sure is not had, or had
And yet unknown, is as not had at all.
In plain then, what forbids he but to know,
Forbids us good, forbids us to be wise?
Such prohibitions binde not. But if Death
Bind us with after-bands, what profits then
Our inward freedom? In the day we eate
Of this fair Fruit, our doom is, we shall die.
How dies the Serpent? hee hath eat'n and lives,
And knows, and speaks, and reasons, and discernes,
Irrational till then. For us alone
Was death invented? or to us deni'd
This intellectual food, for beasts reserv'd?
For Beasts it seems: yet that one Beast which first
Hath tasted, envies not, but brings with joy
The good befall'n him, Author unsuspect,
Friendly to man, farr from deceit or guile.
What fear I then, rather what know to feare
Under this ignorance of Good and Evil,
Of God or Death, of Law or Penaltie?
Here grows the Cure of all, this Fruit Divine,
Fair to the Eye, inviting to the Taste,
Of vertue to make wise: what hinders then
To reach, and feed at once both Bodie and Mind?
    So saying, her rash hand in evil hour
Forth reaching to the Fruit, she pluckd, she eat:
Earth felt the wound, and Nature from her seat
Sighing through all her Works gave signs of woe,
That all was lost.

Charles Tomlinson

(English, 1927–)

Paring the Apple

There are portraits and still-lifes.

And there is paring the apple.

And then? Paring it slowly,
From under cool-yellow
Cold-white emerging. And . . . ?

The spring of concentric peel
Unwinding off white,
The blade hidden, dividing.

There are portraits and still-lifes
And the first, because "human"
Does not excel the second, and
Neither is less weighted
With a human gesture, than paring the apple
With a human stillness.

The cool blade
Severs between coolness, apple-rind
Compelling a recognition.

Charles Simic

(1938–)

Watermelons

Green Buddhas
On the fruit stand.
We eat the smile
And spit out the teeth.

Wang I

(Chinese, Second Century, A.D.)

The Lychee-Tree

(A FRAGMENT)

Sombre as the heavens when morning clouds arise,
Bushy as a great broom held across the sky,
Vast as the spaces of a lofty house,
Deep fretted as a line of stony hills.
Long branches twining,
Green leaves clustering,
And all a-glimmer like a mist that lightly lies
Across the morning sun;
All spangled, darted with fire like a sky

Of populous stars.
Shell like a fisherman's red net;
Fruit white and lustrous as a pearl . . .
Lambent as the jewel of Ho, more strange
Than the saffron-stone of Hsia.
Now sigh we at the beauty of its show,
Now triumph in its taste.
Sweet juices lie in the mouth,
Soft scents invade the mind.
All flavours here are joined, yet none is master;
A hundred diverse tastes
Blend in such harmony no man can say
That one outstrips the rest. Sovereign of sweets,
Peerless, pre-eminent fruit, who dwellest apart
In noble solitude!

                                   —*Translated by Arthur Waley*

Claude McKay

(American, 1890–1948)

The Tropics in New York

Bananas ripe and green, and ginger-root,
    Cocoa in pods and alligator pears,
And tangerines and mangoes and grape fruit,
    Fit for the highest prize at parish fairs,

Set in the window, bringing memories
    Of fruit-trees laden by low-singing rills,
And dewy dawns, and mystical blue skies
    In benediction over nun-like hills.

My eyes grew dim, and I could no more gaze;
  A wave of longing through my body swept,
And, hungry for the old, familiar ways,
  I turned aside and bowed my head and wept.

William Carlos Williams

(American, 1883–1963)

This Is Just to Say

I have eaten
the plums
that were in
the icebox

and which
you were probably
saving
for breakfast

Forgive me
they were delicious
so sweet
and so cold

Helen Chasin

(American,?–)

The Word *Plum*

The word *plum* is delicious

pout and push, luxury of
self-love, and savoring murmur

full in the mouth and falling
like fruit

taut skin
pierced, bitten, provoked into
juice, and tart flesh

question
and reply, lip and tongue
of pleasure.

Anonymous Egyptian

Prayer to the God Thot

The tall palm tree sixty feet high
heavy with fruit:
the fruit contains kernels,
the kernels water.
You who bring water to the remotest place

come and save me because I am humble.
O Thot, you are a sweet well
for him who starves in the desert.
A well that remains closed to the talkative

but opens up to the silent.
When the silent man approaches the well reveals itself;
when the noisy man comes you remain hidden.

Tayeb Salih

(Sudanese, 1929–)

From *The Wedding of Zein*

A HANDFUL OF DATES

I must have been very young at the time. While I don't remember exactly how old I was, I do remember that when
people saw me with my grandfather they would pat me on
the head and give my cheek a pinch—things they didn't do to
my grandfather. The strange thing was that I never used to
go out with my father, rather it was my grandfather who
would take me with him wherever he went, except for the
mornings when I would go to the mosque to learn the Koran.
The mosque, the river and the fields—these were the land-
marks in our life. While most of the children of my age
grumbled at having to go to the mosque to learn the Koran, I
used to love it. The reason was, no doubt, that I was quick at
learning by heart and the Sheikh always asked me to stand up
and recite the *Chapter of the Merciful* whenever we had visitors, who would pat me on my head and cheek just as people
did when they saw me with my grandfather.

Yes, I used to love the mosque, and I loved the river too.
Directly we finished our Koran reading in the morning I
would throw down my wooden slate and dart off, quick as a
genie, to my mother, hurriedly swallow down my breakfast,
and run off for a plunge in the river. When tired of swimming about I would sit on the bank and gaze at the strip of
water that wound away eastwards and hid behind a thick
wood of acacia trees. I loved to give rein to my imagination

and picture to myself a tribe of giants living behind that wood, a people tall and thin with white beards and sharp noses, like my grandfather. Before my grandfather ever replied to my many questions he would rub the tip of his nose with his forefinger; as for his beard, it was soft and luxuriant and as white as cotton-wool—never in my life have I seen anything of a purer whiteness or greater beauty. My grandfather must also have been extremely tall, for I never saw anyone in the whole area address him without having to look up at him, nor did I see him enter a house without having to bend so low that I was put in mind of the way the river wound round behind the wood of acacia trees. I loved him and would imagine myself, when I grew to be a man, tall and slender like him, walking along with great strides.

I believe I was his favourite grandchild: no wonder, for my cousins were a stupid bunch and I—so they say—was an intelligent child. I used to know when my grandfather wanted me to laugh, when to be silent; also I would remember the times for his prayers and would bring him his prayer-rug and fill the ewer for his ablutions without his having to ask me. When he had nothing else to do he enjoyed listening to me reciting to him from the Koran in a lilting voice, and I could tell from his face that he was moved.

One day I asked him about our neighbour Masood. I said to my grandfather: "I fancy you don't like our neighbour Masood?"

To which he answered, having rubbed the tip of his nose: "He's an indolent man and I don't like such people."

I said to him: "What's an indolent man?"

My grandfather lowered his head for a moment, then looking across at the wide expanse of field, he said: "Do you see it stretching out from the edge of the desert up to the Nile bank? A hundred feddans.* Do you see all those date palms? And those trees—sant, acacia, and sayal? All this fell into Masood's lap, was inherited by him from his father."

---

*A little more than a hundred acres.

Taking advantage of the silence that had descended upon my grandfather, I turned my gaze from him to the vast area defined by his words. "I don't care," I told myself, "who owns those date palms, those trees of this black, cracked earth—all I know is that it's the arena for my dreams and my playground."

My grandfather then continued: "Yes, my boy, forty years ago all this belonged to Masood—two-thirds of it is now mine."

This was news to me, for I had imagined that the land had belonged to my grandfather ever since God's Creation.

"I didn't own a single feddan when I first set foot in this village. Masood was then the owner of all these riches. The position has changed now, though, and I think that before Allah calls me to Him I shall have bought the remaining third as well."

I do not know why it was I felt fear at my grandfather's words—and pity for our neighbour Masood. How I wished my grandfather wouldn't do what he'd said! I remembered Masood's singing, his beautiful voice and powerful laugh that resembled the gurgling of water. My grandfather never used to laugh.

I asked my grandfather why Masood had sold his land.

"Women," and from the way my grandfather pronounced the word I felt that "women" was something terrible. "Masood, my boy, was a much-married man. Each time he married he sold me a feddan or two." I made the quick calculation that Masood must have married some ninety women. Then I remembered his three wives, his shabby appearance, his lame donkey and its dilapidated saddle, his *galabia* with the torn sleeves. I had all but rid my mind of the thoughts that jostled in it when I saw the man approaching us, and my grandfather and I exchanged glances.

"We'll be harvesting the dates today," said Masood. "Don't you want to be there?"

I felt, though, that he did not really want my grandfather to attend. My grandfather, however, jumped to his feet and I saw that his eyes sparkled momentarily with an intense brightness. He pulled me by the hand and we went off to the harvesting of Masood's dates.

Someone brought my grandfather a stool covered with an ox-hide, while I remained standing. There was a vast number of people there, but though I knew them all, I found myself for some reason watching Masood: aloof from that great gathering of people he stood as though it were no concern of his, despite the fact that the date palms to be harvested were his own. Sometimes his attention would be caught by the sound of a huge clump of dates crashing down from on high. Once he shouted up at the boy perched on the very summit of the date palm who had begun hacking at a clump with his long, sharp sickle: "Be careful you don't cut the heart of the palm."

No one paid any attention to what he said and the boy seated at the very summit of the date palm continued, quickly and energetically, to work away at the branch with his sickle till the clump of dates began to drop like something descending from the heavens.

I, however, had begun to think about Masood's phrase "the heart of the palm." I pictured the palm tree as something with feeling, something possessed of a heart that throbbed. I remembered Masood's remark to me when he had once seen me playing about with the branch of a young palm tree: "Palm trees, my boy, like humans, experience joy and suffering." And I had felt an inward and unreasoned embarrassment.

When I again looked at the expanse of ground stretching before me I saw my young companions swarming like ants around the trunks of the palm trees, gathering up dates and eating most of them. The dates were collected into high mounds. I saw people coming along and weighing them into measuring bins and pouring them into sacks, of which I counted thirty. The crowd of people broke up, except for Hussein the merchant, Mousa the owner of the field next to ours on the east, and two men I'd never seen before.

I heard a low whistling sound and saw that my grandfather had fallen asleep. Then I noticed that Masood had not changed his stance, except that he had placed a stalk in his mouth and was munching at it like someone surfeited with food who doesn't know what to do with the mouthful he still has.

Suddenly my grandfather woke up, jumped to his feet and walked towards the sacks of dates. He was followed by Hussein the merchant, Mousa the owner of the field next to ours, and the two strangers. I glanced at Masood and saw that he was making his way towards us with extreme slowness, like a man who wants to retreat but whose feet insist on going forward. They formed a circle round the sacks of dates and began examining them, some taking a date or two to eat. My grandfather gave me a fistful, which I began munching. I saw Masood filling the palms of both hands with dates and bringing them up close to his nose, then returning them.

Then I saw them dividing up the sacks between them. Hussein the merchant took ten; each of the strangers took five. Mousa the owner of the field next to ours on the eastern side took five, and my grandfather took five. Understanding nothing, I looked at Masood and saw that his eyes were darting about to left and right like two mice that have lost their way home.

"You're still fifty pounds in debt to me," said my grandfather to Masood. "We'll talk about it later."

Hussein called his assistants and they brought along donkeys, the two strangers produced camels, and the sacks of dates were loaded on to them. One of the donkeys let out a braying which set the camels frothing at the mouth and complaining noisily. I felt myself drawing close to Masood, felt my hand stretch out towards him as though I wanted to touch the hem of his garment. I heard him make a noise in his throat like the rasping of a lamb being slaughtered. For some unknown reason, I experienced a sharp sensation of pain in my chest.

I ran off into the distance. Hearing my grandfather call after me, I hesitated a little, then continued on my way. I felt at that moment that I hated him. Quickening my pace, it was as though I carried within me a secret I wanted to rid myself of. I reached the river bank near the bend it made behind the wood of acacia trees. Then, without knowing why, I put my finger into my throat and spewed up the dates I'd eaten.

—Translated by Denys Johnson-Davies

Alphonse Daudet

(1840–1897)

The Fig and the Sluggard

AN ALGERIAN LEGEND

In the indolent and pleasure-loving town of Blidah, some years before the French invasion, lived a worthy Moor, by name Sidi Lakdar, and by his fellow-citizens nicknamed, "The Sluggard."

Now you must know that the Algerian Moors are the laziest people on earth, and the residents of Blidah especially so, probably on account of the perfume of orange and lemon blossoms, with which the place fairly reeks. But in laziness and listlessness, not one among all the Blidians could hold a candle to Sidi Lakdar. This worthy man had elevated his pet vice to the dignity of a profession. Others were embroiderers, coffee-house keepers, spice merchants; Sidi Lakdar was a sluggard.

At the death of his father, he had inherited a little garden on the outskirts of the town. The low, white walls were tumbling to ruin, the vine-covered gate could not be closed, and a few fig-trees and bananas grew amid the spring-moistened herbage. There he was wont to pass his days, stretched out at full length, silent, motionless, with red ants running through his beard. When he was hungry, he stretched out one hand and picked up a fig or a banana from the ground near by. If it had been necessary to get up and pick fruit from where it grew, he would have died of hunger. So in his little garden the figs ripened and rotted and the birds got a good share of them.

This actually unbridled laziness made Lakdar very popular all through the country. He received the homage due to a saint. When the women of the town, on their way to eat sweetmeats in the cemetery, passed by the little enclosure, they pulled up their mules to a slower pace and talked in muffled tones behind their white masks. The men made pious obeisance, and every day, when school was over, the garden walls swarmed with boys, in striped silk blouses and red caps, who tried their best to disturb the sluggard's repose. They called Lakdar by name, jeered, played tricks on him, pelted him with orange skins,—all for nought. The sluggard never budged. Once in a while he would call from his bed in the grass: "Look out now! I'm going to get up!" But he never got up.

Well, it so happened that on a certain day one of these brats, coming to get some fun out of the sluggard, was as it were touched with grace, and conceived a passion for a similar existence. He announced to his father that he should not go to school any more, and that he was going to be a sluggard.

"Sluggard? You?" said the father, an industrious turner of pipe-stems, as busy as a bee, and who was always seated before his wheel at cock-crow. "Sluggard? You? That is an idea!"

"Yes, father; I want to be a sluggard, like Sidi Lakdar."

"Not much, my lad. You'll be a turner, like your father, or a scribe at the Kadi's court, but a sluggard, never. Get along to school, or I'll dress you down with this choice new strip of wild-cherry. Clear out, you blockhead!"

Yielding to the argument of the wild-cherry stick, the lad did not insist, but feigned obedience. Instead of going to school, however, he made his way to a Moorish bazaar, crept from the sight of a merchant between two piles of Smyrna rugs, and stayed there all day, lying on his back, watching the Moorish lanterns, the blue cloth bags, and the gold-embroidered vestments which sparkled in the sun, and inhaling the insinuating perfume of attar of rose and of the warm woollen burnooses. Thus did he pass the time that he should have spent at school.

A few days went by and the news of this thing came to the ears of the boy's father, who vainly scolded, stormed, blasphemed the name of Allah, and polished off his son's anatomy with all the wild-cherry sticks in the shop,—all to no purpose. The lad simply said: "I'm going to be a sluggard; I'm going to be a sluggard,"—and then went to some snug corner and sought repose.

Discipline was suspended, and after consulting with the scribe, Ali, the father decided what course to pursue.

"See here," he said to his son; "if you really want to be a first-class sluggard, I'm going to take you to Lakdar. He shall put you through an examination, and if he finds that you have genuine talent for the trade, I'll get him to take you as apprentice."

"That suits me," replied the boy.

And so, not later than the next day, freshly scented with vervain, and with heads newly shaved, they went in search of the sluggard in his little garden.

The gate was open as always. The two entered without knocking, and as the vegetation grew thick and high they had some difficulty in discovering the master of the enclosure. Finally, however, they came upon him as he lay beneath the fig-trees, surrounded by a multitude of birds and a welter of weeds,—a bundle of yellow rags which received them with a grunt.

"Allah be with you, Sidi Lakdar," said the father, bowing low and placing his hand upon his breast. "Here is my son, who desires to be a sluggard. I've brought him to you to be examined, that you may see if he has the right qualifications.

If he has, I should like you to take him as apprentice. I'll pay whatever is right."

Without speaking, Sidi Lakdar signed to them to sit down by him on the grass. The father sat down, the lad relaxed full length,—that of itself was a good beginning. They remained thus, in silence.

It was mid-day—very light and very warm. The little garden slept peacefully. Nothing was to be heard but the crackling of the flowering beans as their pods split open in the sun, the murmur of the water flowing through the herbage, and the over-fed birds as they fluttered among the foliage and opened or closed their wings. From time to time, a too ripe fig would break loose and tumble from branch to branch. Then Sidi Lakdar would put out his hand and with a weary air convey the fruit to his mouth. The lad, however, indulged in no such exertion. The finest figs fell about him, but he never even lifted his head. The host, out of the corner of his eye, took note of this magnificent indolence, but said nothing.

An hour, two hours, passed thus. You can imagine that the poor pipe-stem turner began to find the visit rather tiresome; still, he did not dare to protest, so he sat there, motionless, eyes fixed, legs crossed, himself affected by the spirit of sloth which seemed to pervade the garden like the heat and the odor of half-baked bananas and oranges.

All at once a big fig fell from the tree and landed on the lad's cheek. A lovely fig, it was, bismillah!—rosy, nectarious, perfumed like a honey-comb. To bring it into his mouth, the lad had only to touch it with a finger, but such an exertion as that involved seemed to him altogether too fatiguing, so he lay there quietly with the fruit embalming his cheek. At last, however, the temptation was too strong; he glanced toward his father and said in a doleful voice,—

"Papa—papa; put it in my mouth."

At these words, Sidi Lakdar, who was holding a fig in his hand, threw it to a long distance, and exclaimed angrily to the father,—

"This is the child you ask me to take as apprentice? Why,

he is master to me; I ought to take lessons of him!"
  And falling on his knees, with forehead to the ground
before the recumbent boy, he said,—
  "I salute thee, O Father of the Lazy!"

May Sarton

(American, 1912–)

The Fig

Under the green leaf hangs a little pouch
Shaped like a gourd, purple and leathery.
It fits the palm, it magnetizes touch.
What flesh designed as fruit can this fruit be?

The plump skin gives a little at the seam.
Now bite it deep for better or for worse!
Oh multitude of stars, pale green and crimson—
And you have dared to eat a universe!

D. H. Lawrence

(English, 1885–1930)

Figs

The proper way to eat a fig, in society,
Is to split it in four, holding it by the stump,
And open it, so that it is a glittering, rosy, moist, honied,
    heavy-petalled four-petalled flower.

Then you throw away the skin
Which is just like a four-sepalled calyx,
After you have taken off the blossom with your lips.

But the vulgar way
Is just to put your mouth to the crack, and take out the flesh
    in one bite.

Every fruit has its secret.

The fig is a very secretive fruit.
As you see it standing growing, you feel at once it is
    symbolic:
And it seems male.
But when you come to know it better, you agree with the
    Romans, it is female.

The Italians vulgarly say, it stands for the female part; the
    fig-fruit:
The fissure, the yoni,
The wonderful moist conductivity towards the centre.

Involved,
Inturned,
The flowering all inward and womb-fibrilled;
And but one orifice.

The fig, the horse-shoe, the squash-blossom.
Symbols.

There was a flower that flowered inward, womb-ward;
Now there is a fruit like a ripe womb.
It was always a secret.
That's how it should be, the female should always be secret.

There never was any standing aloft and unfolded on a bough
Like other flowers, in a revelation of petals;
Silver-pink peach, venetian green glass of medlars and sorb-
     apples,
Shallow wine-cups on short, bulging stems
Openly pledging heaven:
Here's to the thorn in flower! Here is to Utterance!
The brave, adventurous rosacæ.

Folded upon itself, and secret unutterable,
And milky-sapped, sap that curdles milk and makes *ricotta*,
Sap that smells strange on your fingers, that even goats won't
     taste it;
Folded upon itself, enclosed like any Mohammedan woman,
Its nakedness all within-walls, its flowering forever unseen,
One small way of access only, and this close-curtained from
     the light;
Fig, fruit of the female mystery, covert and inward,
Mediterranean fruit, with your covert nakedness,
Where everything happens invisible, flowering and
     fertilisation, and fruiting
In the inwardness of your you, that eye will never see
Till it's finished, and you're over-ripe, and you burst to give
     up your ghost.

Till the drop of ripeness exudes,
And the year is over.

And then the fig has kept her secret long enough.
So it explodes, and you see through the fissure the scarlet.
And the fig is finished, the year is over.

That's how the fig dies, showing her crimson through the
    purple slit
Like a wound, the exposure of her secret, on the open day.
Like a prostitute, the bursten fig, making a show of her
    secret.

That's how women die too.

The year is fallen over-ripe,
The year of our women.
The year of our women is fallen over-ripe.
The secret is laid bare.
And rottenness soon sets in.
The year of our women is fallen over-ripe.

When Eve once knew *in her mind* that she was naked
She quickly sewed fig-leaves, and sewed the same for the
    man.
She'd been naked all her days before,
But till then, till that apple of knowledge, she hadn't had the
    fact on her mind.

She got the fact on her mind, and quickly sewed fig-leaves.
And women have been sewing ever since.
But now they stitch to adorn the bursten fig, not to cover it.
They have their nakedness more than ever on their mind,
And they won't let us forget it.

Now, the secret
Becomes an affirmation through moist, scarlet lips
That laugh at the Lord's indignation.

What then, good Lord! cry the women.
We have kept our secret long enough.
We are a ripe fig.
Let us burst into affirmation.

They forget, ripe figs won't keep.
Ripe figs won't keep.

Honey-white figs of the north, black figs with scarlet inside,
    of the south.
Ripe figs won't keep, won't keep in any clime.
What then, when women the world over have all bursten into
    self-assertion?
And bursten figs won't keep?

Paul Valéry

(French, 1871–1945)

Pomegranates

LES GRENADES

Hard pomegranates sundered
By excess of your seeds,
You make me think of mighty brows
Aburst with their discoveries!

If the suns you underwent,
O pomegranates severed,
Wrought your essence with the pride
To rend your ruby segments,

And if the dry gold of your shell
At instance of a power
Cracks in crimson gems of juice,

This luminous eruption
Sets a soul to dream upon
Its secret architecture.

—Translated by Kate Flores

William Fahey

(1923–)

Peaches

Clustered in a walled garden, nude Persian houri bending
over a well.

All pink and yellow and dimpled and juicily cleft as Renoir's
dappled baigneuses, *oeils-de-boeuf d'or.*

Or aspiring odoriferously, they lie heaped in pyramids like
sun-warmed Aztec temples.

To eat one: cunnilingus with pubescent cherubim.

And then the gardener's grandmother in the wrinkled pit.

Dannie Abse

(Welsh, 1923–)

Peachstone

I do not visit his grave. He is not there.
Out of hearing, out of reach. I miss him here,
seeing hair grease at the back of a chair
near a firegrate where his spit sizzled,
or noting, in the cut-glass bowl, a peach.

For that night his wife brought him a peach,
his favourite fruit, while the sick light glowed,
and his slack, dry mouth sucked, sucked, sucked,
with dying eyes closed—perhaps for her sake—
till bright as blood the peachstone showed.

Robert Herrick

(1591–1674)

Cherry-ripe

Cherry-ripe, ripe, ripe, I cry,
Full and fair ones, come and buy.
If so be you ask me where

They do grow? I answer, There,
Where my Julia's lips do smile,
There's the land or cherry isle,
Whose plantations fully show
All the year, where cherries grow.

Walter de la Mare

(1873–1956)

Bread and Cherries

"Cherries, ripe cherries!"
The old woman cried,
In her snowy white apron,
And basket beside;
And the little boys came,
Eyes shining, cheeks red,
To buy bags of cherries
To eat with their bread.

Lucien Stryk

(American, 1924–)

Cherries

Because I sit eating cherries
which I did not pick
a girl goes bad under

the elevator tracks, will
never be whole again.
Because I want the full bag,

grasping, twenty-five children
cry for food. Gorging,
I've none to offer. I want

to care, I mean to, but not
yet, a dozen cherries
rattling at the bottom of my bag.

One by one I lift them to
my mouth, slowly break
their skin—twelve nations

bleed. Because I love, because
I need cherries, I
cannot help them. My happiness,

bought cheap, must last forever.

Pablo Neruda

(1904–1973)

A Lemon

Out of lemon flowers
loosed
on the moonlight, love's
lashed and insatiable
essences,
sodden with fragrance,
the lemon tree's yellow
emerges,
the lemons
move down
from the tree's planetarium.

Delicate merchandise!
The harbors are big with it—
bazaars
for the light and the
barbarous gold.
We open
the halves
of a miracle,
and a clotting of acids
brims
into the starry
divisions:
creation's
original juices,
irreducible, changeless,

alive:
so the freshness lives on
in a lemon,
in the sweet-smelling house of the rind,
the proportions, arcane and acerb.

Cutting the lemon
the knife
leaves a little
cathedral:
alcoves unguessed by the eye
that open acidulous glass
to the light; topazes
riding the droplets,
altars,
aromatic façades.

So, while the hand
holds the cut of the lemon,
half a world
on a trencher,
the gold of the universe
wells
to your touch:
a cup yellow
with miracles,
a breast and a nipple
perfuming the earth;
a flashing made fruitage,
the diminutive fire of a planet.

—Translated by Ben Belitt

Stephen Crane

(American, 1871–1900)

The Cry of a Huckleberry Pudding

A DIM STUDY OF CAMPING EXPERIENCES

A great blaze wavered redly against the blackness of the night in the pines. Before the eyes of his expectant companions, a little man moved with stately dignity as the creator of a huckleberry pudding.

"I know how to make'm," he said in a confident voice, "just exactly right."

The others looked at him with admiration as they sat down to eat.

After a time, a pudgy man whose spoon was silent, said: "I don't like this much."

"What?" cried the little man, threateningly.

"I don't seem to get on with it," said the pudgy man. He looked about for support in the faces of his companions. "I don't like it, somehow," he added slowly.

"Fool!" roared the little man, furiously. "You're mad because you didn't make it. I never saw such a beast."

The pudgy man wrapped himself in a great dignity. He glanced suggestingly at the plates of the two others. They were intact.

"Ho," cried the little man, "you're all idiots."

He saw that he must vindicate his work. He must eat it. He sat before them and, with ineffable bliss lighting his countenance, ate all of the huckleberry pudding. Then he laid aside his plate, lighted his pipe, and addressed his companions as unappreciative blockheads.

The pipe, the fire, and the song of the pines soothed him after a time, and he puffed tranquilly. The four men sat staring vacantly at the blaze until the spirits of the tent at the edge of the fire circle, in drowsy voices, began to call them. Their thoughts became heavily fixed on the knee-deep bed of hemlock. One by one they arose, knocked ashes from their pipes, and treading softly to the open flaps, disappeared. Alone, the campfire spluttered valiantly for a time, opposing its music to the dismal crooning of the trees that accented the absence of things congenial and alive. A curious moon peered through locked branches at imperturbable bundles of blankets which lay in the shadows of the tent.

The fragrant blackness of the early night passed away, and gray ghost-mists came winding slowly up from the marshes and stole among the wet tree trunks. Wavering leaves dotted with dewdrops glowed in a half-light of impending dawn. From the tent came sounds of heavy sleeping. The bundles of blankets clustered on the hemlock twigs.

Suddenly from off in the thickets of the gloom, there came a cry. It seemed to crash on the tent. It smote the bundles of blankets. There was instant profound agitation, a whirling chaos of coverings, legs, and arms; then, heads appeared. The men had heard the voice of the unknown, crying in the wilderness, and it made their souls quaver.

They had slumbered through the trees' song of loneliness and the lay of isolation of the mountain grass. Hidden frogs had muttered ominously since nightfall, and distant owls, undoubtedly perched on lofty branches and silhouetted by the moon, had hooted. There had been an endless hymning by leaves, blades, and unseen live things, through which these men, who adored Wagner, had slept.

But a false note in the sounds of night had convulsed them. A strange tune had made them writhe.

The cry of the unknown instantly awoke them to terror. It is mightier than the war yell of the dreadful, because the dreadful may be definite. But this whoop strikes greater fear from hearts because it tells of formidable mouths and great, grasping claws that live in impossibility. It is the chant of a phantom force which imagination declares invincible, and awful to the sight.

In the tent, eyes aglitter with terror gazed into eyes. Knees softly smote each other, and lips trembled.

The pudgy man gave vent to a tremendous question. "What was that?" he whispered.

The others made answer with their blanched faces. The group, waiting in the silence that followed their awakening, wriggled their legs in the agony of fright. There was a pause which extended through space. Comets hung and worlds waited. Their thoughts shot back to that moment when they had started upon the trip, and they were filled with regret that it had been.

"Oh, goodness, what was that?" repeated the pudgy man, intensely.

Suddenly, their faces twitched and their fingers turned to wax. The cry was repeated. Its burden caused the men to huddle together like drowning kittens. They watched the banshees of the fog drifting lazily among the trees. They saw eyes in the gray obscurity. They heard a thousand approaching footfalls in the rustling of the dead leaves. They groveled.

Then, they heard the unknown stride to and fro in the forest, giving calls, weighted with challenge, that could make cities hearing, fear. Roars went to the ends of earth, and snarls that would appall armies turned the men in the tent to a moaning mass with forty eyes. The challenges changed to wailings as of a fever-torn soul. Later, there came snorts of anger that sounded cruel, like the noise of a rampant bull on a babies' playground. Later still, howls, as from an abandoned being, strangling in the waters of trouble.

"Great Scott!" roared the pudgy man, "I can't stand this."

He wriggled to his feet and tottered out to the dying fire. His companions followed. They had reached the cellar of fear. They were now resolved to use weapons on the great destruction. They would combat the inevitable. They peered among the trees, wherefrom a hundred assaulting shadows came. The unknown was shrieking.

Of a sudden, the pudgy man screamed like a wounded animal.

"It's got Billie," he howled. They discovered that the little man was gone.

To listen or to wait is the most tense of occupations. In their absorption they had not seen that a comrade was missing.

Instantly, their imaginations perceived his form in the clutch of a raging beast.

"Come on," shouted the pudgy man. They grasped bludgeons and rushed valiantly into the darkness. They stumbled from gloom to gloom in a mad rush for their friend's life. The keynote of terror kept clanging in their ears and guided their scrambling feet. Tangled thickets tripped them. Saplings buffeted heroically, and stones turned away. Branches smote their heads so that it appeared as if lightning had flapped its red wings in their faces.

Once, the pudgy man stopped. The unknown was just ahead.

The dim lights of early dawn came charging through the forest. The gray and black of mist and shadow retreated before crimson beams that had advanced to the treetops.

The men came to a stand, waving their heads to glance down the aisles of the wilderness.

"There he is," shouted the pudgy man. The party, rushing forward, came upon the form of the little man, quivering at the foot of a tree. His blood seemed to be turned to salt. From out his wan, white face his eyes shone with a blue light. "Oh, thunderation," he moaned. "Oh, thunderation."

"What!" cried his friends. Their voices shook with anxiety.

"Oh, thunderation," repeated he.

"For the love of Mike, tell us, Billie," cried the pudgy man, "what is the matter."

"Oh, thunderation," wailed the little man. Suddenly he rolled about on the ground and gave vent to a howl that rolled and pealed over the width of the forest. Its tones told of death and fear and unpaid debts. It clamored like a song of forgotten war, and died away to the scream of a maiden. The pleadings of fire-surrounded children mingled with the calls of wave-threatened sailors. Two barbaric tribes clashed together on a sunburnt plain; a score of barekneed clansmen crossed claymores amid gray rocks; a woman saw a lover fall; a dog was stabbed in an alley; a steel knight bit dust with bloody mouth; a savage saw a burning home.

The rescuing party leaned weakly against trees. After the little man had concluded, there was a silence.

Finally, the pudgy man advanced. He struggled with his astonished tongue for a moment. "Do you mean to say, Billie," he said at last, "that all that tangled chaos emanated from you?"

The little man made no reply, but heaved about on the ground, moaning: "Oh, thunderation."

The three men contemplating him suddenly felt themselves swell with wrath. They had been terrorized to no purpose. They had expected to be eaten. They were not. The fact maddened them. The pudgy man voiced the assembly.

"You infernal little jay, get up off'n the ground and come on," he cried. "You make me sick."

"Oh, thunderation," replied the little man.

The three men began to berate him. They turned into a babble of wrath.

"You scared us to death."

"What do you wanta holler that way for?"

"You're a bloomin' nuisance. For heaven's sake, what are you yellin' about?"

The little man staggered to his feet. Anger took hold of him. He waved his arms eloquently.

"That pudding, you fools," he cried.

His companions paused and regarded him.

"Well," said the pudgy man, eventually, "what in blazes did you eat it for then?"

"Well, I didn't know," roared the other, "I didn't know that it was that way."

"You shouldn't have eaten it, anyhow. There was the sin. You shouldn't have eaten it anyway."

"But I didn't know," shouted the little man.

"You should have known," they stormed. "You've made idiots of us. You scared us to death with your hollerin'."

As he reeled toward the camp, they followed him, railing like fishwives.

The little man turned at bay.

"Exaggerated fools," he yelled. "Fools, to apply no salve but moral teaching to a man with the stomachache."

Andrew Digby

(English, 1965–)

Blackberries

Their blackness is too complete,
It hurts the eyes to look:
Tiny clusters of jet,
Constellations of inky beads

Hanging early in the evening
Like black lanterns. Remember:
You stood in shorts before your grandfather's anger,
Fought for handfuls of thorns, broken nests

And a few sour fruit, uselessly
Pelting us with those too hard to eat.
Dizzying negatives, too black
To look at, a suffocating darkness

Which compels you to eat;
And having eaten suffer
The bitter taste that lingers on the tongue.

Sir Charles Sedley

(English, 1639?–1701)

Song

Smooth was the Water, calm the Air,
  The Evening-Sun deprest,
Lawyers dismist the noisie Bar,
  The Labourer at rest,

When *Strephon*, with his charming Fair,
  Cross'd the proud River *Thames*,
And to a Garden did repair,
  To quench their mutual Flames.

The crafty Waiter soon espy'd
  Youth sparkling in her Eyes;
He brought no Ham, nor Neats-tongues dry'd,
  But Cream and Strawberries.

The amorous *Strephon* ask'd the Maid,
  What's whiter than this Cream?
She blush'd, and could not tell, she said:
  Thy Teeth, my pretty Lamb.

What's redder than these Berries are?
  I know not, she reply'd:
Those lips, which I'll no longer spare,
  The burning Shepherd cry'd.

And strait began to hug her:
    This Kiss, my Dear,
Is sweeter far
    Than Strawberries, Cream and Sugar.

William Fahey

(1923–)

Tangerines

Jewels from the gilded land, an El Dorado of orange nuggets.
We found them in the first sharp days of autumn, the fruit-
erer warming his hands at them, heaped in a stall. The skin
thick and fleshy when we peeled it away, like the hunter's bag
in the Schwarz-wald of the Brothers Grimm. The fruit hung
in a yellow webbing. . . .

And the perfume rising on the cold air . . .

William Cowper

(1731–1800)

The Bee and the Pine-apple

A bee allur'd by the perfume
Of a rich pine-apple in bloom,
Found it within a frame inclos'd,
And lick'd the glass that interpos'd.
Blossoms of apricot and peach,
The flow'rs that blow'd within his reach,
Were arrant drugs compar'd with that,
He strove so vainly to get at.
No rose could yield so rare a treat,
Nor jessamine were half so sweet.
The gard'ner saw this much ado,
(The gard'ner was the master too)
And thus he said—Poor restless bee!
I learn philosophy from thee,
I learn how just it is and wise,
To use what Providence supplies,
To leave fine titles, lordships, graces,
Rich pensions, dignities, and places,
Those gifts of a superior kind,
To those for whom they were design'd.
I learn that comfort dwells alone
In that which Heav'n has made our own,
That fools incur no greater pain,
Than pleasure coveted in vain.

Norbert Krapf

(American, 1943–)

Paw Paw

Ungainly sapling
everyone overlooks

leaves clumsy as
an overgrown athlete

in jest they
dub you
"the Hoosier banana."

As a boy I roamed
the hills of Dubois
County for the plump
fruit I found
a miraculous cross
between the yeoman
potato and the
noble banana.

I stood in thickets,
turned your flat
seeds with my tongue,
and sucked the juices
off those magic stones.

'Possums, squirrels,
raccoons and foxes
have the last laugh:

they gobble your
fruit before two-
legged animals
can touch it.

Persimmon

Patron of barren
woods and over-
grown fields

bark pocked
into squares
and rough diamonds

sparsely groomed
with toothless leaves

yet revisited like
a shrine by
almost every
bird and mammal

for the wrinkled
orange fruit
that puckered
my green mouth

but tickled my
ripe stomach
as a pudding.

Jonathan Swift

(1667–1745)

Apples

Come buy my fine wares,
Plumbs, apples, and pears,
A hundred a penny,
In conscience too many:
Come, will you have any?
My children are seven,
I wish them in Heaven;
My husband a sot,
With his pipe and his pot,
Not a farthing will gain them,
And I must maintain them.

Desserts

Charles Dickens

(1812–1870)

From *A Christmas Carol*

There never was such a goose. Bob said he didn't believe there ever was such a goose cooked. Its tenderness and flavor, size and cheapness, were the themes of universal admiration. Eked out by apple-sauce and mashed potatoes, it was a sufficient dinner for the whole family; indeed, as Mrs. Cratchit said with great delight (surveying one small atom of a bone upon the dish), they hadn't ate it all at last! Yet every one had had enough, and the youngest Cratchits in particular, were steeped in sage and onion to the eyebrows! But now the plates being changed by Miss Belinda, Mrs. Cratchit left the room alone—too nervous to bear witnesses—to take the pudding up, and bring it in.

Suppose it should not be done enough! Suppose it should break in turning out! Suppose somebody should have got over the wall of the backyard, and stolen it, while they were merry with the goose—a supposition at which the two young Cratchits became livid! All sorts of horrors were supposed.

Hallo! A great deal of steam! The pudding was out of the copper. A smell like a washing-day! That was the cloth. A smell like an eating-house and a pastrycook's next door to each other, with a laundress's next door to that! That was the pudding! In half a minute Mrs. Cratchit entered—flushed, but smiling proudly—with the pudding, like a speckled cannon-ball, so hard and firm, blazing in half of half a quartern of ignited brandy, and bedight with Christmas holly stuck into the top.

Oh, a wonderful pudding! Bob Cratchit said, and calmly too, that he regarded it as the greatest success achieved by Mrs. Cratchit since their marriage. Mrs. Cratchit said that now the weight was off her mind, she would confess she had her doubts about the quantity of flour. Everybody had something to say about it, but nobody said or thought it was at all a small pudding for a large family. It would have been flat heresy to do so. Any Cratchit would have blushed to hint at such a thing.

At last the dinner was all done, the cloth was cleared, the hearth swept, and the fire made up. The compound in the jug being tasted, and considered perfect, apples and oranges were put upon the table, and a shovel full of chestnuts on the fire. Then all the Cratchit family drew round the hearth, in what Bob Cratchit called a circle, meaning half a one; and at Bob Cratchit's elbow stood the family display of glass. Two tumblers and a custard-cup without a handle.

These held the hot stuff from the jug, however, as well as golden goblets would have done; and Bob served it out with beaming looks, while the chestnuts on the fire sputtered and cracked noisily. Then Bob proposed,—

"A Merry Christmas to us all, my dears. God bless us!"

Giuseppi Tomasi di Lampedusa

(1896–1957)

From *The Leopard*

At the end of the meal appeared a rum jelly. This was the Prince's favorite pudding, and the Princess had been careful to order it early that morning in gratitude for favors granted. It was rather threatening at first sight, shaped like a tower with

bastions and battlements and smooth slippery walls impossible to scale, garrisoned by red and green cherries and pistachio nuts; but into its transparent and quivering flanks a spoon plunged with astounding ease. By the time the amber-colored fortress reached Francesco Paolo, the sixteen-year-old son, who was served last, it consisted only of shattered walls and hunks of wobbly rubble. Exhilarated by the aroma of rum and the delicate flavor of the multicolored garrison, the Prince enjoyed watching the rapid demolishing of the fortress beneath the assault of his family's appetites. One of his glasses was still half full of Marsala. He raised it, glanced around the family, gazed for a second into Concetta's blue eyes, then said, "To the health of our Tancredi." He drained his wine in a single gulp.

—Translated by Archibald Colquhoun

Edmond Rostand

(French, 1868–1918)

From *Cyrano de Bergerac*

ACT II, SCENE IV

Ragueneau, Lise, the Musketeer, Cyrano (sitting, writing at a small table), the poets (dressed in black, their stockings falling down, covered in mud).

*   *   *

SECOND POET *(grabbing a cake)*. What rhymes have you composed recently, Ragueneau? . . .

RAGUENEAU *(to the second poet)*. I have set a recipe in verse.

THIRD POET *(sitting down close to a tray of choux pastries).* Let us hear these verses!

FOURTH POET *(gazing at a brioche which he has taken).* This *brioche* has put its cap on crooked. *(He decapitates it in a second bite.)*

FIRST POET. This gingerbread pursues the starving poet with its almond eyes beneath angelic angelica brows! *(He takes the piece of gingerbread.)*

SECOND POET. We are listening.

THIRD POET *(gently squeezing a cream puff between his fingers).* This pastry is dribbling cream. It is laughing.

SECOND POET *(whilst biting the large pastry lyre).* This is the first time I've ever truly been fed by *lyricism!*

RAGUENEAU *(ready to recite, coughs, steadies his cap and assumes a pose).* A recipe in verse . . .

*   *   *

RAGUENEAU. How to make *tartelettes amandines.*

> Beat several eggs until
> They froth and foam;
> Into this *mousse*, blend
> Choicest citron juice
> And the finest almond
> Milk that you can use.
>
> Take light puff paste and place
> In tartlet cases;
> Let nimble fingers glaze
> With brandied apricot
> Each edge. Then drip,
> Drop by tiny droplet,

Your cream into these wells.
Well, to an oven take 'em,
And in the oven bake 'em,
Till golden as gallants,
In merry troupes they're seen:
Your *tartelettes amandines*!

THE POETS *(their mouths full)*. Exquisite! Delicious!

A POET *(choking)*. Humph!

(They move to the back of the stage, eating. Cyrano, who has been looking on, walks towards Ragueneau.)

CYRANO. Can't you see how your soothing voice has lulled them into stuffing themselves?

RAGUENEAU *(in a low voice, smiling)*. Yes, I can see . . . but I don't watch them in case I put them off; for reciting my verses like this makes me doubly happy: I can satisfy my own little foible, whilst letting those who are hungry eat!

—*Translated by Judith Palmer*

William Makepeace Thackeray

(English, 1811–1863)

From *A Little Dinner at Trimmins's*

[Fubsby's was] a shop into which [Fitzroy Trimmins] had often cast a glance of approbation as he passed; for there are not only the most wonderful and delicious cakes and confections in the window, but at the counter there are almost sure to be three or four of the prettiest women in the whole of this world, with little darling caps of the last French make, with beautiful wavy hair, and the neatest possible waists and aprons.

Yes, there they sit; and others, perhaps, besides Fitz have cast a sheep's-eye through those enormous plate-glass window panes. I suppose it is the fact of perpetually living among such a quantity of good things that makes those young ladies so beautiful. They come into the place, let us say, like ordinary people, and gradually grow handsomer and handsomer, until they grow out into the perfect angels you see. It can't be otherwise: if you and I, my dear fellow, were to have a course of that place, we should become beautiful too. They live in an atmosphere of the most delicious pine-apples, blanc-manges, creams (some whipt, and some so good that of course they don't want whipping), jellies, tipsy-cakes, cherry-brandy— one hundred thousand sweet and lovely things. Look at the preserved fruits, look at the golden ginger, the outspreading ananas, the darling little rogues of China oranges, ranged in the gleaming crystal cylinders. *Mon Dieu!* Look at the strawberries in the leaves. Each of them is as large nearly as a lady's reticule, and looks as if it had been brought up in a nursery to itself. One of those strawberries is a meal for those young ladies behind the counter: they nibble off a little from the side; and if they are very hungry, which can scarcely ever happen, they are allowed to go to the crystal canisters and take out a rout-cake or macaroon. In the evening they sit and tell each other little riddles out of the bonbons; and when they wish to amuse themselves, they read the most delightful remarks, in the French language, about Love, and Cupid, and Beauty, before they place them inside the crackers. They always are writing down good things into Mr. Fubsby's ledgers. It must be a perfect feast to read them. Talk of the Garden of Eden! I believe it was nothing to Mr. Fubsby's house; and I have no doubt that after those young ladies have been there a certain time, they get to such a pitch of loveliness at last that they become complete angels, with wings sprouting out of their lovely shoulders, when (after giving just a preparatory balance or two) they fly up to the counter and perch there for a minute, hop down again, and affectionately kiss the other young ladies, and say, "Good-bye, dears! We shall meet again *là haut.*"

Osip Mandelstam

(Russian, 1891–1938)

"Ice cream!" Sun. Light airy cakes.

"Ice cream!" Sun. Light airy cakes.
A clear glass tumbler of water, icy cold.
Our dreams take flight, into a chocolate world
Of rosy dawns on milky Alpine peaks.

But as the teaspoon tinkles, it is sweet
In some little summerhouse amid the dry acacias,
To gaze, then take gratefully from tearoom Graces,
Little whorled cups with crumbly things to eat . . .

The street-organ's playmate suddenly appears,
The ice-cream cart, with multicolored covering—
The chest is full of lovely frozen things,
With greedy attentiveness, a small boy peers.

And what will he choose? The gods themselves can't say:
A diamond tart? A wafer filled with cream?
But under his slender spoon the divine ice,
Glittering in the sun, will soon melt away.

—Translated by Robert Tracy

Marcel Proust

(French, 1871–1922)

From *Swann's Way*

Many years had elapsed during which nothing of Combray, save what was comprised in the theatre and the drama of my going to bed there, had any existence for me, when one day in winter, as I came home, my mother, seeing that I was cold, offered me some tea, a thing I did not ordinarily take. I declined at first, and then, for no particular reason, changed my mind. She sent out for one of those short, plump little cakes called "petites madeleines," which look as though they had been moulded in the fluted scallop of a pilgrim's shell. And soon, mechanically, weary after a dull day with the prospect of a depressing morrow, I raised to my lips a spoonful of the tea in which I had soaked a morsel of the cake. No sooner had the warm liquid, and the crumbs with it, touched my palate than a shudder ran through my whole body, and I stopped, intent upon the extraordinary changes that were taking place. An exquisite pleasure had invaded my senses, but individual, detached, with no suggestion of its origin. And at once the vicissitudes of life had become indifferent to me, its disasters innocuous, its brevity illusory—this new sensation having had on me the effect which love has of filling me with a precious essence; or rather this essence was not in me, it was myself. I had ceased now to feel mediocre, accidental, mortal. Whence could it have come to me, this all-powerful joy? I was conscious that it was connected with the taste of tea and cake, but that it infinitely transcended those savours, could not, indeed, be of the same nature as theirs. Whence did it come? What did it signify? How could I seize upon and define it?

* * *

And suddenly the memory returns. The taste was that of the little crumb of madeleine which on Sunday mornings at Combray (because on those mornings I did not go out before church-time), when I went to say good day to her in her bedroom, my aunt Léonie used to give me, dipping it first in her own cup of real or of lime-flower tea. The sight of the little madeleine had recalled nothing to my mind before I tasted it; perhaps because I had so often seen such things in the interval, without tasting them, on the trays in pastry-cooks' windows, that their image had dissociated itself from those Combray days to take its place among others more recent; perhaps because of those memories, so long abandoned and put out of mind, nothing now survived, everything was scattered; the forms of things, including that of the little scallop-shell of pastry, so richly sensual under its severe, religious folds, were either obliterated or had been so long dormant as to have lost the power of expansion which would have allowed them to resume their place in my consciousness. But when from a long-distant past nothing subsists, after the people are dead, after the things are broken and scattered, still, alone, more fragile, but with more vitality, more unsubstantial, more persistent, more faithful, the smell and taste of things remain poised a long time, like souls, ready to remind us, waiting and hoping for their moment, amid the ruins of all the rest; and bear unfaltering, in the tiny and almost impalpable drop of their essence, the vast structure of recollection.

—*Translated by C. K. Scott Moncrieff and Terence Kilmartin*

Gustave Flaubert

(French,1821–1880)

From *Madame Bovary*

It was under the cart shed that the table had been laid. On it were four sirloin roasts, six chickens fricasseed, a casserole of veal, three legs of mutton, and in the center a beautiful suckling pig flanked by four fresh-casing sausages flavored with sorrel. At the corners were carafes of brandy. The bottles of sweet cider swelled with thick foam around the corks, and all the glasses, in anticipation, had been filled to the brim with wine. Large platters of yellow cream, that trembled at the slightest jarring of the table, were brought forward, their smooth surface decorated with the newlyweds' initials in arabesques of spun sugar. A pastry chef had been found at Yvetot for the pies and sweets. Since this was his début in the region he took particular care with everything and himself brought in for dessert a tiered extravaganza which elicited cries of astonishment. First, at the base was a square of blue cardboard shaped like a porticoed temple, ringed round by colonnades and stucco statuettes, the niches set with constellations of gold paper stars; then, on the second level was a dungeon made of Savoy cake surrounded by delicate fortifications built of angelica, almonds, raisins and quartered oranges; finally, on the topmost layer, which was a green rocky meadow with jam lakes and nutshell boats, one could see a little Cupid balancing in a chocolate swing supported by poles terminating in two natural rose buds, for knobs, at the very peak.

Guy de Maupassant

(French, 1850–1893)

The Cake

Let us say that her name was Madame Anserre so as not to reveal her real name.

She was one of those Parisian comets which leave, as it were, a trail of fire behind them. She wrote verses and novels; she had a poetic heart, and was rarely beautiful. She opened her doors to very few—only to exceptional people, those who are commonly described as princes of something or other.

To be a visitor at her house constituted a claim, a genuine claim to intellect: at least this was the estimate set on her invitations.

Her husband played the part of an obscure satellite. To be the husband of a comet is not an easy thing. This husband had, however, an original idea, that of creating a State within a State, of possessing a merit of his own, a merit of the second order, it is true; but he did, in fact, in this fashion, on the days when his wife held receptions, hold receptions also on his own account. He had his special set who appreciated him, listened to him, and bestowed on him more attention than they did on his brilliant partner.

He had devoted himself to agriculture—to agriculture in the Chamber. There are in the same way generals in the Chamber—those who are born, who live, and who die, on the round leather chairs of the War Office, are all of this sort, are they not? Sailors in the Chamber,—viz., in the Admiralty,—colonizers in the Chamber, etc., etc. So he had studied agriculture, had studied it deeply, indeed, in its relations to the other sciences, to political economy, to the Fine Arts—we dress up the Fine Arts with every kind of science, and we even call the horrible railway bridges "works of art." At length he reached the point when it was said of him: "He is a man of ability." He was quoted in the technical reviews; his wife had succeeded in getting him appointed a member of a committee at the Ministry of Agriculture.

This latest glory was quite sufficient for him.

Under the pretext of diminishing the expenses, he sent out invitations to his friends for the day when his wife received hers, so that they associated together, or rather did not—they formed two distinct groups. Madame, with her escort of artists, academicians, and ministers, occupied a kind of gallery, furnished and decorated in the style of the Empire. Monsieur generally withdrew with his agriculturists into a smaller portion of the house used as a smoking-room and ironically described by Madame Anserre as the Salon of Agriculture.

The two camps were clearly separate. Monsieur, without jealousy, moreover, sometimes penetrated into the Academy, and cordial hand-shakings were exchanged; but the Academy entertained infinite contempt for the Salon of Agriculture, and it was rarely that one of the princes of science, of thought, or of anything else, mingled with the agriculturists.

These receptions occasioned little expense—a cup of tea, a cake, that was all. Monsieur, at an earlier period, had claimed two cakes, one for the Academy, and one for the agriculturists, but Madame having rightly suggested that this way of acting seemed to indicate two camps, two receptions, two parties, Monsieur did not press the matter, so that they used only one cake, of which Madame Anserre did the honors at the Academy, and which then passed into the Salon de Agriculture.

Now, this cake was soon, for the Academy, a subject of observation well calculated to arouse curiosity. Madame Anserre never cut it herself. That function always fell to the lot of one or other of the illustrious guests. The particular duty, which was supposed to carry with it honorable distinction, was performed by each person for a pretty long period, in one case for three months, scarcely ever for more; and it was noticed that the privilege of "cutting the cake" carried with it a heap of other marks of superiority—a sort of royalty, or rather very accentuated viceroyalty.

The reigning cutter spoke in a haughty tone, with an air of marked command; and all the favors of the mistress of the house were for him alone.

These happy individuals were in moments of intimacy described in hushed tones behind doors as the "favorites of the cake," and every change of favorite introduced into the Academy a sort of revolution. The knife was a scepter, the pastry an emblem; the chosen ones were congratulated. The agriculturists never cut the cake. Monsieur himself was always excluded, although he ate his share.

The cake was cut in succession by poets, by painters, and by novelists. A great musician had the privilege of measuring the portions of the cake for some time; an ambassador succeeded him. Sometimes a man less well known, but elegant and sought after, one of those who are called according to the different epochs, "true gentleman," or "perfect knight," or "dandy," or something else, seated himself, in his turn, before the symbolic cake. Each of them, during this ephemeral reign, exhibited greater consideration toward the husband; then, when the hour of his fall had arrived, he passed on the knife toward the other, and mingled once more with the crowd of followers and admirers of the "beautiful Madame Anserre."

This state of things lasted a long time; but comets do not always shine with the same brilliance. Everything gets worn out in society. One would have said that gradually the eagerness of the cutters grew feebler; they seemed to hesitate at times when the tray was held out to them; this office, once so much coveted, became less and less desired. It was retained for a shorter time; they appeared to be less proud of it.

Madame Anserre was prodigal of smiles and civilities. Alas! no one was found any longer to cut it voluntarily. The newcomers seemed to decline the honor. The "old favorites" reappeared one by one like dethroned princes who have been replaced for a brief spell in power. Then, the chosen ones became few, very few. For a month (oh, prodigy!) M. Anserre cut open the cake; then he looked as if he were getting tired of it; and one evening Madame Anserre, the beautiful Madame Anserre, was seen cutting it herself. But this appeared to be very wearisome to her, and, next day, she urged one of her guests so strongly to do it that he did not dare to refuse.

The symbol was too well known, however; the guests stared at one another with scared, anxious faces. To cut the cake was nothing, but the privileges to which this favor had always given a claim now frightened people; therefore, the moment the dish made its appearance the academicians rushed pellmell into the Salon of Agriculture, as if to shelter themselves behind the husband, who was perpetually smiling. And when Madame Anserre, in a state of anxiety, presented herself at the door with a cake in one hand and the knife in the other, they all seemed to form a circle around her husband as if to appeal to him for protection.

Some years more passed. Nobody cut the cake now; but yielding to an old inveterate habit, the lady who had always been gallantly called "the beautiful Madame Anserre" looked out each evening for some devotee to take the knife, and each time the same movement took place around her, a general flight, skillfully arranged and full of combined maneuvers that showed great cleverness, in order to avoid the offer that was rising to her lips.

But, one evening, a young man presented himself at her reception—an innocent, unsophisticated youth. He knew nothing about the mystery of the cake; accordingly, when it appeared, and when all the rest ran away, when Madame Anserre took from the manservant's hands the dish and the pastry, he remained quietly by her side.

She thought that perhaps he knew about the matter; she smiled, and in a tone which showed some emotion, said:

"Will you be kind enough, dear Monsieur, to cut this cake?"

He displayed the utmost readiness, and took off his gloves, flattered at such an honor being conferred on him.

"Oh, to be sure, Madame, with the greatest pleasure."

Some distance away in the corner of the gallery, in the frame of the door which led into the Salon of the Agriculturists, faces which expressed utter amazement were staring at him. Then, when the spectators saw the newcomer cutting without any hesitation, they quickly came forward.

An old poet jocosely slapped the neophyte on the shoulder.

"Bravo, young man!" he whispered in his ear.

The others gazed at him with curiosity. Even the husband appeared to be surprised. As for the young man, he was astonished at the consideration which they suddenly seemed to show toward him; above all, he failed to comprehend the marked attentions, the manifest favor, and the species of mute gratitude which the mistress of the house bestowed on him.

It appears, however, that he eventually found out.

At what moment, in what place, was the revelation made to him? Nobody could tell; but, when he again presented himself at the reception, he had a preoccupied air, almost a shamefaced look, and he cast around him a glance of uneasiness.

The bell rang for tea. The manservant appeared. Madame Anserre, with a smile, seized the dish, casting a look about her for her young friend; but he had fled so precipitately that no trace of him could be seen any longer. Then, she went looking everywhere for him, and ere long she discovered him in the Salon of the Agriculturists. With his arm locked in that of the husband, he was consulting that gentleman as to the means employed for destroying phylloxera.

"My dear Monsieur," she said to him, "will you be so kind as to cut this cake for me?"

He reddened to the roots of his hair, and hanging down his head, stammered out some excuses. Thereupon M. Anserre took pity on him, and turning toward his wife, said:

"My dear, you might have the goodness not to disturb us.

We are talking about agriculture. So get your cake cut by Baptiste."

And since that day nobody has ever cut Madame Anserre's cake.

Ludwig Bemelmans

(American, 1898–1962)

From "Pêche Melba"

. . . I knew all the nuns now and they had all faces of reptiles, of ugly birds—of rodents to me—and ugly hands with awful scaly gray nails like the claws of a hawk.

The first thing upon rising was to lie prone and kiss the floor, and when I refused to do this I was taken to the little Mother Superior. She fixed me with her bird stare and screeched at me. She said she demanded absolute obedience without exception, and that I now prostrate myself before her and kiss the floor. She sat in a chair in front of me and she pointed at the floor with a bony finger and she yelled, "Instantly, and here, you get down and do as I tell you." Her mouth worked with the lips pressed together. She looked at me, I looked at her and when I said that never, never would I get down on the floor, and certainly never on this dirty floor, she came forward out of her chair, and smacked me in one practiced motion—left-right left-right—with both sides of her hand.

I jumped at her and grabbed her by the throat above the white stiff collar of her habit.

At this the Sisters almost fainted. Two tried to pull me

off, the others cried out and reached in the air and for their hearts, and crossed themselves and yammered. I let go of her. She was paler than usual and her thin mouth worked again, and now one of the nuns was able to speak and she said that I had committed a mortal sin. She was a vulgar person from around the neighborhood, judging by the way she spoke. She had pronounced the word *péché*, which is for sin, like *pêche*, which is for peach, and I said:

"Yes, pêche Melba, tarte aux pêches, compote of peaches, peach ice cream, vanilla ice cream, chocolate ice cream, chocolate soufflé, tarte aux pommes, and tarte aux cerises—damn you all, old skins of cows and to hell with you, let yourself be enculé par les Cosaques."

"Out with her, out with her, out of my sight with this creature," screeched the Monster Mother Superior.

They all were in a state of terrible excitement and the priest was called. He came limping in and blinked also like a half-dead old bird.

"What happened?"

He was told the things he could be told.

"That is the one—there."

"Yes, that is the one," they said, and he looked at me, but I think he knew that he had better not touch me and he said:

"Shame—shame on you—"

He gave a long lecture and said that my parents would be informed and that it was a disgrace that a child of such family as mine behaved as I did, and to put me in a room by myself so that I would not spoil the others—the good children. And so I found myself separated from the group and I went to bed without supper, which was no particular punishment here as the food stank, like everything, of poverty, and there never was any dessert—and that is why I had read off the litany of peaches Melba, and pie and soufflés, for certainly the God who let peaches and plums grow, did not want them not to be eaten.

Robert Graves

(English, 1895–1985)

Treacle Tart

The news travelled from group to group along the platform of
Victoria Station, impressing our parents and kid-sisters almost as much as ourselves. A lord was coming to our prep
school. A real lord. A new boy, only eight years old. Youngest son of the Duke of Downshire. A new boy, yet a lord.
Lord Julius Bloodstock. Same name! Crikey!

Excitement strong enough to check the rebellious tears of
home-lovers, and make our last good-byes all but casual.
None of us having had any contact with the peerage, it was
argued by some, as we settled in our reserved Pullman car-
riage, that on the analogy of policemen there couldn't be boy-
lords. However, Mr. Lees, the Latin Master (declined: *Lees,
Lees, Lem, Lei, Lei, Lee*) confirmed the report. The lord was
being driven to school that morning in the ducal Rolls-Royce.
Crikey, again! *Cricko, Crickere, Crikey, Crictum!*

Should we be expected to call him "your Grace," or
"Sire," or something? Would he keep a coronet in his tuck-
box? Would the masters dare cane him if he broke school
rules or didn't know his prep?

Billington Secundus told us that his father (the famous
Q.C.*) had called Thos a "tuft-hunting toad-eater," as meaning that he was awfully proud of knowing important people,
such as bishops and Q.C.s and lords, To this Mr. Lees turned
a deaf ear, though making ready to crack down on any fur-

---

*Queen's Counsel, a top-ranking trial lawyer appointed by the Queen.

ther disrespectful remarks about the Rev. Thomas Pearce, our Headmaster. None came. Most of us were scared stiff of Thos; besides, everyone but Billington Secundus considered pride in knowing important people an innocent enough emotion.

Presently Mr. Lees folded his newspaper and said: "Bloodstock, as you will learn to call him, is a perfectly normal little chap, though he happens to have been born into the purple—if anyone present catches the allusion. Accord him neither kisses nor cuffs (*nec oscula, nec verbera*, both neuter) and all will be well. By the way, this is to be his first experience of school life. The Duke has hitherto kept him at the Castle under private tutors."

At the Castle, under private tutors! Crikey! *Crikey, Crikius, Crikissime!*

We arrived at the Cedars just in time for school dinner. Thos, rather self-consciously, led a small, pale, fair-haired boy into the dining-hall, and showed him his seat at the end of the table among the other nine new-comers. "This is Lord Julius Bloodstock, boys," he boomed. "You will just call him Bloodstock. No titles or other honorifics here."

"Then I prefer to be called Julius." His first memorable words.

"We happen to use only surnames at Brown Friars," chuckled Thos; then he said Grace.

None of Julius's table-mates called him anything at all, to begin with, being either too miserable or too shy even to say "Pass the salt, please." But after the soup, and half-way through the shepherd's pie (for once not made of left-overs) Billington Tertius, to win a bet, leant boldly across the table and asked: "Lord, why didn't you come by train, same as the rest of us?"

Julius did not answer at first, but when his neighbours nudged him, he said: "The name is Julius, and my father was afraid of finding newspaper photographers on the platform. They can be such a nuisance. Two of them were waiting for us at the school gates, and my father sent the chauffeur to smash both their cameras."

This information had hardly sunk in before the third course appeared: treacle tart. Today was Monday: onion soup, shepherd's pie and carrots, treacle tart. Always had been. Even when Mr. Lees-Lees-Lem had been a boy here and won top scholarship to Winchester. "Treacle. From the Greek *theriace*, though the Greeks did not, of course . . ." With this, Mr. Lees, who sat at the very end of the table, religiously eating treacle tart, looked up to see whether anyone were listening; and noticed that Julius had pushed away his plate, leaving the oblong of tough burned pastry untouched.

"Eat it, boy!" said Mr. Lees. "Not allowed to leave anything here for Mr. Good Manners. School rule."

"I never eat treacle tart," explained Julius with a little sigh.

"You are expected to address me as 'sir,'" said Mr. Lees.

Julius seemed surprised. "I thought we didn't use titles here, or other honorifics," he said, "but only surnames?"

"Call me 'sir,'" insisted Mr. Lees, not quite certain whether this were innocence or impertinence.

"Sir," said Julius, shrugging faintly.

"Eat your tart," snapped Mr. Lees.

"But I never eat treacle tart—sir!"

"It's my duty to see that you do so, every Monday."

Julius smiled. "What a queer duty!" he said incredulously.

Titters, cranings of necks. Then Thos called jovially down the table: "Well, Lees, what's the news from your end? Are the summer holidays reported to have been wearisomely long?"

"No, Headmaster. But I cannot persuade an impertinent boy to sample our traditional treacle tart."

"Send him up here," said Thos in his most portentous voice. "Send him up here, plate and all! Oliver Twist asking for less, eh?"

When Thos recognized Julius, his face changed and he swallowed a couple of times, but having apparently lectured the staff on making not the least difference between duke's

son and shopkeeper's son, he had to put his foot down. "My
dear boy," he said, "let me see you eat that excellent piece of
food without further demur; and no nonsense."

"I never eat treacle tart, Headmaster."

Thos started as though he had been struck in the face. He
said slowly: "You mean perhaps: 'I have lost my appetite,
sir.' Very well, but your appetite will return at supper time,
you mark my words—and so will the treacle tart."

The sycophantic laughter which greeted this prime
Thossism surprised Julius but did not shake his poise. Walking to the buttery-table, he laid down the plate, turned on his
heel, and walked calmly back to his seat.

Thos at once rose and said Grace in a challenging voice.

"Cocky ass, I'd like to punch his lordly head for him,"
growled Billington Secundus later that afternoon.

"You'd have to punch mine first," I said. "He's a . . . the
thing we did in Gray's *Elegy*—a village Hampden. Standing
up to Lees and Thos in mute inglorious protest against that
foul treacle tart."

"You're a tuft-hunting toad-eater."

"I may be. But I'd rather eat toads than Thos's treacle
tart."

A bell rang for supper, or high tea. The rule was that
tuckbox cakes were put under Matron's charge and distributed among all fifty of us while they lasted. "Democ-
racy," Thos called it (I can't think why); and the Matron, to
cheer up the always dismal first evening, had set the largest
cake she could find on the table: Julius's. Straight from the
ducal kitchens, plastered with crystallized fruit, sugar icing
and marzipan, stuffed with raisins, cherries and nuts.

"You will get your slice, my dear, when you have eaten
your treacle tart," Matron gently reminded Julius. "*Noblesse
oblige.*"

"I never eat treacle tart, Matron."

It must have been hard for him to see his cake devoured
by strangers before his eyes, but he made no protest; just
sipped a little tea and went supperless to bed. In the dor-

mitory he told a ghost story, which is still, I hear, current in
the school after all these years: about a Mr. Gracie (why
"Gracie"?) who heard hollow groans in the night, rose to
investigate and was grasped from behind by an invisible
hand. He found that his braces had caught on the door knob;
and, after other harrowing adventures, traced the groans to
the bathroom, where Mrs. Gracie . . .

Lights out! Sleep. Bells for getting up; for prayers; for
breakfast.

"I never eat treacle tart." So Julius had no breakfast, but
we pocketed slices of bread and potted meat (Tuesday) to slip
him in the playground afterwards. The school porter inter-
vened. His orders were to see that the young gentleman had
no food given him.

Bell: Latin. Bell: Maths. Bell: long break. Bell: Scripture.
Bell: wash hands for dinner.

"I never eat treacle tart," said Julius, as a sort of response
to Thos's Grace; and this time fainted.

Thos sent a long urgent telegram to the Duke, explaining
his predicament: school rule, discipline, couldn't make excep-
tions, and so forth.

The Duke wired back non-committally: "Quite so. Stop.
The lad never eats treacle tart. Stop. Regards. Downshire."

Matron took Julius to the sickroom, where he was allowed
milk and soup, but no solid food unless he chose to call for
treacle tart. He remained firm and polite until the end, which
came two days later, after a further exchange of telegrams.

We were playing kick-about near the Masters' Wing,
when the Rolls-Royce pulled up. Presently Julius, in overcoat
and bowler hat, descended the front steps, followed by the
school porter carrying his tuck-box, football boots and hand-
bag. Billington Secundus, now converted to the popular view,
led our three cheers, which Julius acknowledged with a gracious tilt of his bowler. The car purred off; and thereupon, in
token of our admiration for Julius, we all swore to strike
against treacle tart the very next Monday, and none of us eat
a single morsel, even if we liked it, which some of us did!

When it came to the point, of course, the boys sitting close to Thos took fright and ratted, one after the other. Even Billington Secundus and I, not being peers' sons or even village Hampdens, regretfully conformed.

From *Punch* (circa 1860)

TRIFLE

Air—"The Meeting of the Waters"

There's not in the wide world so tempting a sweet
As that Trifle where custard and macaroons meet;
Oh! the latest sweet tooth from my head must depart
Ere the taste of that Trifle shall not win my heart.

Yet it is not the sugar that's thrown in between
Nor the peel of the lemon so candied and green;
'Tis not the rich cream that's whipp'd up by a mill:
Oh, no! it is something more exquisite still.

'Tis that nice macaroons in the dish I have laid,
Of which a delicious foundation is made;
And you'll find how the last will in flavor improve.
When soak'd with the wine that you pour in above.

Sweet *plateau* of Trifle! how great is my zest
For thee, when spread o'er with the jam I love best;
When the cream white of eggs—to be over thee thrown.
With a whisk kept on purpose—is mingled in one!

Vincent Clemente

(American, 1932–)

The Lobstermen's Restaurant in Jamesport

I wonder what it's like
at 4 in the morning, the lobstermen,
only them and the three German sisters
who cook in the back. Smell of coffee
morning fries eggs just right
they never stick to the pan.
But I would be out of place, an intruder
though I love the sea with a love
close to passion. But these men
know it better, out there alone
I can imagine how they talk to it
though I don't know what they say.

I break no rule of camaraderie
it's well into the afternoon,
they're long into port and I only stop
for the strawberry rhubarb pie
and always the same question
from one of the three: **How does it taste
going down?** And always the same reply:
Better it couldn't be.
And nothing could be closer to the truth.
I'm sure it's in the lard, the lard
they mix in with the dough
and the cinnamon to appease the bitter rhubarb.
Better it couldn't be.

How pleased they are to get it out of me
a stranger passing through from Stony Brook
but coming into strangeness:
might as well be Hawthorne's Salem
the sea has such a presence here,
like an old uncle's firm hand from behind
on the fin of your shoulder, so firm
it almost hurts.
But I pay my way. I always have.
True, no sea yarns, no talk of currents
and tides. True, I can't repair a net
mend a lobster pot. But I know pie,
especially strawberry rhubarb, and this
so pleases them it makes me one like them.
We share a truth together: about the lard and the cinnamon,
as sure as the seasons . . . as sure as the tides.

William Goyen

(American, 1915–)

Tapioca Surprise

Before the rainstorm broke on the little town that unusual
autumn afternoon, the whole world seemed to turn apple
green, as if it were sick, and not a thing stirred, no leaf or
limb or anything. And then, in the green stillness that was
like the sick town holding its breath, there descended upon
the telephone wires in front of Opal Ducharm's house a flock
of blackbirds to sit all in a quiet row there. "Blackbirds at
even', misery and grievin'," Mrs. Ducharm recited at her

window, where she happened to be to watch Mrs. Sangley across the street. Rentha Sangley had just appeared on her porch with her head and face swaddled in an ostentatious bandage, so that she looked like some nun, and she was sweeping the leaves in the still moment before the storm would break. The whole town seemed to be waiting, except Rentha Sangley, who was showing off her bandage to the neighborhood to try to get sympathy.

And then it turned very dark and a little wind started and Mrs. Ducharm saw Rentha Sangley go in her house. The blackbirds flurried and broke their pattern, and they left the telephone wire swinging. The leaves, some of them big and tough as hides, began rolling and flying; and one leaf rushed in through the door Mrs. Opal Ducharm opened, and lay still on her rug. She slammed the door and stared at the leaf and recited, sensitive to omens, "Leaf on the floor, trouble galore . . ." and picked up the leaf.

Now big raindrops slapped on the sidewalks, and right away there was a steady colorless pour. This meant, without one doubt, that The Paradisers—of which Opal Ducharm was President—could not meet on the high school football field to practice their special number. And that they would have to miss another time of practicing for when the Grand Paradiser, Hester Shrift, would come next week to review the performance of their Fife and Drum Corps that was so renowned throughout the very state . . . and because of her, since she had organized and trained Paradisers all over the country. "You blackbirds, you leaf. This is what you were telling me, and maybe even more," Opal Ducharm said, going right to her phone. She did have a feeling of everything all wrong and ominous, the way she sometimes did.

She tried her phone again. No, it still would not work! But thank goodness Maudie Rickett had called in time—she was the last to get through before the phone had gone deaf on the other end, when the sky had first begun to gather and threaten. "Maudie," Opal had said, "We'll all come on, in spite of if it rains, to my house and see what we can drum up—socially. It's necessary to the morale of the organization to *assemble*—in *some* way—despite *natural* interferences. You call your list and tell it of the change." And then she had started calling her list—for even the President had a list— when of all things this deafness smote the other end of her phone. She couldn't get a person to answer, no one said a thing. Now how could that be? Then she tried, hung up and tried again, but she could never get anyone, not even Central.

Of all times to have this unusual thing happen to the phone! She would just have to run across to Rentha Sangley's and use her phone. This would also be an excellent chance to find out the meaning of her big bandage, what kind of accident or trouble had beset her *this* time. She ran through rain and flying leaves and knocked on Rentha Sangley's door, using not her knuckles but the special knocker that was a woodpecker carved by Mr. Sangley before he passed.

Rentha Sangley appeared. It seemed her eyes were the only unbandaged thing left upon her face. "I saw your bandage from my window, and *what* happened to you, you poor thing?" But before Mrs. Sangley could get a word out edgewise through the wrappings, Opal Ducharm put first things first and said, "Rentha, honey, could I use your phone in an emergency?"

"It was a little cyst," Rentha said, showing Opal the phone. "I could have had bloodpoison or a cancer, and lucky to have neither." She walked painfully but proudly under the burden of the bandage, almost as if she were wearing a new big hat. "Dr. Post cut it out yesterday, using a little chloroform on me."

But Opal Ducharm already had Central on the phone and she was explaining the crazy condition of her phone—which was more serious than any cyst cut out. "I'll run right home, honey," she said to the telephone operator, whom she knew personally. "I'm across the street at Rentha Sangley's and you try ringing me at home. This is an emergency."

"I do hope you'll be healed up soon, Rentha," Opal commiserated, and went for the door. "I have to hurry now to my phone."

"Oh I'll be all right," she said, weakly and with a pained face. And then she bellowed towards the kitchen, "Grandma Sangley you stay out of my hard sauce!"

"How is Grandma Sangley?" Opal Ducharm asked, opening the door.

"Into everything. And me encumbered like this . . ."

But Opal was already running down the steps and out into the rain. I just hope all the ladies will know not to go to the football field but to come to my house, she said to herself, running.

As she opened her door she heard the thrilling sound of her phone ringing. This must be the operator. She ran and answered, but there was nothing. Opal Ducharm said hello again. Still no response from the other end. Yet there was the feeling of somebody there, like somebody hiding in a house and not answering your call. What a kind of a phone to have! she declared. And today of all days. Then she said into the phone:

"Now honey, don't you say a word because I can't hear you, you'll be just wasting your sweet breath. You may be that little operator I just talked to over at Rentha Sangley's phone but I can't tell, I mean how could I?; and you may be a Paradiser and if you are, then this phone is broken on your end, I don't know why, but just listen to me, this is for *you*. This is Opal Ducharm, President of the Paradisers, Unit No. 22, as you know, and since it's just pouring down bullfrogs, as you *know*, we cannot practice for our special performance for the Grand Paradiser Hester Shrift at the high school football field but will convene at my house for a get-together instead. Don't talk, don't talk! I can hear your little clicking but don't try to talk, honey, because I can't hear you. Just listen to me. We have to *postpone* because of this downpour. Just come on straight to my house instead of to the football field. *And call your list.* Do you hear? *Call your list* and tell it of the change." She waited, but there was not a sound, not even the little clicking, and so she banged down the receiver and was so unnerved she wanted to cry. But the phone rang again, and again there was no sound. She went through her speech again. This happened over and over, and each time she told again the story of the meeting at her house until she was hoarse. I just hope some word has got through to the Paradisers, she said.

To calm herself and to forget her anxiety, she stood at the door and called Sister, her sweet cat. Sister arrived miraculously, the way she always did, out of silence and nowhere, tail high in the air, and brushing against everything, dawdling to torment Opal. She seized her and squeezed her harder than she meant, until Sister's claws came out of her; and then she kissed Sister's purple ears. She sat down with her and felt a claw in her thigh. "Why sweet Sister," she said, "you act like you despise me." And then she spoke a long whispered confidence to her and felt the claw loosen. Opal was hungry. But she would wait for the Tapioca. Still, at this moment, she did not know which she loved more: Tapioca or Sister.

And then it was four o'clock and time for the meeting— and rain rain rain.

But the usually expert machinery of the list-calling did not work so smoothly and everyone was confused. There were some women at the football field, drenched in the rain, and some no place at all, so far as the callers could make out, for no one answered any place that was called. The result was only a fragment of Paradisers at Opal Ducharm's house, twelve women out of twenty-eight . . . two lonely squads. "We'll just have a little social," Opal Ducharm said, trying to make the most of a bad situation—which was one of the tenets of the Paradisers—for they had a whole philosophy of life; they did not just blow fife and beat drum. "Anyway I *feel* like a relaxin' social," Opal said. "But one word," she added. "Be sure to get your dresses in shape. We will all, of course, wear our white formals. With white corsages. This must, as you know, be perfect for the Grand Paradiser."

The ladies all sat around talking about their troubles and afflictions, the way they loved to do. Opal Ducharm went to her kitchen and started preparing refreshments, which was this time Tapioca. She could hear Moselle Lessups telling about her dentist, Dr. Gore, who was all the scandal in the town because he had been discovered practicing without a license. "He *knows* his profession," she was declaring, "and I don't care *what* they say about his certificate, whether it's forged or not. He can tell you what every tooth in your head is up to. And in a fascinatin' way. And holds a little mirror up so you can see his work in progress. Some people don't like to see, just want to close their eyes till it's all over. But if you *know*, it helps, I think.

"'You see, Mrs. Lessups,' Dr. Gore showed me in the little tooth mirror, 'a big molar is pushin some little ones away from it. It found the vacancy left by the tooth you had pulled out and it has tried to lean over into this vacant place. Do you understand?' he says. 'Yes,' I said . . . 'but . . .' 'We can't have that big old molar doin this to all those other little teeth,' he says, 'can we?' with such a tenderness and real interest and affection for the teeth. 'But what will we do?' I says. 'Pull it right out,' he says. 'It's no good to you,' he says, just as though he suddenly despised my big molar. 'It's just crowdin all those other smaller ones and jammin them all together in too little a space.' 'Well,' I says, 'Dr. Gore, I don't want all my good teeth pushed to the front like old Boney Vinson's down at the Station!' I says and laughed. 'But use deadening because you know how nervous I am.'"

The ladies listened and wagged their heads.

Then Paradiser Clover Sugrew gave one of her imitations that quietened the room down for a few minutes until Mrs. Mack McCutcheon burst up from her chair over everybody and went off into one of her exaggerations that nobody could stop—you just had to let her go on through with it to the end, like a rock that suddenly, for no good reason, started falling down a hill. It was about her Napropath for her nervous headaches.

"It is caused by one little nerve!" she cried, before anybody hardly knew what the score was, "made like a . . . oh, we all have it, you have it and I have, this little nerve . . .

let's see, what's its name, never *can* remember it, ought to, it's the cause of all my misery, ought to know it better'n my own name—aw shoot, can't think of its name now . . . but *any*way, this little ever-what-it-is nerve just stops working— on my Junction Board . . . which is situated right back here at the bottom of my neck and right between my shoulders. Don't look so *morbid*, you all, you all have one too, we all have, all have a Junction Board so don't look so morbid. Any- way . . . imagine your Junction Board as like a switchboard— this is what the Napropath tells me—all the nerves are there, they are all there, switchin on, switchin off, pluggin in calls to the brain. Well, when *it* stops workin—'why, please tell me,' I asked my Napropath; and he shrugged his shoulders to say, 'That's the mystery, Mrs. McCutcheon; now drop your chin'; when *it* stops, then (wouldn't you know), two *other* nerves—the, let's see—oh don't know their names either. *Anyway*—we've all got these, too—these two nerves runnin down your chest on either side—*then* the headache starts. But the most *peculiar* thing is that I have a *tramp nerve*. It just wanders around, can never tell where it'll be next— aren't our bodies a miracle? The good Lord made such a mas- terpiece when he made these bodies, works of art, a mystery for all to behold . . . .''

Mrs. Mack McCutcheon stopped abruptly and what came in over her dead silence was Mrs. Randall's voice saying, "all I said was 'I never in my life!' and turned and walked right out of Neiman-Marcuses with me a new hat on."

As Mrs. Randall was the one who had money and drove to Dallas to buy all her clothes, the subject of her exclamation was urgently important to the other ladies. They listened to her. She was telling about the little male milliner in Neiman- Marcuses. "I tell you I never in my life heard anybody be able to talk about a hat the way he does. He said, 'This is *your* hat, Mrs. Randall, I knew it the moment I put it on your head. This hat is a nice statement on your head. Not sayin too much, just enough. Just the right kind of a state- ment for you to make goin down the street—not a shriek, not a sigh, but a good-size, sure and strong positive yes!, Mrs. Randall.' How he can talk about a hat, that Lucien Silvero, brought in by Neiman-Marcuses from New York!"

Opal Ducharm was whipping her cream for the Tapioca Surprise and listening when she could to all the stories that were like a stitching party in her living room. Then she put her bowl of firm cream on the table and turned to the bowls of Tapioca looking very special, ready for the cream.

A noise was behind her and she turned round to find Sister the cat upon the table over her cream. She could not clap her hands fast enough, however, to stop Sister from dragging her tongue across the top. Then she cried, softly so the ladies could not hear, "Shoo, you Sister!" and Sister sprang away and ran to sit by the door, where she casually began cleaning her face and whiskers. "You hateful Sister!" Opal whispered as she smoothed over the little rut left by the cat's tongue. "Now you go outdoors!"—and she opened the door for the cat.

Opal Ducharm put the cream on the Tapioca, it looked so delicious, and then she stood at her kitchen door with the tray and said with real charm, "Surprise, Paradisers!"; and all the conversation stopped. The ladies loved the surprise refreshments at the meetings, and all tried to be original.

The surprise was passed round and admired, and all the Paradisers crooned with delight. And then they all started in on it.

When Opal Ducharm went to the kitchen to get her bowl, she spied through her window what looked like a sprawled cat in the driveway. She ran out to Sister and found her truly dead and not sleeping or playing possum. Sister was lying over on her side, drawn long and limp; and her paws were thrust out from her as if she had died trying to hold away whatever kind of death had taken her. Round her black lips were speckles of whipcream and some was still hanging on her whiskers. And then Opal saw the whole picture in a flash. "Poisoned by the cream!" she gasped. Just like those fifty-four people that got bacteria in the banana cream pie at the

Houston cafeteria. She rushed up the steps through the door and as she ran she was beholding the image of twelve Paradisers lying flung down like the cat, poisoned dead: Ora Stevens, Moselle Lessups, Clover Sugrew, and all the others, drawn out and limp on her living room floor, all the fifes and drums stilled forever. She flew to the living room, flung out her hands and cried, "Stop the Surprise! Stop! Stop! It is deadly poison and has just killed the cat!" and knocked flying to the floor a spoonful that Esther Borglund was just about to devour. And then she told the bewildered Paradisers about her discovery of the cat, dead in the driveway with the cream on her whiskers and how earlier she had caught Sister with her tongue in the bowl of cream. The ladies were stunned, but Opal shouted, "Get your purses and we'll all run to Victory Hospital just around the corner, that's the quickest thing;" and to Myrtle Dubuque who was already on the phone she yelled "Myrtle that phone's dead, too, dead as Sister and dead as we'll all be if we don't hurry hurry . . ."; and they all rushed out. By grace, the Paradiser Lieutenant was there—it was Johnny Sue Redundo—and with her whistle, which she blew at once and, as if by magic, organized rout into loose squads which lurched without their usual and State-renowned precision, but as valiantly as they could, towards Victory Hospital.

At Victory Hospital the Head Registered Nurse, Viola Privins, was doing all she knew to keep the ladies calm until Dr. Sam Berry could help them—applying cold towels, taking pulses, giving antidotes. Mrs. Cairns had a thermometer in her mouth and many of the ladies had hypos for shock. Cots were put up in the hall by the Emergency Room like the time of the Flu epidemic, but most of the ladies were just too sick to lie down. In fact, the ladies were getting sicker and sicker; some thought they were ready to have a convulsion; and Mrs. Randall, the sickest of all, kept seeing her face writhing and going purple in her mirror. (She had just gobbled up most of her dish of Tapioca, she loved it so.) One Paradiser fainted, and the fattest—it was Ora Starnes—had to be laid out her full length and weight in the Emergency Room, where she was brought to with a cold cloth and ammonia. But when she opened her eyes upon a nurse helping in a stabbed and bleeding derelict, she snuffed out again quick as a candle and hogged the only emergency table.

There was the question as to who should go in to the stomach pump first, since there was only one pump. Some said the officers should go, others suggested alphabetical order, Mrs. Lessups insisted that those who ate the most should go, and Leta Cratz said the sanest thing of all when she shouted, "The sickest should be first—Mrs. Randall is nearly dyin!"

In the midst of all this pandemonium, Myrtle Dubuque, the secretary of the Paradisers and elected that because she was so calm all the time, was moving up and down among the Paradisers, patting them and saying, "Honey, be calm!" She was as steady as if she were taking down the minutes of a rowdy business meeting.

Finally Opal Ducharm, the President, took hold of the situation and reminded all that the motto of the Paradisers was Charity, Unselfishness and Service—and went in first to the pump, which had just arrived with Dr. Berry, with exemplary dignity even in pain. This inspired others to self-effacement except Sarah Galt (who was only a probationary member anyway) who said she was not going to wait any longer and was going to call her personal family physician.

The ladies started going in to Dr. Berry, one by one, and he was efficient and sweet with each patient. But you can imagine what confusion little Victory Hospital was in. It was just the time for the patients' supper but not a one got it. Everything was delayed, compresses, pulses, pills and bedpans; and red lights begged from most every room. But there was no nurse to answer. "This would be the worst tragedy in the town since the time the grandstand collapsed at the May Fete," a little student nurse, Lucy Bird, said. Mrs. Laura Vance, the richest woman in the town and in Victory Hospital for one of her rest cures, put on her Japanese Kimona (from her actual trip to Japan) and came out to assist. But by this time half the town was there. "What is it?" somebody asked Lew Tully who was in, again, for a drying out. "Beats me, but from what I can tell, somebody tried to poison and then rape twelve Paradisers."

"Why'd he want to poison 'em?"

"Why'd he want to rape 'em?" answered Lew.

Paradisers came running in who, in spite of the expert machinery of the list-calling, could not be reached when there was important official information about the organization to be relayed, but had immediately heard, without the slightest difficulty of being reached, of the tragedy of the Tapioca. But most of them were of no help at all, they just got in the way; and Myra Pugh got a hypo she didn't merit, in the scramble. Volunteers came from all over, even Jack the Ant Killer was there—why, nobody knew, but he thought he could help; and Mack Sims of the Valley Gold Dairy was there because he had sold the cream and was afraid the Paradisers might get out an injunction against him for poisoning them, especially if anybody died. Some husbands came, but not Jock Du- charm, this was his day in Bewley, selling his product; and anyway those who did come just got in the way, except Mr. Cairns, a real businessman with sense, who immediately called Honey Grove Hospital, twenty miles away, for their stomach pump, and it was coming by ambulance imme- diately. A reporter from The Bee came in and Opal Ducharm appointed Grace Kunsy to act as temporary publicity chair- man since the regular one, Ora Starnes, was just too sick to say one word for the papers.

By the time several of the ladies had survived the ordeal of the stomach pump and were standing around or lying on the cots, feeling saved and relieved, if languorous, the panic began to subside a little, and it appeared that the women would all come through. Opal Ducharm was complaining that there should be more stomach pumps in a hospital this size and that the Paradisers should have a Bazaar to raise funds for these. She put it on the agenda for the next meeting.

So no one died, and with the help of the volunteers, it was finally over, every stomach was purged, and about nine o'clock that night Dr. Sam Berry pronounced them all out of danger. The women were told to rest for a while, but not a one would stay at Victory Hospital. Mrs. Delancy, the smoker of the group, had another cigarette, and they all went home.

Poor Opal Ducharm, of course, felt the sting of the near-tragedy most severely, for it seemed her fault, and yet it couldn't be. She got home weak and exhausted.

"It just makes me sick, I declare to my soul," she was saying to herself as she opened the door, when there was Jock, her husband. "And where in the name of the Savior have you been?" she yelled, knowing perfectly well that it was his day in Bewley.

"I just got in about twenty minutes ago, Opal. You know today was my day to go to Bewley."

And when Opal saw that Jock was not going to be sympathetic, this was going to be too much. But then he never did care anything about the Paradisers, wouldn't even become an Auxiliary, and wear the special tie-clasp, like the other husbands, but bowled instead. "If they want me in the Auxiliary let 'em meet another night besides Tuesdays. That's my bowling night," he said. This was a source of great hurt and shame to Opal who, after all, *was* the President.

"Well you shouldn't have gone to Bewley today! You missed something near-fatal. You could have helped, which you never do, so never mind."

"Helped what?"

"I had to have my stomach pumped, that's all. But never mind."

"You know I sell my product in Bewley on Tuesdays, Opal. And what did you swallow, for Christ's sakes?"

"Something poisoned. But never mind."

"Well Opal, we'll get back to the poison in a minute, but what I'm trying to tell you is that Sister is dead."

"Oh don't remind me of that because she was poisoned too!"

"Poisoned? Well I don't know about you, Opal, but that damned cat wasn't poisoned. What I'm trying to tell you is that Ruta Tanner just left here. She came to tell you that when she drove in the driveway during your meeting she believes she hit a cat. She felt a thud and saw something lying on its side in the driveway. Now how much closer can you get to the fact that she ran over Sister and killed her?"

"Oh to my Savior!" Opal wailed. "But why didn't Ruta come in here and tell me? It would have saved us all from so much suffering!"

"She said she was too upset to come in and disturb the meeting with such bad news. And especially seeing as how, since she's on probation for driving drunk under the influence of martinis at the Thanksgiving Special March, she felt too humiliated to come in on a meeting. If you ask me, she's been hitting the gin like a bat outta hell since you all expelled her—or whatever the hell you did. She said to tell you that she tried to call you from Pig Stand No. 2 but your 'phone wouldn't work. Anyways, I called her a dumb hit-and-run-driver and said I was going to sue her and that lounge-lizard husband of hers with the beer-belly. I don't want to get mixed up in it, lemme alone. I've been in Bewley all day tryin to sell my product to a bunch of numbskulls."

"Oh where is poor Sister now?" Opal shrieked and tore at the divan which Sister's claws had already shredded in places.

"I just put her in an A&P shopping bag and will bury her directly. What else can I do, for God's sake? If you don't get hold of yourself you're going to have to have more than your stomach pumped. Your brains, for Christsakes. Anyway," he said, under his breath as he went to the refrigerator to get a beer, "there'll be less cat hair all over everything in the house . . . *including* my blue suit which by now *looks* like Sister. I was about ready to give it to her."

Opal Ducharm could have been humiliated by this comment, but she was now going through such various feelings that she didn't know which to settle for. At first she felt elated because nobody was poisoned, and then she thought of

Sister killed and was heart-broken. She started to call the poor exhausted women all pumped half to death for nothing, but she remembered her dead phone and felt rage. Then she really got just plain fed-up with the whole thing and in a second decided to eliminate every feeling but one, her appetite, and started for the kitchen.

"Well," she said. "I know what *I'm* going right to the icebox and do. That's eat me a good big helping of that Tapioca. There's an awful lot left and I didn't even get to taste of it."

And from the refrigerator she drew out a finger wrapped with whipcream and smacked it up with a brave tongue in a kind of toast to the killed cat and to the whole affair, and, bringing a mound of the good Tapioca, came in and sat down by Jock.

"When I've quieted down and can stand to recall it, I'll tell you the whole terrible thing," she advised Jock.

"Whenever you're ready," Jock said. "Shall I wait—or bury the cat?"

Charles E. Fritch

(American, 1927–)

The Misfortune Cookie

With an ease born of long practice, Harry Folger cracked open the Chinese cookie and pulled the slip of paper free. He smoothed it out on the table and read the message printed there:

YOU WILL MEET AN OLD FRIEND!

Harry chuckled to himself. It was inevitable that he would

meet an old friend. He met them every day—on his way to work, at the office, in his apartment building—even in the various Chinese restaurants he frequented.

He bit into the cookie, crunched the remnants between his teeth, and washed them down with a swig of the now luke-warm tea. He enjoyed the fortune cookie as much as the for-tune itself. But then he enjoyed everything about the Chinese food that he always ate, without ever tiring of it—the chow mein, the chop suey, the chicken fried rice, the won ton, the egg foo yung, the—oh, why go on? Heaven, to Harry Folger, was eating in a Chinese restaurant.

And as he was leaving the place, he met an old friend.

Her name was Cynthia Peters, or had been until she'd married. She was not old in the chronological sense, however, but a young woman not yet in her thirties. Harry had fond memories of the tempestuous affair he had experienced with the lady when both were younger, and frequently his dreams were filled with such pleasant recollections.

"Cynthia!" he said, surprised but pleased.

"Harry!" she exclaimed, tears of sudden happiness well-ing in her hazel-green eyes.

And Harry knew that despite the fact they were both married, he was going to have an affair with her.

When he finally got around to thinking about it, Harry marveled at the coincidence of his meeting old friend Cynthia right after a fortune cookie had forewarned him of such an occurrence. It was a coincidence, of course, for it could be nothing else. Harry enjoyed reading the messages—written, he always assumed, by coolie labor somewhere in Hong Kong—but he did not believe them to contain the absolute truth.

Not just then, he didn't.

The meeting places of himself and Cynthia were, needless to say, Chinese restaurants. Her husband, she told him, was a beast who made her life miserable. His wife, he informed her, was a bitch with whom he was quite unhappy. On one of these occasions, after a delicious meal of sweet and sour spareribs, Harry cracked open his fortune cookie to discover this message:

WATCH OUT! SOMEONE IS FOLLOWING YOU!

He looked up to discover Cynthia's irate husband entering the restaurant. There was barely time enough to spirit her out the rear exit. There would have been no time at all if the Chinese fortune cookie hadn't alerted Harry to the imminent danger.

Coincidence again, Harry decided—until he received a similarly worded message an instant before his wife (who hated Chinese food) entered the restaurant where he and Cynthia were eating, and once again Harry escaped in the nick of time.

As a result, Harry began taking the messages more seriously. He was hoping for some invaluable tip on the stock market or some winning horse in Saturday's race, but none came. For the most part, except for emergencies, the messages were bland bits of wisdom and random advice.

With one noticeable exception.

It occurred as he and Cynthia (who, like him, loved Chinese food) were finishing off the remaining morsels of Mandarin duck and she was telling how suspicious her husband was getting and how sure she was that Harry's own wife must not be blind to the secret rendezvous. At that precise moment, Harry cracked open a crisp fortune cookie, pulled out the slip of paper and read:

YOU ARE GOING TO DIE!

Harry gulped and almost choked on the piece of cookie in his mouth. It was ridiculous, of course. Then his attitude changed abruptly to one of indignation. What the hell kind of message was that for some underpaid coolie in Hong Kong to stuff into a fortune cookie? He thought of complaining to the manager, but he changed his mind. Instead, he decided he didn't feel well. He took Cynthia home, letting her off in front of her apartment.

As he was about to drive off, he heard a noise at the opposite window. He looked to see Cynthia's husband pointing a gun at him. He gasped, flung open the car door and scrambled out, bumping into his wife, who also had a gun in her hand.

Harry ran. He was vaguely aware that two guns fired simultaneously, but he felt no pain and was not about to stop his flight. He ran, not pausing for breath until he was a good four blocks away. Then he leaned against a building, dragging in lungfuls of air, to take inventory. There didn't seem to be any holes in him, nor was there any sign of blood.

Thank God, he thought, for the lousy aim of the two irate spouses.

Even so, he was shaking uncontrollably. He had to go someplace and relax. They might still be after him, and he'd be safer in a crowded place. He looked up at the building to see where he was.

He was standing in front of a Chinese restaurant.

It was one he'd never been to before, and his curiosity was aroused. Also his appetite, although he'd eaten a Chinese meal only an hour before. Besides, he always felt secure in such a place.

Harry Folger walked in, sat at a table. Surprisingly, he was the only person there. When a waiter appeared, Harry ordered the number-two dinner. He ate it, enjoying each mouthful, forgetting the unpleasant episode in the street. Then he cracked open his fortune cookie and read the message that had been tucked inside.

The words didn't register at first. When they did, he looked up in sudden panic—to see the waiter grinning derisively with a skull face. Harry looked around wildly for a way out, but there were no doors or windows in the restaurant, no way to get out now or ever.

He started screaming.

When he tired of that, he felt hungry again. He ordered another meal, ate it. The message in the fortune cookie this time was exactly as the first.

He had another meal after that one, and another after that, and another after that—and each time the message in the fortune cookie was the same. It said:

YOU'RE DEAD!

Robert Herrick

(1591–1674)

The Honeycomb

If thou hast found an honeycomb,
Eat thou not all, but taste on some;
For if thou eat'st it to excess,
That sweetness turns to loathsomeness.
Taste it to temper; then 'twill be
Marrow and manna unto thee.

John Keats

(English, 1795–1821)

From *The Eve of St. Agnes*

XXX

And still she slept an azure-lidded sleep,
In blanched linen, smooth, and lavender'd,
While he from forth the closet brought a heap
Of candied apple, quince, and plum, and gourd;
With jellies soother than the creamy curd,
And lucent syrops, tinct with cinnamon;
Manna and dates, in argosy transferr'd
From Fez; and spiced dainties, every one,
From silken Samarcand to cedar'd Lebanon.

XXXI

These delicates he heap'd with glowing hand
On golden dishes and in baskets bright
Of wreathed silver: sumptuous they stand
In the retired quiet of the night,
Filling the chilly room with perfume light.—
"And now, my love, my seraph fair, awake!
Thou art my heaven, and I thine eremite:
Open thine eyes, for meek St. Agnes' sake,
Or I shall drowse beside thee, so my soul doth
ache."

Louis Simpson

(1923–)

Chocolates

Once some people were visiting Chekhov.
While they made remarks about his genius
the Master fidgeted. Finally
he said, "Do you like chocolates?"

They were astonished, and silent.
He repeated the question,
whereupon one lady plucked up her courage
and murmured shyly, "Yes."

"Tell me," he said, leaning forward,
light glinting from his spectacles,
"what kind? The light, sweet chocolate
or the dark, bitter kind?"

The conversation became general.
They spoke of cherry centers,
of almonds and Brazil nuts.
Losing their inhibitions
they interrupted one another.
For people may not know what they think
about politics in the Balkans,
or the vexed question of men and women,

but everyone has a definite opinion
about the flavor of shredded coconut.
Finally someone spoke of chocolates filled with liqueur,
and everyone, even the author of *Uncle Vanya,*
was at a loss for words.

As they were leaving he stood by the door
and took their hands.
                In the coach returning to Petersburg
they agreed that it had been a most
unusual conversation.

M.F.K. Fisher

(1908–)

R Is for *Romantic*

. . . And for a few of the reasons that gastronomy is and always has been connected with its sister art of love.

Or perhaps instead of reasons, which everyone who understands anything about digestion and its good and bad endocrinological effects will already know, I should discuss here, with brief discretion, a few direct results of the play of the

468   FOOD FOR THOUGHT

five senses, properly stimulated by food upon human passion. The surest way, if not the best, is to look backward.

Passion, here at least, means the height of emotional play between the two sexes, not the lasting fire I felt for my father once when I was about seven and we ate peach pie together under a canyon oak, and not the equally lasting fire I felt for a mammoth woman who brought milk toast to me once in the dusk when I was seventeen and very sick, and not the almost searing gratitude I felt for my mother when she soothed me with buttered carrots and a secret piece of divinity fudge once when I had done wrong and was in Coventry, and not the high note of confidence between two human beings that I felt once on a frozen hillside in France when a bitter old general broke his bread in two and gave me half.

This other kind of passion that I speak of, romantic if ever any such brutal thing could be so deemed, is one of sex, of the come-and-go, the preening and the prancing, and the final triumph or defeat, of two people who know enough, subconsciously or not, to woo with food as well as flattery.

The first time I remember recognizing the new weapon I was about eight, I think. There was a boy named Red, immortal on all my spiritual calendars, a tall, scoffing, sneering, dashing fellow perhaps six months older than I, a fellow of withdrawals, mockery, and pain. I mocked back at him, inadequately, filled with a curious tremor.

He followed me home every afternoon from school, a good half-block behind, and over the giggles of my retinue of girl friends came his insults and his lewd asides to a train of knee-britched sycophants. We must have looked very strange to the relicts of the Quaker settlers of our little town, who pulled aside their parlor curtains at our noise, but if our pipings were audible to their ancient ears they would not have felt too shocked, for as I recall it all we said, in a thousand significantly differing tones, was, Oh, yeah? Huh! Oh, *yeah?*

My friends gave me advice, as doubtless Red's gave him, and our daily march continued until February 14 that year without much variation. Then Red presented me with the biggest, fanciest, and most expensive Valentine in the class box: we knew, because it still said "50¢" on the back, in a spidery whisper of extravagance marked down thoughtfully in indelible pencil by the bookstore man and left carefully unsmeared by my canny lover.

I stalked on sneeringly every afternoon, virginal amid my train of damsels, the knights behind, hawking and nudging.

I was won, though, being but human and having, at eight as now, a belly below my heart. Red, through what advice I can never know, a few days later slipped into my desk the first nickel candy bar I had ever seen, called, I think, a Cherriswete.

It was a clumsy lump of very good chocolate and fondant, with a preserved cherry in the middle, all wrapped up in a piece of paper that immediately on being touched sent off waves of red and gilt stain. It was, to me, not only the ultimate expression of masculine devotion, but pure gastronomical delight, in a household where Grandmother disapproved of candy, not because of tooth decay or indigestion, but because children liked it and children should perforce not have anything they liked.

I sniffed happily at the Cherriswete a few times and then gave each girl in my retinue a crumb, not because I liked her but because of her loyalty. Then I took it home, showed it to my little sister, spun it a few times more past her nose to torture her, and divided it with her, since even though young and savage we loved each other very much.

My heart was full. I knew at last that I loved Red. I was his, to steal a phrase. We belonged together, a male and female who understood the gastronomical urge.

I never saw him again, since his father was transferred by Standard Oil from Brea to Shanghai that week end, but he has had much more influence on me with that one Cherriswete than most men could have in twenty years of Pol Roger and lark tongues. Sometimes I wonder if he is still tall, freckled, and irreverent—and if he remembers how to woo a woman. Often I thank him for having, no matter how accidentally, taught me to realize the almost vascular connection between love and lobster pâté, between eating and romance.

Samuel Ferguson

(Irish, 1810–1886)

The Lapful of Nuts

Whene'er I see soft hazel eyes
    And nut-brown curls,
I think of those bright days I spent
    Among the Limerick girls;
When up through Cratla woods I went,
    Nutting with thee;
And we pluck'd the glossy clustering fruit
    From many a bending tree.

Beneath the hazel boughs we sat,
    Thou, love, and I,
And the gather'd nuts lay in thy lap,
    Beneath thy downcast eye:
But little we thought of the store we'd won,
    I, love, or thou;
For our hearts were full, and we dare not own
    The love that's spoken now.

Oh, there's wars for willing hearts in Spain,
    And high Germanie!
And I'll come back, ere long, again,
    With knightly fame and fee:
And I'll come back, if I ever come back,
    Faithful to thee,
That sat with thy white lap full of nuts
    Beneath the hazel tree.

Imants Ziedonis

(Russian, 1933–)

Do Not Eat, O My Child, When a Song Is Sung!

Do not eat, O my child, when a song is sung! Never eat, O my child, when a song is sung! There, in the song, someone's soul is imploring and begging—perhaps it feels hungry at that moment—do not eat, never eat, O my child, when a song is sung.

Do not drink, O my child, do not drink when a song is sung. It is an oriole singing there, asking for rain, begging the leaves for a dew-drop—it is the oriole begging and imploring there, it sings in hunger, tormented by thirst.

We are a tribe of eaters. O my child, yet put down your spoon on the table; when a song is sung, put down your spoon on the table, O my child. Heed not, O my child, this big grown up man who is eating, do not learn from him: he has long since gobbled up all his songs, and now cannot tell a song from a potato.

The same door lets through a spoon and a song.

Will the spoon stop before your mouth when a song is sung?

O my child, take your spoon by the hand, quietly lead it aside—let the song pass first, O my child!

—*Translated by Dorian Rottenberg*

Permissions

"The Egg" from *The Best of Clarence Day* by Clarence Day. Copyright ©
1948 by Mrs. Katherine B. Day. Reprinted by permission of Alfred A.
Knopf, Inc.

"Cheese" from *Fruits & Vegetables* by Erica Jong. Copyright © 1968,
1970, 1971 by Erica Mann Jong. Reprinted by permission of Henry Holt
and Company.

"The Shrimp Served at the Party Were Gigantic! Here's an Embarrassing
Yarn About It" appears courtesy of Marvin Cohen.

"In Sicily" from Elio Vittorini, *A Vittorini Omnibus.* Copyright © 1973
by New Directions Publishing Corporation. Reprinted by permission of
the publisher.

Selections from *The Leopard* by Guisippe Tomasi di Lampedusa, trans-
lated by Archibald Colquhoun. Translation copyright © 1960 by William
Collins & Co. Ltd., and Pantheon Books, Inc. Reprinted by permission of
Pantheon Books, a division of Random House, Inc.

"The Pizza" by Cheryl Pallant. Reprinted by permission of the author.

"Caviare at the Funeral" and "Chocolates" from *Caviare at the Funeral.*
Copyright © 1980 by Louis Simpson. Reprinted by permission of Frank-
lin Watts, Inc.

"A Bride" from *The Jade Mountain: A Chinese Anthology* by Wang
Chien, translated by Walter Bynner from the text of Kiang Kang-Hu.
Copyright 1929 and renewed copyright © 1957 by Alfred A. Knopf, Inc.
Reprinted by permission of the publisher.

"Soup" from *A Return to a Place Lit by a Glass of Milk* by Charles
Simic. Copyright © 1974 by Charles Simic. Reprinted by permission of
George Braziller, Inc., New York.

"Soup," "Preparations," and "Jack Watts" from *Selected Poems 1970–
1985* (Poetry Wales Press, 1986) and *Poems—Selected and New* (Story
Line Press, 1986). Copyright © 1986 by Tony Curtis. Reprinted by permission of the author.

"The Brothers" reprinted with permission of Macmillan Publishing Company from *The Art of Eating* by M.F.K. Fisher. Copyright 1954 by
M.F.K. Fisher.

"Meat" by Walter de la Mare, reprinted by permission of the Society of
Authors, and the Literary Trustees of Walter de la Mare.

"How Gargamelle, Bigswoln With Gargantua, Ate an Abundance of Tripe"
from *Gargantua and Pantagruel* by François Rabelais, translated by Jacques
Le Clerc, (1936).